My best years in the Navy were sp[...] Watching him lead our staffs ma[...] watched Captain Ryan mold the[...] cient, motivated, tactically aggressive unit that fought the Global War on Terrorism and Operation Iraqi Freedom from the Mediterranean. He was the best leader I served with at sea in my career.

—Scott Fry, VADM (Ret)
Senior Vice President, Alion Science and Technology

In my career, I have been led by and witnessed over one hundred senior officers from different services and different countries, and Captain Dave Ryan remains the absolute best! This book is a must-have in your collection if you are leader of people. Whether in the military or (especially) in the civilian sector, if you are running a squad or large division, this book is something you will come back to over and over again, while making a difference in the lives of those you lead.

—Captain Ted LeClair, USN
Senior Vice President and Director, Natixis Advisor Academy

Leadership doesn't just happen. You need to experience it, study it, and think about how you will exercise it. Dave Ryan and the instructors at CLS have helped a generation of Naval Officers to think deeply about how we would lead in our commands. They made us better leaders!

—William Landay, VADM (Ret)
President, WE LANDAY Consulting LLC

DELIVER UP HONOR

DELIVER UP HONOR

DAVID RYAN

**FORWARD WRITTEN BY ADMIRAL JIM STAVRIDIS,
FORMER NATO SUPREME ALLIED COMMANDER.**

YorkshirePublishing
www.yorkshirepublishing.com
Write Now.

ISBN Hardcover: 978-1-946977-64-9
ISBN Paperback: 978-1-946977-65-6
Deliver Up Honor
Copyright © 2016 by David Ryan

Yorkshire Publishing
3207 South Norwood Avenue
Tulsa, Oklahoma 74135
www.YorkshirePublishing.com
918.394.2665

CONTENTS

....

DELIVER UP HONOR

APPENDICES

FOREWORD

There are thousands of books of leadership. *Deliver Up Honor* is at the top of my list because it is written by a man who has lived leadership at every significant level in our military and excelled every step of the way.

Navy Captain Dave Ryan started as an enlisted recruit and served with distinction throughout a long and superb career in the US Navy, including command of an award-winning Destroyer, a deployed Destroyer Squadron, chief of staff of Sixth Fleet and, most importantly to the genesis of this book, as a founding writer and instructor of the US Navy's Command Leadership School. His reputation throughout his long career in the Navy was as one of the very best of the best, chosen for the toughest assignments, and delivering outstanding results at every step. It was perfectly logical that he would be chosen personally to stand up the first formal leadership school of the US Navy.

Given the challenge in 1995 by then chief of Naval Operations, Admiral Mike Boorda, Dave Ryan—alongside three other post-command officers—essentially codified two hundred years of naval leadership and distilled it into a course that endures today in Newport, Rhode Island. Every man and woman sent to command in the US Navy has passed through the doors of the Command Leadership School for more than two decades, and the successful results in both peace and war speak for themselves. In this remarkable book, the reader has firsthand access to every aspect of that course.

Quoting the great leaders of past centuries, filled with both scholarly analysis and deeply grounded in practical leadership, *Deliver Up Honor* sets the benchmark for leaders today—in the military, business, diplomacy, politics, medicine, or any other walk of life. In crisp, clear prose, it provides a charted course to sail and become a more compassionate, effective, and inspirational leader.

In the end, the best leaders inspire others to reach deep within themselves and become part of something greater than their individual lives. This is something Captain Dave Ryan has done at every step of his extraordinary life, and we are lucky to have his wisdom, experience, and scholarship captured in such a clear and vibrant volume.

—James Stavridis
Admiral, US Navy
Supreme Allied Commander at NATO 2009-2013
Dean, The Fletcher School of Law
and Diplomacy, Tufts University

PREFACE

Deliver Up Honor incorporates academic and personal exposure gained through my experience designing, writing, implementing, and teaching the Navy's Command Leadership Course. The book draws on many sources, conversations with combat veterans too numerous to mention, and the most telling books and quotes from military heroes past and acknowledged leaders present. Specifically, it is an extension of one of my Command Leadership School topics entitled "Leadership in Combat and Crisis."

It was my great fortune to have been provided an opportunity to research, gather, and review eight of the most significant military combat studies in existence at that time. The lessons and insights gained from that exercise and the experience of facilitating the CLS are something that will stay with me always. Those studies, combined with the additional research listed and stated throughout, give the book the credibility needed when discussing leadership in combat or crisis, and the *honor* that is required from the leader and those led in what is considered the most trying of human experiences.

General George S. Patton stated, "Success in war lurks invisible in that vitalizing spark, intangible, yet as evident as lightning—the warrior's soul… It is the cold glitter of the attacker's eyes, not the point of the questioning bayonet that breaks the line. It is the fierce determination of the driver to close with the enemy, not the mechanical perfection of the tank that conquers the trench. It is the cataclysmic ecstasy of the conflict in the flier, not the perfection of the machine gun, which drops the enemy in flames. Yet volumes are devoted to arms; only pages to inspiration."

My book is dedicated to all those who understand that the most essential dynamic of combat power is *inspirational leadership*. It has always been and will always be.

In the last analysis, it is about crossing the line between fear and courage. It is about "delivering up honor."

INTRODUCTION

....

What is the relationship between "battle-mindedness" and "inspirational leadership?" Who should be responsible for getting a command or organization ready for its missions? There is this historically referred to idea of the need to be both mentally and physically ready for combat. How is this achieved? How has it been achieved?

Some believe that due to the Title Ten, senior level responsibility to "train and equip," that perhaps the system and not the commanding officer or leader should be ultimately responsible to build this battle-mindedness and combat readiness. Fundamental requirements for success by this approach would mean that the system is competent enough to determine and execute proper mission (combat/tactics) training and provide an adequate resource infrastructure to effect its application.

The system, as opposed to commanding officer choice above, could violate the triad of responsibility, authority, and accountability. That is, Title Ten US Code 5947/ART 113, 0802, Navy Regs., clearly articulates that commanding officers, by law, have the responsibility and will certainly be held accountable. But have COs been afforded the commensurate authority? If so, are they executing that authority? Do they currently possess the prerequisite skills in tactics and leadership to direct their command training and develop battle-mindedness?

Let's consider a hypothesis: *Most commanding officers and leaders of military organizations are capable of tactically preparing and leading their men and women into combat. They understand the methods needed to provide their people that which will bind them together to withstand the strongest of challenges. We have created a long line of commanders prepared to lead and act in combat and stress environments.*

True or false?

It is important to remember that a hypothesis is simply something to be considered to be true for the purpose of investigation or argument. In this book, we will explore the relationship between inspirational leadership and the combat performance of leaders and those they are to lead. We will discuss leaders, those led, situations they find themselves in, and methods of communications.

Are commanding officers capable of leading their commands into harm's way? Do they know how to give and take hard knocks and are their crews prepared to do that? What does a command like that look like? How can that climate be created? How and where can one learn these skills?

The above are all good questions worthy of open dialogue. Sailors, airmen, and marines have a right to expect competent and confident leadership. The law mentioned above demands, "Take all measures," but do the current training system and our leadership development efforts support this concept? Will they provide what is needed?

For those who are to lead, the responsibility is for the here and now. Things need to be done. Things can be done. Some things are being done. Some COs are already making a big difference and fighting for their right to lead. They have learned things. They have thought things through. They understand their strengths and weaknesses.

Points to ponder for the book:

> To give the soldier a correct concept of battle is a far different thing from encouraging him to think about war. The latter is too vast a canvas. It includes too much detail, which is confusing to his mind and immaterial to his personal problem.
>
> We have surpassed all other armies and outstripped common sense in our effort to teach the man something about war. He is counseled about war's causes, which is a good thing on those rare occasions when the instruction is in qualified hands. He is told about how soldiers and sailors of other nations observe courtesy and foster tradition. He is even bored by lectures on strategy and logistics of high command.
>
> But he does not get what he most requires, the simple details of common human experience on the field of battle. As a result, he goes to the supremely testing experience of his lifetime almost as a total stranger.

Those facts, which are denied him, should be made his not only for the sake of personal survival but in the interest of unit efficiency. The price for failure is paid up and down the line.

It is true that the individual soldier in the more recent periods of warfare has been trained to regulate his movements on the field of battle according to the nature of the ground. He has been schooled to maneuver with his weapons in such a way that his employment of the ground will give his weapons maximum effectiveness and himself a degree of protection. That is the desirable physical equation for each man going into combat with the purpose of firing against the enemy— to find an efficient site for the weapon which at the same time provides a relatively secure site for the firer.

Surely, it will be said, this is the heart of the matter—the relating of the weapon to the ground and the soldier to the weapon and the ground, and the relating of all weapons within the formation to each other and to the ground, so that there will be maximum fire power and maximum defensive strength within the position.

My answer to this fundamental proposition in the tradition of military logic is that it is absolutely false.

The heart of the matter is to relate the man to his fellow soldier as he will find him on the field of combat, to condition him to human nature as he will learn to depend on it when the ground offers him no comfort and weapons fail. Only when the human, rather than material, aspects of operation are put uppermost can tactical bodies be conditioned to make the most of their potential unity. (Lord Moran, *Anatomy of Courage*)

The above quote is a clear example of the philosophy that the actions of each of us affect the lives of all of us. This philosophy, combined with realistic and somewhat uncomfortable training, has historically provided inspiration and commitment, vice mere compliance to mission and task. It is the strength of unity brought by the combat element of comradeship, the historic idea that intrinsic values are fear inhibitors and action enablers. The Marine Corps's crucible "band of brothers" approach captures this philosophy of battle-mindedness.

History may sometimes be conveniently overlooked today. History will tell you it is never different in the fundamentals. The difference is in the details. If I were to bet, I would bet on history. Honor, courage, and commitment do not happen in the classroom or in port, nor is it the training infrastructure's responsibility to provide it, nor do we need anyone's permission to build it in our commands or organizations. All we need is the effort, energy, and courage to do it. Commanding officers and leaders must be competent and confident in their leadership and war-fighting skills. They must know the right stuff. They must understand the strengths and limits of their equipment and the series of systems that support them, and that they in turn support. It is about systems knowledge. It is also about leadership training that when applied correctly builds the desire in people to want to learn their equipment and jobs and to develop the will to win. This has been proven to lead to the courage and stamina that are indispensable in the most trying of circumstances. Leadership is the enabler of all this. *It is the prime mover.*

More insight from Lord Moran's *Anatomy of Courage*:

> What I advocate, in brief, is the substitution of reality for romance in all discussions of the battlefield, and the introduction into training in the maximum measure possible of the same element which steadies a command during its trial by fire. It is that way with any fighting man. He is sustained by his fellows primarily and by his weapons secondarily. Having to make a choice in the face of the enemy, he would rather be unarmed and with comrades around him than altogether alone, though possessing the most perfect of quick-firing weapons.
>
> …Men who have been in battle know from first-hand experience that when the chips are down, a man fights to help the man next to him, just as a company fights to keep pace with its flanks. Things have to be that simple. An ideal does not become tangible at the moment of firing a volley or charging a hill. When the hard and momentary choice is life and death, the words once heard at an orientation lecture are clean forgot, but the presence of a well-loved comrade is unforgettable. In battle the most valued thing at hand is that which becomes most stoutly defended. All values are interpreted in terms of the battlefield itself.

COs must continue to fight for their authority and know what to do when they get it. How will we help them to act? Why not put our COs through a decision in combat or crisis course to teach and test their tactical competence, a "how to think" course, not a PQS or checklist "what to think" course? We need to prepare ourselves, and those we are to lead, to be both mentally and physically ready for combat or crisis. Preparing to go into harm's way is no trivial task. Commanding officers and those they are to lead must be prepared to cross the line between fear and courage. Once that critical line is crossed, they must understand the nature and purpose of war and act and wield power based on their previous long and realistic intensive training.

So battle-mindedness is a combination of all the above, understanding (1) the purpose and nature of war; (2) the system we employ to win our wars; (3) the fundamental leadership that provides direction, purpose and motivation, and looks to make decisions and manage risk; (4) the ability of the leader to build *unity* so all understand clearly that the actions of each of them really do effect the lives of all of them; (5) in a combat or stressful situation, to provide all something that relegates any personal bias to a position of secondary importance.

How best to do all this is a decision *you* must make. How it's been done and what elements are associated with this fundamental leadership responsibility are provided in the following pages. Everything that is done and everything that is not done is either additive to or subtractive from how both the leader and those led will react in combat or stress. Leaders must be able to make decisions under great stress, based on less-than-perfect information, knowing that the consequences may be significant for their country, crew, and self.

For when sailors, airmen, or marines turn to you for direction, when their eyes turn to you, that is not the time to realize that *you* are ill-prepared to *act*.

DELIVER UP HONOR

Figure 1.

CHAPTER 1

ASSIGNMENT

Leadership: The most essential dynamic of combat power is competent and confident officer and chief petty officer leadership. Leaders inspire sailors with the will to win. They provide purpose, direction, and motivation in combat. Leaders determine how maneuver, firepower, and tactics are used, ensuring these elements are effectively employed against the enemy. Thus, no peacetime duty is more important for leaders then studying their profession, understanding the human dimension of leadership, becoming tactically and technically proficient, and preparing for war. These help them understand the effects of battle on sailors, units, and leaders. The regular study and teaching of military doctrine, theory, history, and biographies of military leaders are invaluable.

Commanders are selected for their tasks because of their moral character, firm willpower, and professional ability. They must imbue their commands with their ideas, desires, and methods. The personal and professional influence of their competence has a positive bearing on the outcomes of battles and campaigns.

Professional competency, personality, and the will of strong Leaders represent a significant part of any unit's combat power. While leadership requirements differ with the unit size and type, all leaders must demonstrate character and ethical standards. Leaders are first Sailors, Airmen, and Marines. They must know, understand and prepare their subordinates. They must act with courage and conviction in crisis or battle. They must build trust and teamwork. During missions, they have put their people where they need to be and they themselves positioned to make decisions or to influence the action by their personal presence.

Strong leaders and trained, dedicated sailors, airmen, marines are the greatest combat multipliers. When opposing forces are nearly equal, the moral qualities of sailors and leaders–sense of duty, courage, loyalty, and discipline, combined with stamina and skill–provide the decisive edge. Once the force is engaged, superior combat power derives from the courage and competence of those led, the excellence of their training, the capability of their equipment, the soundness of their tactics, doctrine, battle orders, and fighting instructions, and, above all, the quality of their leadership. (Stockdale, James B., *Leadership In Response To Changing Societal Values*)

I'm not sure leadership can be defined better than the above thoughts. Having said that, then all leaders must be able to answer the fundamental question: what have I prepared myself and those I am to lead to do? For it is stated:

Mahan states in *The Influence of Sea Power upon History*,

> There is not in modern naval history a more striking warning to the officers of every era, than this battle of Toulon. Coming as it did after a generation of comparative naval inactivity, it tried men's reputations by fire. The lesson, in the judgment of the author, is the danger of disgraceful failure to men who have neglected to keep themselves prepared, not only in knowledge of their profession, but in the sentiment of what war requires. The average man is not a coward; but neither is he endowed by nature only with the rare faculty of seizing intuitively the proper course at a given moment. He gains it, some more, some less, by experience or by reflection. If both have been lacking to him, indecision will follow; either from not knowing what to do, or from failure to realize that utter self-devotion of himself and his command are required.

I had finished my command tour and was sitting in class at the Naval War College. I had gotten a phone call from my detailer, as we had been in discussions concerning my next assignment. It would be shore duty, as I was now waiting to make captain and hopefully screen for major command. I returned the call and he said something like, "You've been chosen for an assignment." Having been a Naval Military Personnel Command detailer or assignment officer, I knew that the word "chosen" had a kind of non-negotiable stigma attached to it. Typically, it meant either it was an important job, or that you were the only one left to fill it. Not sure even today which was true, only that for me it turned out to be very important. He indicated I was to be assigned along with three other post-command officers to design, author, and teach a two-week command leadership course. We would set up shop in the old OCS (officer candidate school) building at NETC Newport and were to convert Perry hall, which used to contain the SWOS (surface warfare officers' school) trainer—or the moving triangles as we used to call it—(nothing like the new trainers today; ships were small equilateral triangles, you needed a vivid imagination back then). The effort was fully funded, and we had some four months to put the course flow together and brief it to Admiral Boorda and his executive board for approval. I reported November 25, 1994, briefed Admiral Boorda in April 1995, and the first course came on line May 1995. It was an amazingly fulfilling time.

Yellow stickers had just come on to the market and we filled up the OCS building with them. We brainstormed and talked through many ideas. The four musketeers as we called ourselves were the following: John Meyer who commanded USS Hewitt (DD-966), Rodger Krull who commanded USS Santa Fe (SSN 763), Marc Purcell who commanded VF-111, and myself, who commanded USS Callaghan (DDG-994). Two SWOs, an aviator, and a submariner. After we beat to death "why us," we got to work. We read everything we could get our hands on. We looked at the main theme guidance provided to us from Admiral Boorda. We diagrammed an overarching skeleton course theme. We came up with possible topics. We kept sorting them out, lumping them together forming units. We decided that in the end, the bottom line is about how you and your command perform in a combat or crisis situation. It's about the leader, those led, situations they find themselves in and how and what is communicated.

We then took our major themes and some lumped topics to form a rough course flow. We did significant historical research, as it was important to include customs and traditions and refresh our link to US naval heritage. I remembered that when I was naval aide to the commandant of the Marine Corps, General P. X. Kelley, he often referred to his responsibilities under Title Ten. I had never heard about it or read it before, but Title Ten became one of our more important points of the course. We began stating, "It's your responsibility under the law," a powerful statement and a key learning point made at every opportunity. It was a sort of unifying theme for the four of us, and we began to realize the importance of what we were being asked to do. This would not be a mundane and resting shore duty prior to our next sea assignment, certainly no chance to improve my golf handicap! We were to write a course directed by the CNO to assist proven leaders to live up to their responsibilities "under the law." It was a daunting task. The never-ending brain sessions would make my head hurt, bringing the "too hard" and "why me" discussions to the forefront again and again.

Finally, however, we turned the corner on all that, when we put the flow together and stood back to pick it apart, as we had done so many times before. Only then did it register and truly feel that we had generated a real leadership framework. It was a feeling I will remember always. We all looked each other in the eyes and, without saying a word, nodded the realization that we had shared in a creation that was perhaps the most significant thing we had achieved individually or collectively. I have often wondered that if it had been four other post-command officers locked in room for four months, given such a task, what would they have generated? I would like to think that it would have been fairly similar. For in the end, it was truly not about us, but what we had collectively shaped from what had always been understood and accomplished by so many before us throughout naval history. In essence, it's about *inspirational leadership*.

Here is what "The Law" 10 US Code 5947 states:

> All Commanding officers…are required to show in themselves a good example of virtue, patriotism and subordination; to be vigilant in inspecting the conduct of all persons who are placed under their command; to guard against and suppress all dissolute and immoral practices, and to correct…all persons who are guilty of them; and to take all necessary and proper measures, under the laws, regulations and customs of naval service, to promote and safeguard the morale, the physical well-being and the general welfare of the officers and enlisted persons under their command.

The "law" as we came to refer to it says to take *all* measures, not some, but *all*. It is the report card of a commanding officer's tour, and it is difficult to get an "A" grade. We considered how you could prepare yourself and your command/organization to take all measures.

What would a command/organization capable of doing that look like?

More brainstorming followed, many more yellow stickers in various groupings. We put together the Command Leadership School (CLS) logo (figure 1), having unearthed many historical links, like the command pin. The pin has six stars on it representing the US Navy's six original frigates: *United States*, *Constellation*, *Constitution*, *Chesapeake*, *Congress*, and *President*. These frigates were approved by an Act of Congress on March 27, 1794, and built at a cost of $ 688,888.82, a pretty good price for six ships by today's standards. Those stars were a historical connection dating all the way back to the first commanding officers. Sad to say that I spent my whole command tour not knowing that, and not sure where I could have learned it other than by doing my own research. I should have known more naval history prior to my command tour. Those fortunate enough to have been given the opportunity and responsibility of command have a special commitment to those who have gone before us, including familiarizing ourselves with our navy's history, customs, and traditions. We must value what we guard and fully appreciate why we do so.

And so it was that we refreshed our collective memories as to many forgotten but still motivational customs and traditions in CLS. On a personal note, however, I never did understand why my navy, so steeped in heritage and history, would not have ensured the names of those six original ships still remain on active duty. Whether six ships or six hundred, surely those six names should remain in commission? I can only imagine the relative ease of the commanding officer to build unity on a ship whose name dates back to one of the originals, its wardroom resonating with memorabilia. We name ships for all kinds of reasons and obvious political purposes. We even name them for people who have contributed little to our navy, let alone having served in her. Underlining again the importance of inspiration, perhaps the new LCS class ships present an opportunity to reestablish all six back in service to their country. It should be done, and with much fanfare too.

We took a mission approach to the school, with the CNO's directives firmly in mind. Many more yellow stickers quickly resulted, we should have bought stock in them! The mission statement was agreed on, and when I say agreed, that is how it was with us. Early on, we took several personality tests, including the Myers-Briggs test; not sure if that's used today, but from my perspective, it was very interesting and explained why we had all been working so well together. The test explained why one thought seemed to be able to be addressed from many different approaches, yet after thorough discussion could be agreed to by all. We had already been working in close quarters for some time, but I don't recall any heated moments beyond the earlier "why me" discussion. The test basically places personas into four quadrants, depending on test responses. As it turned out, the four of us placed in different quadrants, each complementing the others. It certainly made a believer out of me as to the importance of knowing your people well and listening to understand rather than refute. The ability to see and discuss things from all angles was one of our great strengths.

As I mentioned, Admiral Boorda gave us four main themes. He wanted the course to be

- lean, hard hitting, intense;
- fleet relevant;
- navy-developed;
- leadership skills, *not program-focused*.

He desired the course to draw from and share leadership experiences. Two additional themes were added during the development:

- Ethics and core values throughout
- Integration of a senior leadership seminar

CHAPTER 2

THE WORK

Four months were spent going over the major points to be covered. We took the points and organized them into common themes. These became topics, and in turn units, which evolved into a natural flow progression. This we agreed would be additive or subtractive when it came time for the leader to lead his organization in a combat or crisis situation.

We likened it to Colonel Joshua L. Chamberlain leading the men of the Twentieth Maine at the battle of Gettysburg. Having earlier fought at Antietam and Fredericksburg, his brilliant charge saved the day at Little Round Top on the afternoon of July 2, 1863.

In the leadership course, we actually ended up playing that scene from the movie *Gettysburg* to illustrate the point that when eyes turn to you in anticipation of inspirational leadership and direction, that is not the time to fail to act. If you do, eyes will turn quickly to someone else. You will never regain your men's trust after that kind of failure. You must cross the line between fear and courage and act. That piece of wisdom became an important theme for the course. I will refer to that point throughout this book.

We would continue to revisit each topic over and over again in order to maintain a building foundation to the key points made in each individual topic. We would emphasize those points, or tie-ins, at the end and beginning of each individual topic, a focus on what should have been gained thus far, as a quick review prior to introducing the next additive leadership topic. All these to be added up into a kind of step-ladder, a building process for the student to understand all the variables involved in the relationship between the leader and those led. The ability of the leader to address these points in himself and those led would be key in minimizing fear, stress, and risk, but maximizing loyalty, confidence, and commitment.

For every topic, the key points in the course flow were outlined. We introduced the concept that there are really two main things the CO, or any leader for that matter, must deal with in his command or organization to get the bottom line accomplished, namely, dealing with people and dealing with the environment, the technical, political, or cultural issues.

First, we started by dividing the blackboard into two basic columns under the heading "Leadership" and began filling in our yellow sticker topic headings of those things we knew needed to be covered in the course. On the dealing with people side, we would talk about Title Ten responsibilities, breaking down the "law" and scrutinizing what needed to be covered.

Good examples are as follows:

- *Virtue*. We knew we needed to address values like integrity and their roles in ethical decision-making.

- *Patriotism*. We had to discuss the Constitution, love of country, naval heritage, and loyalty issues.

- *"Guard against and suppress all dissolute and immoral practices."* We had to look at the importance of setting the correct example, instilling discipline, etc.

- *"To take all measure to promote and safeguard the morale, physical well-being."* We needed to talk about developing subordinates, training, and safety.

Considering Title Ten, we came up with some "must" core topics:

- Responsibility, authority, and accountability
- Leader/manager
- Ethics and core values
- Personal vision
- Developing subordinates
- Safety
- Leadership in combat and crisis

Based on our maritime heritage of being prepared for battles at sea, this last topic became our bottom line statement.

Everything you do or don't do is either additive or subtractive toward how both you and those you lead perform in combat or crisis.

As it turned out, most of those were topics presented to the 0-6 working group. They were the first ones we worked on. The need to allow for self-evaluation was also recognized. We had to cover the leader's ability to understand and develop command relationships and to stress the required skill of clear communication. We would introduce the concept that everything you do or fail to do communicates a message to your command or organization. How your message gets communicated would be the outcome of your previously developed mission, vision, and goals. How you would communicate these leadership thoughts and the desired direction for your command or organization would be contained and outlined in your command philosophy. This philosophy would be how you intend to achieve your personal definition of a successful command or organization.

Included in the appendix A are the command philosophy and command goals that I used on the Callaghan. It is just a simple example, not anywhere near perfect, but it accomplished what I wanted to have my command become. We are all a product of those who have led us, and in Steve Woodall, I had the privilege of working for one of the finest examples of integrity and leadership. Steve was my XO on USS *Alywin* and went on to command USS *King* and USS *Mobile Bay*. He taught me a great deal, and much of what

I used in my command tour came from him. Particularly memorable on the Callaghan was being under his tactical command in a three-ship surface action group steaming in close formation and at flank speed in the Persian Gulf. He remains my very good friend and one of the best leaders I had in my thirty years in the navy.

Captain John Byers remains my best friend and mentor. He was my commanding officer on Spartanburg County (LST 1192), when I was the engineer. Because of his leadership example and integrity, I decided to stay in the navy and take the command exam. Without his inspirational leadership, I would have never been afforded the privilege to command Callaghan.

So as we proceeded through the topics, we tried hard to focus on the leader-led relationships and build the key points. We spent significant time at the end of each topic and at the beginning of each new topic going over the flow and key points, making an additive linear and logical connection into the next topic. Our constant challenge was to feed off one another as we covered all those criteria that historical combat studies indicated were either additive or negative for the leader and those he led in combat; all this building towards our Unit 8, which would be entitled "Leadership in Combat and Crisis." This last topic fell to me to write and teach. Along with my command tour and being one of the fathers of CLS, I consider it my most significant naval accomplishment.

In discussing the flow, we realized that what we were really developing was the idea covered early on in this book about the need to learn and develop the "how to think" leadership skill, as opposed to simply being told "what to think." The latter is the notion that if I needed to know something, somebody should tell me. That idea certainly does not conform to the "take all measures" introduced by "the law." There is a distinct relationship between responsibility, authority, and accountability that needs to be understood. Once you accept the responsibility, it is then a choice as to how you wield the required authority to execute your mission. Only then can and should you be held accountable; important to remember, however, that accountability can be either positive or negative.

Although you do not know how you will handle your responsibility, authority, and accountability until you actually take command, you can think through what these terms mean, their relationship to each other, and their impact on everything you do in command. It is important to put yourself through this thought process prior to assuming command, because how you interpret and put these terms into practice will define what kind of a commanding officer you will be on a daily basis. In thinking this through, consider your motivations for going to command, how you define a successful command tour, and how you intend to live up to your responsibilities for your command under the law. Once you have sorted this out, you are well on your way toward putting together your plan for your command tour.

> The ultimate confluence of responsibility, authority, and accountability is reached in the Commanding Officer of a ship at sea. (Admiral George W. Anderson Jr., USN)

"Command and authority are very closely intertwined. Command is the authority (the legal basis) of a person in the military to exercise control of subordinates through the chain of command. Authority, therefore, is the legitimate power of leaders to control and direct the subordinates under them and cause subordinates to react to their commands, if in fact those commands are within the scope of the leader's position.

Directly related to authority is responsibility. Naval officers receive certain responsibilities along with each assignment. Some responsibilities, such as discipline, morale, training, and troop well-being, are inherent in every job assigned. Others come from the authority bestowed on officers, petty officers, and noncommissioned officers alike. Responsibilities also originate from guidelines such as orders, regulations, directives, and manuals.

Commanders are accountable for their own actions and the actions of their personnel, and that accountability is based on the authority delegated and responsibility assigned to commanders as a result of their past performance, experiences, and judgment. Responsibility and authority increase with rank. In the Navy and the Marine Corps, they go hand in hand, and as an officer increases in rank, he must not lose sight of their importance, always remembering that he is 100 percent accountable for all of his actions 24 hours per day." (Montor, Karel, *Fundamentals of Naval Leadership*,)

While the main purpose of the book is to present the leadership in combat and crisis topic, as stated earlier, the whole course flow was designed to prepare both the leader and those he/she was to lead by covering/reviewing all the elements historically needed for success. It strikes me as very important to work these elements through the "wisdom block." As a visual example, I used the process below, the basic idea for which came from Steven Covey. The concept uses the theory behind the liberal arts curriculum, that exposing students to great thinkers and philosophers better prepares them for life, introduces them to values and ethics, and teaches them how to think. It allows them to develop a decision-making process that ensures decisions are made in the wisdom block vice the data block. I put a model together to reflect the process. I have seen this pyramid used for many things since, but here is how we displayed the "how to think idea":

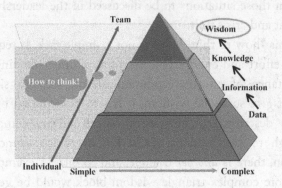

Decision Making

Essentially, you need to collect relevant data and compress it into useful information, then compress useful information into knowledge, then compress useful knowledge into wisdom and make decisions and act from within the wisdom block.

This concept holds for both the individual and team, whether for simple or complex problems, and is even more relevant today than when we introduced it in 1995. With the onslaught of high-tech computers, the ready availability of data is truly amazing, but that only increases the risk of making decisions in the data or information block vice the wisdom block. Of course getting to the wisdom block is even more difficult today due to the volume of data. Inevitably, therefore, making *every* decision in the wisdom block is not possible, so we introduced the concept that leaders need to be able to make decisions based on *less than perfect* information. We also introduced the concept of making decisions and managing risk as a critical leadership skill, as will be seen later in those situations to be discussed in the leadership in combat and crisis unit.

This "how to think" idea is not a simple task. It requires much effort and energy. It is essential to understanding the importance of effective communications, for you simply cannot *give* someone wisdom, it has to be acquired by the process described. You must work yourself and your command through to the wisdom block. For every issue/function/mission, there is *another* triangle, and so on. An example of the more complex triangle wisdom block would be getting you and all your command teams and command itself into your command philosophy wisdom block. In other words, getting all those left side of the equal sign variables correct in your personally defined successful command equation.

Yes, it takes a lot of effort and energy to achieve the concept of "take all measures."

We already introduced the idea that you could think of your command or organization as an equation.

$$A+B+C+X+Y+Z +? = \text{Successful Command}$$

If the right side of the equal sign is your definition of a successful command, then to the left of the equal sign are all the variables that must be assigned a value in order to balance the equation. CLS covered many of those variables to be considered in the two-week course. It was not about programs. It was to get all the variables considered first and the equation solved before any interaction with command elements started. Just time to think and reflect about your command and what you wanted it to be and accomplish. The CO needs to be worried about delivering up that which Col. Chamberlain brought to his organization, in short, *honor*.

I truly believe that because of the significant effort of four post-command officers, we delivered a two-week "how to think" course, which covered all leadership variables needed to deliver up honor, no matter how trying the circumstances.

Inevitably, some of the more important points became recurring themes throughout the course and were used on a continuous basis to make sure the building block design of the course remained evident and understood. Although certified as instructors, we really tried to be facilitators, but facilitators in a "how to think" versus a typical navy "what to think" school.

We spoke to many professors and all indicated that if the learning comes from the student then it will remain and be used. So we designed the course to get the students themselves to reveal the points, and we made sure they were additive from the beginning to the end by continuously building situations and case studies that emphasized them. Of course we were walking a fine line, given that all the "students" were leaders by definition, already placed in positions of great responsibility. So we made sure to "sit in their seats" too, for some had already seen combat, and we needed to be seen to be able to identify with them firsthand and not talk down to them.

In the end, we can *all* be better leaders. *Our* challenge was to facilitate discussions in a linear and logical manner, designed to make sure they would have the opportunity to think about themselves in leadership positions in their command, so they'd be able to say, by their own definition, that their command tour was successful. It was to give them the time to define what a successful tour and command would look like and all the things that they would need to address and consider to assure their vision was achieved. We introduced Title Ten and stressed if it is the report card, how will you get an "A"? What does an organization like that look like, and how will you achieve it? This was a daunting task, made easier however by our school that broke it down into its component parts, all contributing to the next one, presented in a manner that would allow each leader to formulate his/her own pattern of behavior and leadership motivational style, while providing purpose, direction and motivation to those led. It was a most worthwhile two weeks out of their training pipeline.

So we took all the input available to us: a dedicated 0-6 working group, a flag review board, and our own staff; and we developed the course. We were very fortunate to have the administrative help of a thoroughly professional company called AmerInd. They shouldered much of the course administration burden, and we could not have brought the course online without their effort.

We even designed the building from the ground up, using the concept of an adult learning facility provided to us by those knowledgeable in successful methods for teaching adults. Numerous professors were consulted, and much of the credit for the building and design of the schoolhouse physical infrastructure goes to the first director of the school, my good friend, Capt. John Meyer. In addition, we received tremendous support for everything we wanted to do from building construction, classroom design, furniture and computer selection to initial school standup from our reporting senior and mentor, the commanding officer of NETC, Newport, RI, Capt. R. K. Farrell. The Leadership School could not have been brought online without his outstanding support. Every detail was managed to be additive, but everything needed to be done for the first time. As I mentioned, we even designed the school logo, consisting of an old-style anchor we chose from an outdated version of the blue jackets manual, a commissioning pennant, the school banner, and the "at sea and ashore" warfare pins.

We created an adult learning environment supported by an interactive computer-based system. It was quite simply the most technically supported, navy-written and facilitated, adult learning course ever produced in our navy. One of the requirements Admiral Boorda placed on his flag officers was that a flag guest speaker would be required for every class. A significant and additive support requirement for the school. Capt Barnett, one of the later CLS instructors, would capture the flag's remarks and distribute them to the class. I must still have forty or so, and having reviewed them all prior to writing this book, their collective points covered the many aspects of the course. Again, a logical and cohesive command leadership course written by officers who had successfully completed their command tours. It's exactly what Adm. Boorda wanted, and it's what he got.

As you proceed through the book, I will be presenting a look at how the original course was developed and will be sharing eight out of the thirty-five total topics in the eight units of that course. These topics are the ones I consider the core lessons of the school. Of course, converting a verbal lesson plan to a book presentation inevitably necessitated a number of changes, but I am confident these adaptations faithfully still convey how they were originally written and taught in the school.

CHAPTER 3

THE BRIEF

Here is the brief we developed and I presented in April 1995 to Admiral Boorda and his executive board, five months after we had started our brainstorming.

Good afternoon Adm. Boorda and members of the executive board. As a result of the December meeting, I am here to provide a briefing on the command leadership course. During this briefing I will describe the command leadership course, its development, content and flow, and provide insight as to some of the benefits this course will have for prospective commanding officers.

All of the instructors are post-command officers. Capt. Meyer, CDR's Krull, Purcell and I stood the staff up in December. Capt. Barnett joined the staff last week.

COURSE SPECIFICS

We expect officers from all designations including reserves. For the aviation community, PXO's will attend the course. The course will be presented in renovated classrooms at NETC, Newport. A library, auditorium, and staff admin offices round out our facilities.

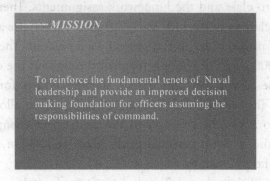

——— MISSION

To reinforce the fundamental tenets of Naval leadership and provide an improved decision making foundation for officers assuming the responsibilities of command.

The course mission statement captures what we feel are the benefits to the students and the Navy, that is to reinforce ethics, core values and individual leadership traits, as well as developing a stronger command decision foundation.

COURSE DEVELOPMENT THEMES

Lean, Hard-hitting, intense

Fleet relevant, Navy-developed

Leadership skills—not program focused

Draw from and share leadership experience

Ethics and core values throughout

Senior leadership Seminar (SLS) and Total Quality Leadership integrated

We believe the course structure, content and challenging requirements will better prepare the PCO's for command. One of the keys will be the individual effort each PCO puts into class and the homework assignments. There will be full classroom days (0730-1730) that will require a good deal of preparation on the part of each student. There are over 1000 pages of reading assigned throughout the course that the instructors will use as starting points for each lesson. The written assignments are designed to allow the PCO to apply the concepts of the course, put thought to paper and develop personal goals, plans and vision, and a command philosophy.

In addition, there will be a capstone case study near the end of the course assigned as a group project and designed to permit the PCO's to tie together all the significant learning points of the course. We will encourage open and honest discussions in the class as we draw on each PCO's experience and ideas to foster as much interaction as possible. The mixture of different designators in a seminar environment with a good deal of facilitated discussion and case study work should provide the appropriate environment to air ideas, issues and concerns. We want the PCO's to test their ideas on how they intend to approach their command tours.

We will draw on a wealth of research conducted on leadership, beefed up with military examples to foster fleet—relevant discussions that apply directly to their command tour. Theory will meet reality, as each PCO will be challenged to think hard about leadership and how they will develop and perpetuate successful organizations committed to mission effectiveness and continuous improvement.

COURSE FLOW DIAGRAM

This diagram shows the course framework and indicates the key elements and topic tie-in points that build on one another. It clearly illustrates how dynamic and effective leadership from the commanding officer and chain of command, along with a commitment to total quality and continuous improvement can promote a positive command climate and significantly enhance mission effectiveness by minimizing fear, stress, and risk while maximizing loyalty, confidence and commitment to meet the challenge of a combat or crisis situation.

SLS INTEGRATION

Once this flow was developed, we realized that the SLS curriculum needed restructuring to provide fleet relevance if we were to obtain commitment to total quality and continuous improvement, vice compliance to what many perceived as just another program. Working with the Cinclantflt and Cincpacflt TQL officers we were able to meet the objectives of this plan. Ultimately, we expect the goals of this plan will be achieved in the Fleet.

COURSE TOPIC OUTLINE

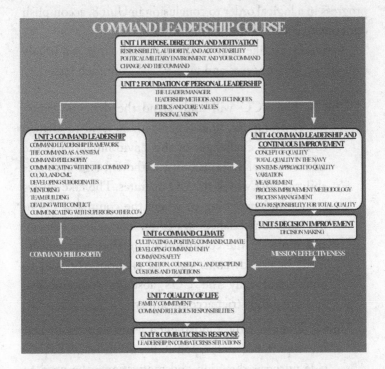

This course topic flow presents the combination of the flow diagram and individual Unit topics. The course is designed on a building block approach to illustrate how effective leadership can be applied to all facets of a command. Individual topic themes do not necessarily come to closure at the completion of the lesson. For example, the fundamental tenets of naval leadership are revisited over and over as continuous themes throughout the course. The insertion of the lesson topics into the course flow allows the course to progress in a logical order to conclusion in Unit 8, accomplish our course objectives and fulfill our mission.

I would now like to walk through each Unit and briefly explain the key concepts and take-aways from each lesson.

Unit 1. The PCO will understand the dynamic external environment, how organizations need to change to meet the challenges of this environment, and the framework of responsibility, authority, and accountability under which the CO operates. The take-aways are an understanding of where the command fits in the various published strategies, methods to educate and motivate the command to mission accomplishment in this dynamic external environment, and to understand fully the CO's absolute responsibility, authority and strict accountability.

Unit 2. Examines the fundamental leadership tenets and the importance and responsibility of the leader to provide purpose, direction and motivation—the need to evaluate individual leadership styles, and their application to a leadership model. This Unit is the foundation for the rest of the course. The take-aways are a deeper understanding of the individual's strengths and weaknesses, an examination of leadership styles, how ethics and core values are an integral part of leadership, and the development of personal goals, plans and vision.

Unit 3. Translates a personal leadership style into the command, and integrates leadership concepts. The take-aways are the formulation of a command philosophy, and methods to improve command relationships and communications up and down the chain of command. This Unit also serves as a bridge to Unit 4.

Unit 4. Introduces the quality philosophy—continuous improvement methods and goals of TQ, with emphasis on leadership responsibilities. The take-aways are an understanding of the benefits of TQ and continuous improvement to mission effectiveness.

Unit 5. Focuses on command-level decision-making and lays the groundwork for making decisions that involve risk sometimes based on less than perfect information as occurs in a combat or crisis situation. This kind of decision-making will be further discussed in Unit 8.

Unit 6. Deals with putting the command philosophy into practice, and the key factors in promoting a positive command climate, such as equal opportunity and the smooth integration of women into the command. The take-aways are the impact of command climate on mission effectiveness, how standards impact command climate—and how actions speak louder than words.

Unit 7. Deals with the external quality of life issues affecting command climate and readiness. The take-aways are the impact on command climate and an understanding of the CO's leadership responsibilities with respect to quality of life.

Unit 8. Deals with the CO and unit response to combat or crisis, factors affecting decision—making, stress, fear, risk assessment, fog of war, the impact of training, trust, confidence, loyalty, courage, and camaraderie on combat or crisis response. This Unit is the sum of all previous units. The take-aways are the tools to prepare the CO and his people to optimize command response and to act decisively.

DEALING WITH ISSUES
Take on all issues (for example)

- Careerism
- No mistakes mentality
- Ethical dilemmas

These are just a few of the many issues we expect will be brought up and discussed openly in this course. The discussion of these kinds of issues will be of significant benefit to the students and we will be prepared to deal head on with them and others as they arise.

I turned off the projector and answered questions. The course was approved.

The two slides below were added to the Adm. Boorda brief and then used for the course introduction in the auditorium on the first day of the school.

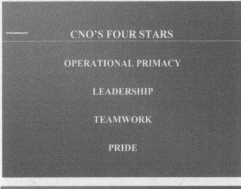

CNO'S FOUR STARS

OPERATIONAL PRIMACY

LEADERSHIP

TEAMWORK

PRIDE

LEADERSHIP CONTINUUM THEMES

VALUES

RESPONSIBILITY, AUTHORITY, AND ACCOUNTABILITY OF LEADERSHIP

UNITY OF COMMAND, NAVY, AND SERVICES

CONTINUOUS IMPROVEMENT

CHAPTER 4

THE COURSE

The CLS classroom was computerized with the newest Dell computers. All the topic study guides, outlines, and readings were available on the computer. In addition, in the desks were the school leadership books considered a must read during the two-week course. We started each new course in our auditorium, where we provided the introduction brief, which was basically the same brief given to Admiral Boorda with the two slides now added. We would go over some admin things, expectations, and so on. We laid out some simple ground rules:

Classroom Ground Rules

1. Full participation.

2. Speak openly, one person at a time.

3. Give and take honest, constructive feedback.

4. Respect ideas and opinions.

5. Share confidential, anonymous experiences.

6. Complete assigned homework.

7. Avoid side discussions.

8. Start on time.

9. Stay on track.

10. Attack issues, not people.

We tried very hard from the outset of the course to dispel any notions that we were there to make them leaders, for they were already leaders. We simply said the navy is affording you two weeks to just think about your command/organization, in a structured manner, allowing you, through discussion and readings, to think about how you will fulfill your responsibilities of command.

We then played General Douglas Macarthur's speech given to the corps of cadets at West Point on May 12, 1962. I was fortunate to be able to convince West Point that the tape would be used for leadership purposes. To hear the general deliver the speech (appendix B) was a motivating and inspiring opportunity. I can't remember how many times I have heard it, but it never fails to stir emotions and inspire. The speech was then followed by remarks by Admiral Arleigh Burke back in 1959, but never more relevant than today. In my opinion, they provided the real charter and mandate for our leadership school. We always opened and closed the school with remarks by Admiral Burke. I will do so with this book as well.

COMMAND LEADERSHIP SCHOOL

The Naval profession becomes more complex with each passing year. New scientific discoveries lead to the development of new weapons systems, which in turn give navies new capabilities. These, in turn, introduce the need for new tactics at sea, and new strategic concepts in the employment of naval forces.

Thus naval officers must always remain flexible in their thinking, readily adaptable to change, and imaginative in the application of new developments to the strengthening of naval capabilities.

There is one element in the profession of arms, however, that transcends all others in importance. This is the human element. No matter what the weapons of the future may be, no matter how they are to be employed in war or international diplomacy, *man* will still be the most important factor in naval operations.

The need for good leadership, therefore, is the constant factor, and in this lies the officer's greatest opportunity for service to his country and to the cause of freedom throughout the world.

As leaders, naval officers are the example to whom others look for guidance, for inspiration, and for a standard upon which to base their own conduct and beliefs.

The bedrock of our national power is the moral strength of our people, the character of our nation, and the ethical values of Americans wherever they may be.

In the eyes of the world, wherever the naval officer may go—indeed in the eyes of his own countrymen as well—the officer represents the finest in the manhood of our great nation.

The badge of naval rank and the insignia of the officer's commission will identify him everywhere with the power of the United States—not only the physical power of military forces, but more importantly the moral power of free men.

This is why it is so important that under great pressure of our continuing need to develop the finest aircraft, the most modern submarines, the most far-ranging carries, and the whole complex of nuclear weapons, we keep uppermost in mind that *leadership* remains our most important task.

No matter what mark an officer may leave in history by his deeds in battle, or in intellectual contributions, or in material inventions, his greatest legacy to his country will be the example he has given as a man and as a leader of men.

Arleigh Burke
Admiral, US Navy
Chief of Naval Operations
Washington, DC
2 January 1959

I think it important at this point to provide those major learning points for each unit and topics as I proceed through the course flow. It will mean more to the reader as the book evolves and as these points are brought up and illustrated. Again, every point represents a distinct data variable, adding them up provides the leadership equation illustrated earlier.

$$A+B+C+X+Y+Z +? = \text{Successful Command}$$

I have outlined how we formed the units. Now let me go over some of the major learning points of the topics that comprise them, as indicated in the course topic outline.

Unit 1

Entitled "Purpose, Direction, and Motivation," we came to those three words by brainstorming the definition of leadership as defined back then by the Fleet Naval Manual. It states:

> "Leadership is that quality inherent or acquired in a person which enables them to achieve accomplishment from their subordinates by virtue of their willingness rather than by force or mere compliance."

The quote gets to the heart of inspirational leadership by example that achieves commitment compared to compliance. It promotes the idea that a leader's main responsibility is to provide purpose, direction, and motivation on a daily basis. Each instructor was assigned students to work with throughout the course as a kind of mentor. A specific mentoring session was held halfway through unit 3. I would take the flow of the course and walk through where we were and emphasize the more important points.

It's *not* about you!

Understanding the triad of responsibility, authority, and accountability, under Title Ten, your leadership responsibility is to provide purpose, direction, and motivation.

Leaders need to understand their environment, political situation, and national interest in the mission. You must be able to explain the reason *why* to your people. Why are you fighting? What part is your organization playing in the big scheme of things?

You have to grasp the impact of change on your organization, the fact that by your taking it over, the organization is necessarily undergoing change. You therefore have a responsibility to develop a plan to both lead and shorten the transition period of that change. In short, you have to be both a transformational and a transactional leader.

Let's look at these roles more closely.

Transactional leadership. This is defined as leadership that maintains status quo but involves an exchange process, whereby followers get immediate, tangible rewards for carrying out the leader's orders.

Transformational leadership. Change, innovation, and long-range improvement; defined as a leadership process that is purposeful and visionary, involving an organized search for changes, analysis, and the capacity to move resources from areas of lesser to greater productivity.

Unit 2

This points out the importance of striking a balance between the leader and manager organizational command functions, recognizing that different leadership styles applied in different situations can develop subordinates more effectively.

Situations usually indicate when you should be directive or when you can delegate. You have to bear in mind the importance of matching the strength of the individual to the task, based on the risk involved if the task is completed unsatisfactorily. Thus a review of all aspects of assignment of people to tasks should be undertaken. Again, the leader-led situation and communication discussion, the importance of building bidirectional trust through a character, value-based leadership style, driving home the importance of understanding *yourself*. This is a significant and key mental drill providing an introspective look. It entails the critical leadership thought sequence below: It all starts with your personal vision.

Personal vision
Personal philosophy
Personal goals
Command vision
Command philosophy
Command goals
Command unity and success

By the time the student finishes unit 2, responsibilities in command should have been revisited, stressing the importance of fulfilling them to their country, organizational service branch, and command. They should have reviewed their own leadership style and traits, personal values, strengths, and weaknesses—likewise, their pattern of behavior and their personal vision and goals for themselves and command. This then transitions to command philosophy development.

At that point, it was a requirement of the school to write a command vision, plus a command philosophy. Provided in appendix C is the best vision statement I received. Also provided for reference in appendix A, is the command philosophy and goals I used on USS *Callaghan* (DDG -994). Had I attended the CLS, mine would have been much better.

We would continue to build the awareness of variables on the left side of the command leadership equation that need to be addressed and correctly executed day in and day out.

Next, we introduced the navy command excellence study, carried out to contrast the difference between superior and average units. The study compared twenty-one operational units (twelve rated superior, nine average) from three warfare communities (air, surface, and submarine) in both the Atlantic and Pacific fleets. Research teams, composed of navy and civilian consultants, spent four to five days at each command, observing and interviewing. They were told which commands were superior and average only after the survey was complete. Twelve themes were discovered in interviews with COs. Personal characteristics or behaviors differentiated those COs of superior commands from those running average commands. Average COs exhibited most of the twelve themes, but not consistently. Superior COs did all these things daily, with both completeness and consistency.

The twelve themes are the following:

Targets key issues
Gets a crew to support command's philosophy
Develops XO
Staffs to optimize performance
Gets out and about
Builds esprit de corps
Remains calm
Develops a strong wardroom
Values chief's quarters
Ensures training is effective
Builds positive external relationships
Influences successfully

While this list may seem simple, the work is in the "how" you will completely accomplish it. Again, time is well spent *anticipating* just how to manage the list adequately prior to actually assuming the command or organizational responsibility. Why? Because the listed items will be assessed and a message communicated by your actions or lack thereof, regardless of whether you have thought about it or not.

The study went on to outline three competencies of leadership.

1. *Diagnosis.* The mental competency to understand the situation and world around you; is a cognitive ability. Being able to identify where you are, where your peo-

ple are, and seeing where you want to go are the first steps of leadership.

2. *Adaptation* is a behavioral competency. Modifying your behavior and adapting to your environment and resources are essential to deciding whether to alter the present state.

3. *Communication* is a process competency.

The study also elaborated that superior leaders develop their subordinates and provided five steps common to successfully training high performers. Although I always liked the five steps, one has to be cautious about a possibly facile categorization into numbers—e.g. five steps, six habits, four traits, etc.—but this one really works. Yes, it sounds easy, but it's difficult to execute, especially the intelligent risk issue, which assumes that the leader is competent enough in his/her abilities to step in and preempt a failure.

Here they are:

1. Tell them what you want them to do.

2. Show them what you want them to do, as they need to see what good performance looks like.

3. Let them try. This involves "intelligent risk" by the leader, that of not turning over too much responsibility too soon.

4. Observe and rate performance, a step often overlooked. They need constructive feedback

5. Manage the consequences: positive (praise), negative (punishment), neutral (no response).

We have talked about the flow of the course and how it led to insertion of various topics into the course outline as shown in figure 2. The mentoring session above followed unit 2, leading to unit 3.

Unit 3

The various topics in this unit were designed to take the purpose, direction, and motivation from unit 1 and combine the insights gained from building unit 2's foundation of leadership and applying command leadership. I will discuss later the command leadership framework we introduced that allows a systems approach to a successful organization.

We allowed the time and provided most elements needed at this point to write a typical leader's command philosophy. The importance of adequate communication was discussed, as was the need to listen with a view to understanding rather than to refute. The discussion of relationships between the key people in any organization in a command case study centered on the CO/XO/CMC triad. We indicated developing subordinates is key. The significance of mentoring those who might one day fulfill the responsibilities of your current position was stressed. How to build teams and deal with conflict within those teams was thoroughly aired, as was how best to communicate with one's superiors.

To reiterate, in unit 3, we take the leader's individual skills and traits discussed in unit 2 to the command itself. Unit 3 then leads to what your actual command philosophy is, hopefully what you desired to happen as written in the course. For the interaction and application of those topics and relationships in unit 3 is in fact the reality of your actions, decisions, and example, in turn the essence of your true philosophy.

Unit 4

Unit 4 develops the relationship between command leadership and continuous improvement, the driver being that the totality of quality definitely improves decision-making. Understanding variation and quality in daily work are true process improvement and mission effectiveness multipliers. I will discuss this in the command leadership framework, which was our attempt to make TQ a tool in the military, which, if applied correctly, should add greatly to mission effectiveness. I'd like to believe it is still being applied in our navy today. Just the simple idea of first describing and then taking the "dumb" out of any of our processes surely remains beneficial.

Unit 5

Focuses on command level decision-making and lays the groundwork for making decisions that involve risk and are based on less than perfect information as occurs in a combat or crisis situation. This unit discusses decision-making and its contribution to mission effectiveness. Discusses how your application of the leadership framework can improve decision-making and result in an improved command mission effectiveness.

Units 6, 7, and 8

Both sides of the leadership course topic outline come together into unit 6, the establishment of your command climate. It is here that the concept of command unity is discussed, the importance of celebrating unity, not diversity. The thrust is that through your inspirational leadership example, you can build unity, which in turn relegates personal bias to a position of secondary importance.

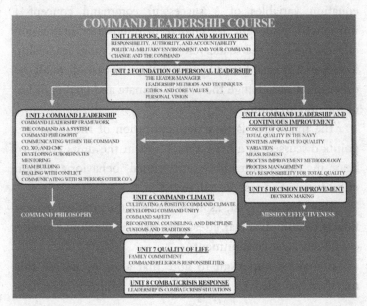

The direct result of correctly building teams and camaraderie leads to the introduction of the critical concept stressed in unit 8, namely that *the actions of each of us affects the lives of all us.*

Also discussed is the relationship between recognition, counseling, and discipline. The importance is underlined as to understanding and providing linkage to customs and traditions, lest we become guardians not valuing what it is we guard.

As you can see by the arrows connecting the units, we tried to make the point that all the units become interactive. Thus a change in any of the topic variables, much like the equation variables of a successful command concept I introduced, could effect a change in philosophy or mission effectiveness. If the leader changes his personal leadership foundation as established by unit 2, this will cascade to all the other units and change the overall climate and quality of life of the organization.

The main idea is that the application of the ideas and points discussed in all the topics and in the units come to bear in the command/organizational behavior, mission effectiveness and response in unit 8.

The ultimate goal, as indicated in the original course flow, is to minimize fear, stress, and risk, yet maximize loyalty, confidence, and commitment.

It may be important to note that after we put all this together, we tried to outline what our ultimate objectives were for the course, so they are listed here for review. I would propose that any course that could achieve such demanding objectives in two weeks, plus achieve it in the wisdom block, would have been a useful course to attend.

CLS TERMINAL OBJECTIVES

1. Describe the impact of US policy on a command.

2. Describe the necessity for leading change and the effect of leadership on the adoption of change.

3. Explain the responsibility, authority, and accountability of a CO to maintain mission effectiveness.

4. Explain the relationship of leadership, ethics, and core values to command effectiveness.

5. Describe the methods a CO uses to implement vision, goals, plans, and philosophy and the contributions of these elements to mission effectiveness.

6. Describe systems theory and its impact on mission effectiveness.

7. Describe the methods a CO employs to maintain mission effectiveness through the effective use of personnel and teams.

8. Describe communication and its impact on mission effectiveness.

9. Explain TQL and its impact on mission effectiveness.

10. Describe command climate and it impact on mission effectiveness.

11. Describe leadership responsibilities for managing personnel diversity and equal opportunity to enhance command readiness.

12. Describe quality of life and its impact on mission effectiveness.

13. Discuss leadership perspective in the combat and crisis environment, to include the effects of fear, stress, and risk management.

From this point on, I will be presenting the core topics from the old CLS. My main purpose is to convey as many key points and themes that become significantly important multipliers when it comes time for the leader to lead his organization in a crisis or combat situation. They should apply to any situation where the risk is great for him/herself and his/her people.

I have previously covered the four key elements: leader-led-situation-communication. The relationship between these factors is critical. My intention is to present eight topics that I consider most critical to the development of the relationship of these four main factors. As mentioned earlier, converting a verbal lesson to a book necessitated numerous changes and new effort, but I believe the theme and message of the original topics remain intact. They are:

Unit 1: 1.2 Navy's role in support of National Security Strategy

Unit 2: 2.3 Ethics and Core Values
2.4 Personal Vision

Unit 3: 3.1 Command Leadership Framework
3.6 Developing Subordinates
3.8 Communicating with superiors and other COs

Unit 6: 6.3 Command Safety

Unit 8: 8.1 Leadership in Combat/Crisis Situations

The first three topics presented are basic tenants for the individual leader.

The application of the framework covered in 3.1:

- Allows an overview of planning from the beginning of your assumption of leadership responsibility.

- Facilitates a way to communicate your plan and incorporate your vision into action.

- Aids in getting your people quickly on board and aligned with your direction.

- Provides an assessment tool, a way to track and measure your progress toward achieving your defined successful command.

You simply must have a measurable plan, and you need to know if you are "getting there."

Command Safety drives to the heart of preparing for specific situations to be discussed when I present the last topic, "Leadership in Combat/Crisis Situations." Understanding today the difference between doing things safely and merely undertaking risk avoidance, remains as important as ever, so the topic focuses directly on the key question: "what have you prepared your subordinates to DO"?

Six of the eight topics are based on original verbal topics, which were written and facilitated by me. The communicating with superiors and other COs was based on a topic written and taught by my good friend Captain John Meyer, who is an assistant dean of leadership at the Naval War College. The other topic, Personal Vision, was a favorite of mine and was written and taught by Capt. Mark Purcell. Most of the Total Quality topics and critical TQ teaching points were written and taught by Captain Roger Krull, who has the knack of taking something difficult and making it easy to understand.

I have tried to provide the major points from all Units and topics. My selected eight topics for this book should provide an opportunity for the reader to reflect on their leadership foundation prior to proceeding to chapter 12.

This book is not about me. It has nothing to do with my career. It is about what was created based on exhaustive leadership research and the added feedback of over six hundred command bound officers during my assignment at the Command Leadership

School. It remains my strongest *vision* that the fundamental leadership tenets embedded in the lesson topics presented in this book become incorporated at every teaching level in every organization and institution throughout the country.

While the book is about a school designed for naval officers about to go to their first command tour, it is not much of a stretch to apply the same leadership time-honored principles put forth to *any* organization, whether military or civilian. As naval officers, we have been asked to adopt the ideas of many civilian-written leadership books into our military principles, and at the end of the day, leadership is leadership. I would hope that the civilian community can do the same. After all, it is still all about getting things done as efficiently and effectively as possible with and through people. The better the leader, the better that is done, and the more successful the company will be. It is about the leader providing purpose, direction, and motivation on a daily basis. Based on the study of history, much of what needs to be considered and done to accomplish this is discussed in this book. How you apply this "how to think" wisdom is up to you.

Strong leadership remains the key to the continued success of our military and this great country. As presented in the old CLS lesson topics:

Leaders must understand the world environment in which they operate. They must be able to answer the question "why?" You can't expect ethical decision-making without first instilling traditional Judeo-Christian values. To build an organization, you must first have created a mental vision and designed a physical plan to achieve it. You cannot expect good followership without leading and developing your subordinates. Perhaps true safety lies in long intense realistic training. Inspirational leadership maximizes loyalty, confidence, and commitment, while minimizing fear, stress, and risk. It's what allows both the leader and those led to cross the line between fear and courage.

I urge leaders everywhere to take these lesson topics to heart and become both a transactional and transformational leader. *Start today! Teach them today! It's important, and it's needed!*

CHAPTER 5

1.2 NAVY'S ROLE IN SUPPORT OF THE NATIONAL SECURITY STRATEGY

In this course we will talk a lot about you as the leader, those that you will lead, situations that you will find yourself in, and types of communications that could be used in these situations. In addition, we will specifically look at the fact that leaders in the military world, as in its civilian counterpart, are responsible for many things. There are, however, some significant differences, and we will discuss those in depth. We will look at the commanding officer's responsibility to provide subordinates these three main things: purpose, direction, and motivation. In the next two hours, we will talk a little about the first of these responsibilities: *to provide purpose.*

Much research on our part has encouraged us to incorporate numerous leadership studies and historical data. Perhaps the best reason for the need to do this can be illustrated by this quote from the former Secretary of the Army, Gen. J. A. Wicham:

If we ignore the historical importance of our profession, the society from which it comes and why it is worth preserving, we run the risk of the guardians not valuing what they guard." (General John A.Wicham, Chief of Staff, Army)

The army's military leadership manual FM 22-100 *(we used the army's manual because work on the navy's was underway, but not ready for use at that time)* includes the following especially relevant statements:

- The geopolitical and social realities of the modern world often obscure the reason for following a particular course of action to achieve national goals.

- Leaders ensure they and their soldiers (sailors too!) clearly understand why their nation is engaged in a particular course of action and how it is essential for protecting America's vital national interests.

Other than in a war environment, these pointers can be emotional and hard for your command to understand. Conversely, a sense of purpose and unity is fairly easy to achieve in a world war environment. An example not easily understood was being unable to pick up Cuban refugees in peril on the high seas. Take a minute to name some such naval operations in '94 or '95.

(At this point, I put a deployment chart up and briefly indicated the various missions we were currently involved in worldwide. For each of these operations, there were specific justifications tied into

national interests that called for our military presence. This led to a discussion as to why is it important for a commanding officer to understand the geopolitical and social realities of the modern world.)

Army studies and the navy's unfinished Persian Gulf study, which we will discuss in unit 8 determined that when soldiers/sailors understand why American forces have been committed, they follow their leaders and risk their lives to accomplish the mission, despite all odds. It is this important concept of *unity of purpose* that we are introducing here and will expand on as we proceed through the course.

These studies go on to reveal that American fighting men and women do best when they know why they are doing something. As leaders in the military, if your people are to give their lives for their country, would you agree that you owe it to them to be able to answer the question *why?*

Navy regulations require that prior going into battle you must tell your subordinates your plans. Why not tell them why as well? You will see examples of this in a later topic.

If you agree that you should be able to tell them why, where or how, can you find the necessary information and what will you say? You need to have thought about that ahead of time.

World Security Overview

- Appreciate how the world has changed
- Understand regional substantive issues
- Armed forces' role to promote stability and thwart aggression

- Strategy is driven by environmental change
- Understand your threat environment
- Mission readiness in today's multipolar regional power-center environment

From a leadership and tactical standpoint, we hope you agree that it's important to understand your operating environment, the basis for what we do in the military, and why we do it. With that said, understanding the environment today in terms of where or what our next military commitment will be is not easy. Together, we will review and get you up to speed on the above points of discussion.

World Security Overview: The Navy's role in support of national security strategy.

- Geopolitical context
- Current deployment situations
- Issues of concern
- Trouble spots
- Regional review

Pacific/Far East
Europe, Africa
SWA/Middle East
Latin America

Conclusion
Impact on US military
Impact on your command

I will provide an unclassified broad-brush national security strategy overview, which should cover the above slide topics.

We'll start with a look at the world from a geopolitical perspective. Let's quickly tie in your readings last night. I hope most of you were able to absorb the required readings for this lesson. If not please do so within this first week so you can bring yourself up to date. *(Appendix E contains all required readings for presented lesson topics).*

The National Security Strategy, February 95.

The version you have is a still a rough draft. It is important that you are aware of how our doctrine reflects the current administration's interpretation of the American people's concerns and expectations. If you have never seen these documents before, you need to review each one, and understand the significant role that this concept of "national interests" plays in determining what we in the military do, how we do it, where we do it, and the resources we have at our disposal.

We will discuss this briefly and some key points and issues of concern as we look at some potential trouble spots. As background, we will take a trip around the world looking at some regional CINC issues, and I'll provide an unclassified force deployment overview. At the end, you should have a good understanding of the impact the world environment has on both the military and on your command.

Let's start by quickly reviewing info sheet 1-1-1. This contains some basic information on how everything flows from the interpretation of what the administration believes is our national interests, from national policy to the employment of forces:

a. *National policy.* This is established jointly by the legislative and executive branches of government. National policy is the foundation and source upon which a supporting structure of strategy, doctrine, and tactics is built.

b. *Strategy.* The art and science of developing and using political, economic, psychological, and military forces as necessary during peace and war to afford the maximum support to policies, in order to increase probabilities and favorable consequences of victory, and lessen the chances of defeat. Strategy is a large-scale concept of how to best achieve theater and/or national objectives. (Reference joint pub. 1-02, page 364).

c. *National security strategy (NSS).* Announces the president's strategy in support of national policy objectives.

d. *National military strategy (NMS).* Furnishes the advice of the Chairman of the Joint Chiefs of Staff (CJCS) to the president, National Security Council (NSC), and the secretary of defense on national military strategy and fiscally constrained force structure required to support attainment of national security objectives (reference AFSC, 1993, pp. 5–8, and Powell, 1992). Doctrine and tactics support national military strategy.

e. *Naval doctrine.* Forms a bridge between the naval components of our nation's NMS and our tactics, techniques, and procedures. Doctrine guides our actions toward well-defined goals and provides the basis for mutual understanding within and between services and our national policy makers. Situational demands influence doctrine and determine proper force composition.

f. *Doctrine.* Fundamental principles by which military forces or elements thereof guide their actions in support of national objectives. Doctrine defines the requirements for all the elements of war (such as people, training, equipment, platforms) to execute tactics. Doctrine is the means by which we want to achieve missions that support a strategic goal or objective. Doctrine is the heart of naval warfare. It governs actions beyond the ordered execution of military options, but is not prescriptive. It is not a set of concrete rules, but rather a basis of common understanding throughout the chain of command.

g. *Tactics.* The employment of units in combat or the orderly arrangement and maneuver of units in relation to each other and/or to the enemy in order to use their full potential. Tactics are the specific techniques and procedures used in employing forces to optimize the chances of successfully accomplishing an assigned mission.

From the commander-in-chief to the combatant commander:

a. *National command authority (NCA)*. Supports the military aspect of national policy through the assignment of military forces. The organization for national security includes the president (as commander-in-chief) and secretary of defense. Actions have been historically limited to the assignment of military forces, the approval of operational plans and/or recommended courses of action, and the decision to execute.

b. *The Joint Chiefs of Staff*. Act as the principal advisor to the NCA and relay NCA direction to the unified/combatant commanders (reference AFSC, 1993, pages 2-2 through 2-16).

c. *Unified/Combatant Command*. A command having broad continuing missions and is composed of forces from two or more military departments (reference AFSC, 1993, page 2–19). Unified/combatant commanders employ forces in support of assigned multinational and national operations. Responsibilities are based on geographical area/region or on function. Example of a unified/combatant command structure:

1) USACOM (United States Atlantic command) whose service components are the following:

   a) US Atlantic fleet
   b) Forces command
   c) Air combat command
   d) Marine forces Atlantic

d. *Navy roles.* The navy has five fundamental roles in support of the national security strategy—projection of power from the sea to land, sea control and maritime supremacy, strategic deterrence, strategic sealift, forward naval presence (reference Dalton 1994, page 49).

Warfare Types

a. *Attrition.* Seeks victory though the cumulative destruction of the enemy's material assets by superior firepower technology.

b. *Maneuver.* Seeks victory by circumventing a problem and attacking it from a position of advantage rather than meeting it straight on.

Command mission. Task or tasks assigned to a command by a superior. Examples are as follows:

a. *Surface combatant.* Escort a specific US flagged tanker (e.g., Exxon Monmouth) from Straits of Hormuz to Kuwait.

b. *Fighter squadron.* Maintain a barcap (barrier combat air patrol) station sixty miles east of Kuwait City to prevent incursion along threat axis

Role. Broad and enduring purpose(s) of a particular unit or type of unit. Examples are the following:

a. *Surface combatant.* Provide forward presence, sea control, and fleet defense in the Persian Gulf.

b. *Fighter squadron.* Provide fleet air defense, strike escort, and tactical reconnaissance in the Persian Gulf.

Function. Specific responsibilities assigned to a command to enable the command to fulfill its established role or roles. Examples are the following:

a. *Surface combatant.* Protect against air attack and fast patrol boat attacks in the Persian Gulf.

b. *Fighter squadron.* Protect neutral and US shipping against air attack in the Persian Gulf.

NSS/NMS/NCA/CINCS/Doctrine/Tactics, etc. This is also the order in which we will discuss them.

I provided an information sheet that looked at the significant role that the UN plays in US national security affairs. The importance of this info sheet was to be able to appreciate the number of significant groups that are involved in this multiregional, multipolar world today, a diplomatic nightmare.

As of mid-1993:

Association of Southeast Asian nations (ASEAN) was formed in 1967 to promote economic, social, and cultural cooperation, and development among the non-communist states of the region. Members in 1993 were Brunei, Darussalam, Indonesia, Malaysia, Philippines, Singapore, and Thailand. Annual ministerial meetings set policy; a central secretariat in Jakarta and specialized intergovernmental committees work in trade, transportation, communications, agriculture, science, finance, and culture.

Caribbean Community and Common Market (CARICOM) was established July 4, 1973. Its function is to further cooperation in economics, health, education, culture, science and technology, tax administration, and the coordination of foreign policy. Members in 1993 were Antigua and Barbuda, Bahamas, Barbados, Belize, Dominica, Grenada, Guyana, Jamaica, Montserrat, St. Kitts and Nevis, St. Lucia, St. Vincent and the Grenadines, Trinidad, and Tobago.

Commonwealth of Independent States (CIS) was created December 1992, upon the disbanding of the Soviet Union. It is made up of ten of the fifteen former Soviet constituent republics.

Members are Armenia, Belarus, Kazakhstan, Kyrgyzstan, Moldova, Russia, Tajikistan, Turkmenistan, Ukraine, and Uzbekistan. The commonwealth is not in itself a state, but an alliance of fully independent states. Commonwealth policy is set through coordinating bodies such as a council of heads of state and council of heads of government. The capital of the commonwealth is Minsk, Belarus.

Commonwealth of Nations, originally called the British commonwealth of nations, is an association of nations and dependencies loosely joined by a common interest based on having been parts of the old British Empire. The British monarch is the symbolic head of the commonwealth. There are fifty self-governing independent nations in the commonwealth, plus various colonies and protectorates. As of 1993, the members were the United Kingdom of Great Britain and Northern Ireland and fifteen other nations recognizing the British monarch, represented by a governor-general, as their head of state: Antigua and Barbuda, Australia, the Bahamas, Barbados, Belize, Canada, Grenada, Jamaica, New Zealand, New Guinea, Saint Kitts and Nevis, Saint Lucia, Saint Vincent and the Grenadines, Solomon Islands, and Tuvalu (a special member), and thirty-four countries with their own heads of state: Bangladesh, Botswana, Brunei Darussalam, Cyprus, Dominica, the Gambia, Ghana, Guyana, India, Kenya, Kiribati, Lesotho, Malawi, Malaysia, the Maldives, Malta, Mauritius, Namibia, Nauru (a special member), Nigeria, Pakistan, Seychelles, Sierra Leone,

Singapore, Sri Lanka, Swaziland, Tanzania, Tonga, Trinidad and Tobago, Uganda, Vanuatu, western Samoa, Zambia, and Zimbabwe.

The commonwealth facilitates consultation among member states through meetings of prime ministers and finance ministers, and through a permanent secretariat. Members consult on economic, scientific, educational, financial, legal, and military matters. Members also try to coordinate policies.

European Community (EC), officially, the European communities, is the collective designation of three organizations with common membership, the European Economic Community (common market), the European Coal and Steel Community, and the European Atomic Energy Community (EURATOM). The twelve full members are: Belgium, Denmark, France, Germany, Greece, Ireland, Italy, Luxembourg, Netherlands, Portugal, Spain, and the United Kingdom. Some sixty nations in Africa, the Caribbean, and the Pacific are affiliated under the Lorne convention.

A merger of the three communities' executives went into effect July 1, 1957, though the component organizations date back to 1951 and 1958. The council of ministers, the commission of the European communities, the European parliament, and the European court. A merger of the three communities' executives went into effect July 1, 1957, though the component organizations date back to 1951 and 1958. The council of ministers, the commission of the European communities, the European parliament, and the European court of justice comprise the permanent structure. The EC aims to integrate the economies, coordinate social developments, and bring about political union of the democratic states of Europe. Effective December 31, 1992, there are no restrictions on the movement of goods, services, capital, workers, and tourists within the community. There are also common agricultural, fisheries, and nuclear research policies.

Leaders of the twelve European community nations met December 1 through 9, 1991, in Maastricht, the Netherlands. Treaties on monetary union and political union and accompanying protocols agreed upon by the leaders:

Committed the EC to launching a common currency for at least some nations by 1999 (Britain and later Denmark were allowed to "opt out" of joining).

Sought to establish common foreign policies for the twelve members.

Laid the groundwork for a common defense policy under the western European Union.

Expanded the policy issues in which the EC would have a voice.

Gave the EC a leading role in social policy (Britain was not included in this plan).

Pledged increased aid for the community's four poorest nations—Ireland, Greece, Spain, and Portugal.

Slightly increased the powers of the 518-member European parliament.

The treaties require ratification by all twelve members before they can go into effect.

European free trade association (EFTA) was created on May 3, 1960, to promote expansion of free trade. Current members are Austria, Finland, Iceland, Liechtenstein, Norway, Sweden, and Switzerland. By December 31, 1966, tariffs and quotas had been eliminated. Members of the association entered into free trade agreements with the EC in 1972 and 1973. In 1992, the EFTA and EC concluded an agreement to create a single-market with free flow of foods, services, and capital, and labor encompassing the 19 nations of the two organizations.

Group of Seven (G-7) is an organization of seven major industrial democracies that meet periodically to discuss world economic and other issues. G-7 was established September 22, 1985. Members are Canada, France, Germany, Italy, Japan, the United Kingdom, and the United States.

International Criminal Police Organization (Interpol) was created on June 13, 1956, to ensure and promote the widest possible mutual assistance between all police authorities within the limits of the law existing in the different countries and in the spirit of the universal declaration of human rights. There were 152 members in 1993.

League of Arab States (The Arab League) was created March 22, 1945. Members in 1993 were Algeria, Bahrain, Djibouti, Egypt, Iraq, Jordan, Kuwait, Lebanon, Libya, Mauritania, Morocco, Oman, the Palestine liberation organization, Qatar,

Saudi Arabia, Somalia, Sudan, Syria, Tunisia, United Arab Emirates, and Yemen. The league promotes economic, social, political, and military cooperation and mediates disputes among the Arab states. It also represents Arab states in certain international negotiations. The league's headquarters is in Cairo.

North Atlantic Treaty Organization (NATO) was created by treaty (signed April 4, 1949) and went into effect august 24, 1940. Members in 1993 were Belgium, Canada, Denmark, France, Germany, Greece, Iceland, Italy, Luxembourg, Netherlands, Norway, Portugal, Spain, Turkey, the United Kingdom, and the United States. The members agreed to settle disputes by peaceful means to develop their individual and collective capacity to resist armed attack, to regard an attack on one as an attack on all; and to take necessary action to repel an attack under article 51 of the United Nations charter.

The NATO structure consists of a council and a military committee of three commands (allied command Europe, allied command Atlantic, allied command channel) and the Canada-US regional planning group.

With the dissolution of the Soviet Union and the end of the cold war in the early 1990s, NATO members sought to modify the organization's mission, putting greater stress on political action and creating a rapid deployment force to react to local crises. Former Warsaw Pact members were no longer considered adversaries, and Hungary gained associate membership in 1991.

Organization of African unity (OAU) was formed on May 25, 1963, by thirty-two African countries (fifty-one members in 1993) to promote peace and security, as well as economic and social development. It holds annual conferences of heads of state. Headquarters are in Addis Ababa, Ethiopia.

Organization of American States (OAS) was formed in Bogotá, Colombia, on April 20, 1948. Headquarters are in Washington, DC. It has a permanent council, inter-American economic and social council, inter-American council for education, science and culture, judicial committee, and Commission on Human Rights. The permanent council can call meetings of foreign ministers to deal with urgent security matters. A general assembly meets annually. A secretary general and assistant are elected for five-year terms. There are thirty-five members, each with one vote in the various organizations: Antigua and Barbuda, Argentina, the Bahamas, Barbados, Belize, Bolivia, brazil, Canada, Chile, Colombia, Costa Rica, Cuba, Dominica, Dominican republic, Ecuador, El Salvador, Grenada, Guatemala, Guyana, Haiti, Honduras, Jamaica, Mexico, Nicaragua, Panama, Paraguay, Peru, St. Kitts and Nevis, St. Lucia, St. Vincent and the Grenadines, Suriname, Trinidad and Tobago, United States, Uruguay, Venezuela. In 1962, the OAS excluded Cuba from OAS activities but not from membership.

Organization for Economic Cooperation and Development (OECD) was established on September 30, 1960, to promote economic and social welfare in member countries and to stimulate and harmonize efforts on behalf of developing nations. The OECD collects and disseminates economic and environmental information. Members in 1993 were Australia, Austria, Belgium, Canada, Denmark, Finland, France, Germany, Greece, Iceland, Ireland, Italy, Japan, Luxembourg, Netherlands, New Zealand, Norway, Portugal, Spain, Sweden, Switzerland, Turkey, the United Kingdom, and the United States. Headquarters are in Paris.

Organization of Petroleum Exporting Countries (OPEC) was created November 14, 1960. The group attempts to set world oil prices by controlling oil production. It is also involved in advancing members' interests in trade and development dealings with industrialized oil-consuming nations. Members in 1993 were Algeria, Gabon, Indonesia, Iran, Iraq, Kuwait, Libya, Nigeria, Qatar, Saudi Arabia, United Arab Emirates, and Venezuela.

Organization of the United Nations. The text of the UN charter may be obtained from the office of public information, United Nations, New York, NY 10017.

General Assembly. The general assembly is composed of representatives of all the member nations. Each nation is entitled to one vote. The general assembly meets in regular annual sessions and in special sessions when necessary.

Special sessions are convoked by the secretary general at the request of the Security Council or of a majority of the members of the UN. On important questions, a two-thirds majority of members present and voting is required. On other questions, a simple majority is sufficient. The general assembly must approve the budget and apportion expenses among members. A member in arrears will have no vote if the amount of arrears equals or exceeds the amount of the contributions due for the preceding two full years.

Security Council. The Security Council consists of fifteen members, five with permanent seats. The remaining ten are elected for two-year terms by the general assembly. They are not eligible for immediate reelection. Permanent members of the council are china, France, Russia, the United Kingdom, and the United States. Nonpermanent members are Cape Verde, Hungary, Japan, Morocco, Venezuela (until December 31, 1993), Brazil, Djibouti, New Zealand, Pakistan, and Spain (until December 31, 1994). The Security Council has the primary responsibility within the UN for maintaining international peace and security. The council may investigate any dispute that threatens international peace and security. Any member of the UN at UN headquarters may participate it its discussions and a nation not a member of UN may appear if it is a party to a dispute. Decisions on procedural questions are made by an affirmative vote of nine members. On all other matters, the affirmative vote of nine members must include the concurring votes of all permanent members. It is this clause which gives rise to the so-called veto power of permanent members. A party to a dispute must refrain from voting. The Security Council directs the various peacekeeping forces deployed throughout the world.

Economic and Social Council. The economic and social council consists of fifty-four members elected by the general assembly for three-year terms of office. The council is responsible under the general assembly for carrying out the functions of the United Nations with regard to international economic, social, cultural, educational, health, and related matters. The council meets usually twice a year.

Trusteeship Council. The administration of trust territories is under UN supervision. The only remaining trust territory is Palau, administered by the US.

Secretariat. The secretary general is the chief administrative officer of the UN. He may bring to the attention of the Security Council any matter that threatens international peace. He reports to the general assembly.

Budget. The general assembly approved a total budget for 1992–92 of $2.36 billion.

International Court of Justice (World Court). The International Court of Justice is the principal judicial organ of the United Nations. All members are *ipso facto* parties to the statute of the court. Other states may become parties to the court's statute. The jurisdiction of the court comprises cases that the parties submit to it and matters especially provided for in the charter or in treaties. The court gives advisory opinions and renders judgments.

Its decisions are binding only between the parties concerned and in respect to a particular dispute. If any party to a cause fails to heed a judgment, the other party may have recourse to the Security Council. The fifteen judges are elected for nine-year terms by the general assembly and the Security Council. Retiring judges are eligible for reelection. The court remains permanently in session, except during vacations. All questions are decided by majority. The court sits in The Hague, Netherlands.

It is important to look at how the world has changed since the "cold war." There has been a significant change to the world order.

- Bipolar world is history.
- Russia suffering severe economic, social, ethnic, and political pressures.
- Shift to multipolar regional power centers.

In one of the topic readings, Adm. Owens talks about the navy's role in this new multipolar environment. He poses these questions:

Is the world still a dangerous place?

- Global Nuclear conflict less likely?
- Conventional regional conflict more likely?
- Small-scale nuclear/WMD detonation more likely?

What are your thoughts for each one?
Dir. CIA says the following, so let's discuss this quote.

> Yes we have slain a large dragon. But we live now in
> a jungle filled with a bewildering variety of poisonous
> snakes, and in many ways, the dragon was much easier
> to keep track of. (Former CIA Director Woolsey)

The understanding of the world and current affairs allows a better understanding of the need for change. Analysis of the world reveals what concerns the US. We'll consider that shortly.

Let's look at the National Security Strategy (NSS) of Engagement and Enlargement Feb 1995:

Focus on three goals:

- To sustain our security with military forces that are ready to fight (enhancing our security).
- To bolster America's economic revitalization (promoting prosperity at home).
- To promote democracy abroad (promoting democracy).

NSS indicates that the US must remain engaged in global affairs.

President Clinton indicates that for the American people to be safer, we must

- deter would-be aggressors,
- open foreign markets,

- promote the spread of democracy abroad,
- encourage sustainable development,
- pursue new opportunities for peace.

The NSS calls on the Preamble of the Constitution to set out the basic objectives:

> To provide for the common defense, promote the general welfare, and secure the blessings of liberty to ourselves and our posterity.

States that to do that the military must accomplish:

- Deterring and defeating aggression in major regional conflicts
- Providing a credible overseas presence
- Countering weapons of mass destruction
- Contributing to multilateral peace operations
- Supporting counter-terrorism efforts and other national security objectives.

The National Military Strategy (NMS) states:

- Fundamental purpose of the armed forces is to fight and win our nation's wars whenever and wherever called upon.

- NSS calls for engagement and enlargement—NMS calls for flexibility (smaller more versatile forces) and selective (we cannot do everything or be everywhere at once).

National Military strategy discusses when we will deploy forces and how, which is built on the three components:

1. Peacetime engagement (six elements)
2. Deterrence and conflict prevention (eight elements)
3. Fight to win (eight elements)

Basic idea behind NMS is to fight to win—called the The Weinberg doctrine—the basic idea was that there will be no more Vietnams—meaning, no more war without the American people's total commitment...

NSS and NMS Forces Built on five foundations:

- Quality men and women
- Force enhancements
- Readiness
- Modernization
- Balance

The Navy's role in support of the NMS:

- Projection of power from sea to land
- Sea control and maritime supremacy
- Strategic sealift
- Forward naval presence

Geopolitical context dictated a change in the navy's doctrine. Contained in the navy's *from the sea 1992*.

What was the main reason for the shift in operational focus?

- End of Cold War/Berlin Wall
- Shift was to regional power

The change was a basic shift from a global to a regional threat. From a global maritime threat toward projecting power and influence across the seas in response to regional challenges.

Next came the revised doctrine.

Forward from the sea of naval forces. Indicates role of naval forces in situations short of war is to be *engaged* in forward areas, with the objectives of preventing conflicts and controlling crisis.

Forward from the sea states that naval forces are the foundation of peacetime forward presence operations and overseas response to crisis.

Overseas Presence

> Without the fleet, the contest would be on our own
> home grounds, and war is one contest it is best to be
> on the visiting team." (Adm. Chester W. Nimitz)

In short, forward deployed naval forces will provide the critical operational linkage between peacetime operations and initial requirement of developing crisis or major regional contingency. Sounds simple enough but in today's rules of engagement environment it may not be that simple.

Two near simultaneous major regional contingencies are still our strategic marching orders. Whether it can be done is linked to lift and acceptable casualties sustained, which have been near zero of late. It's tough, however, to fight a war with zero acceptable casualties. This fact heightens the need for technology and smart weapons to assist in doing more with less and with low risk to forces. *One of the chairman's three revolutionary concerns was to stay ahead in this technology area.*

All this leads to doctrine as provided in your readings in NDP-1.

Information Sheet 1-2-2

This doctrine at the time consisted of two major themes. I provided an information sheet that outlined the current thinking on these two main naval missions as required in 1995.

- Control of the sea
- Navy's role in OOTW

Information Sheet 1-2-2

a. Introduction

This information sheet is designed to assist the student in understanding both wartime and other-than-wartime naval operations.

b. References

1. Dalton, John H., et al. *Forward...from the sea*, proceedings, December 1994, pages 46–49.
2. Naval doctrine publication 1, naval warfare, 1994, pages 31–33, 50–57.

NAVAL OPERATIONS IN WAR

Control of the sea is fundamental to accomplishing our naval roles. It directly supports our ability to project power ashore by encompassing control of the entire maritime area: subsurface, surface, and airspace, in both the open oceans and the littoral regions of the world. Control of the sea allows us to

- protect sea lines of communication,

- deny the enemy commercial and military use of the seas,

- establish an area of operations for power projection ashore and support of amphibious operations, and

- project naval logistic support to forward deployed battle forces.

Control of the sea can be accomplished through decisive operations by

- destroying or neutralizing enemy ships, submarines, aircraft, or mines;

- disabling or disrupting enemy command and control;

- destroying or neutralizing the land-based infrastructure that supports enemy sea control forces;

- seizing islands, choke points, peninsulas, and coastal bases along the littorals;

- conducting barrier operations in choke points that prevent enemy mobility under, on, and above the sea.

By establishing control of the sea in every dimension, thus ensuring access to any adversary's coast from the sea, we open opportunities for power projection, insertion, and resupply. Control of the sea, however, has both spatial and temporal limits. It does not imply absolute control over all the seas at all times. Rather, control of the sea is required in specific regions for particular periods of time, to allow unencumbered operations.

NAVAL OPERATIONS: OTHER THAN WAR

Under international law, nations have a right to use force for individual or collective self-defense against armed attack and to help each other in maintaining internal order against insurgency, terrorism, and other threats. Naval forces operating under the direction of national command authorities and unified commanders implement this international right to

- conduct contingency operations;
- evacuate noncombatant personnel;
- combat terrorism;
- aid host nations through security assistance and foreign internal defense;
- assist other nations in defending themselves;
- enforce United Nations' economic sanctions;
- participate in peace-support operations;
- intercept vessels to prevent uncontrolled immigration;
- plan and conduct disaster relief, humanitarian assistance, and civil support operations;
- coordinate public health operations;
- assist interagency counter drug operations.

Naval forces are organized, trained, and equipped to defend our nation and its interests. We defend our nation by maintaining a visible and credible capability both to fight and to take that fight abroad. Application of our expertise in operations other than war also exercises many of our wartime capabilities and our ability to accomplish our service role in defense of our nation.

Facilitate a discussion of US in her new world policemen role. What problems does this role add to the leadership and readiness role? *This was always a good discussion.*

Five years since fall of Berlin wall, deployed forces to assist in security or humanitarian crises about forty-five times more than the preceding twenty years. A far greater pace than the preceding twenty years. *Most likely even greater today.*

What does this statistic mean to us in military?

It means greater regional instability. *This is certainly true today as well.*

Summary of concerns from the NSS/NMS
Naval operations in operations other than war
(*As it existed in 1995*)

Issues of Concern

- Arms proliferation (WMD/CW/BW)
- Regional aggression
- Tech transfer (SRBM/RBM/NUC)
- Counter terrorism
- Counter narcotics
- Increase military use in OOTW
- Famine/drought/disease
- Maintaining tech edge in declining budget
- Overseas presence in declining budget

NSS/NMS/NDP-1/ETC

It is these concerns, interests, and strategic objectives that drive our deployment schedule and overseas presence in regional areas of critical importance and instability.

Let's take a look at where we are currently deployed and examine it from a regional perspective. We'll tie in some of the regional organizational players and the United Nations from info sheet 1-2-3. You may want to refer to it as we discuss the Cincs' areas of responsibilities. From this drill, we will develop a list of what we can call "where to look," which could indicate those areas most likely to draw US attention in the not too distant future. (*I would again post an unclassified current world deployment look published monthly in the Navy Times.*)

DISCUSSION OF REGIONAL SLIDES

We would walk through each area and discuss each bullet, the class would provide comments based on their experience in these areas and discuss current or possible future concerns.

Regional review: Pacific/Far East; Pacom

- Korean Peninsula
- Japan-US Relations
- PRC-Taiwan
- Spratley Islands
- India-Pakistan

Regional Review: Latin America (Southcom/Usacom)

- Socioeconomic injustices, political instability, insurgency, terrorism

- Significant military challenges? Haiti, Cuba, Peru

- US interests in the area

  20% US Imported Oil

  25% of US Exports

- Chile, Venezuela: Economic Bright Spots?

- Argentina, Brazil, Chile: Arms Exporters

Regional Review: Africa (Eucom/Centcom)

- Diversity: forty-nine countries

- Former "Cold War" playground

- Emerging weak central Govt's 80% independent since 1960

- Difficult problems for government

- Famine/drought/disease/arms

- Tribalism, ethnic competition

- Militant Islamic influence

- Always the question of strategic interest

Regional Review: Europe (EUCOM)

- US role in the Balkans
- Bosnia
- Future of NATO?
- Integration (EC)
- Arms proliferation
- Greece-Turkey

Regional Review: ME/SW Asia (CENTCOM/ EUCOM)

- Future of Iranian threat
- Iraq

Arabs-Israel

- Protecting our friends
- Fundamentalists-Islamists: extremists

At this point in the lecture, based on my thoughts and those expressed from the students during our regional review, we would take a shot at defining our current areas of concern, areas that some of the students might deploy to during their tour of command. At the end of that, I provided the conclusion of the impact of the current operating environment on the US Military in general and our Navy specifically.

Prior to each class, I would research and hand out the upcoming command operating schedule for each student. For many, it was the first time they actually connected themselves to what was about to happen to them and what they would be required to do. Again, the charter of the school was to get their minds into their command. There was always someone going to deploy soon after they assumed command. They were always much more focused.

- More ambiguous threat in the area of declining budget.
- Defining acceptable future risk
- Regional vs. global focus
  - o More influence to CINCS
  - o Non-traditional mission
  - o Crisis response missions
  - o Conventional vs. Nuclear
- Maintain forward presence in key areas
- Coalition warfare
- Downsizing and Reconstruction: how fast can we put it back together

I reviewed this lesson taught in 1995, originally written because until I went to War College after my command tour; I was not aware of how things really fit together. It is, of course, not rocket science, but it has a flow and emphasizes the importance of understanding the role we play in the big scheme of things. Again, the importance to be able to explain the "why" you are doing something in the big picture. Having taught the lesson for several months, I found that the reviews echoed my experience that most of the students had not yet been exposed to most of the documents, how they tied in, or the makeup of the regional areas. They had never been afforded the opportunity to review the documents and gain the big picture of what we do and why we do it. Thus they also found it very helpful.

It was interesting to see what I had written in 1995. While I am not familiar with the current National Security or National Military Strategy guidance, those in 1995 were very well done. It is still relevant today in many areas and predictions, as the world remains a dangerous place. I would hope that my effort here at least sparks an interest in finding out what the documents say that form the basis for "the why" as to what we do today and more importantly what you may be asked to do. A leader must be able to explain "the why."

CHAPTER 6

....

DECISION MAKING FOUNDATION: THE STRENGTH TO WEATHER THE STORM

TOPIC 2.3 ETHICS AND CORE VALUES

In this course, we will talk a lot about you as the leader, those that you will lead, situations that you will find yourself in, and types of communications that could be used in these situations. In addition, we will specifically look at the fact that leaders in the military, as in the civilian world, are responsible for many things. There are, however, some significant differences, and we will discuss those in depth. We will look at the leader's responsibility to provide subordinates these three main things: purpose, direction, and motivation. In the next two hours, we will talk a little about the second of these responsibilities, *to provide direction*.

I. Introduction

The Ethical Perspective

The nation expects its Navy to adhere to the highest standards of professional conduct and to reflect the ideals of American values. The American people demand a high-quality Navy that honors the core values of the Constitution it is sworn to uphold–a strong respect for the rule of law, human dignity and individual rights.

Despite the difficult environments in which Navy forces operate, sailors are expected to obey the laws of naval warfare, to protect civilians and other non-combatants, to limit collateral damage, respect private property, and to treat prisoners of war with dignity. Amid the rigors of combat, the integrity of every sailor—from the highest to the lowest ranks—is of paramount importance. Since lives hinge on accurate reporting, there can be no room for half-truths or falsehoods. Sailors must be counted on to do what is right, even when no one is watching.

Leaders have a special responsibility to subordinates. They must never risk their sailors' lives needlessly. They return their sailors' trust with the greatest care for their well-being, while aggressively pursuing the accomplishment of the mission. Leaders treat subordinates with respect; never do they seek self-gain at the expense of their sailors or their subordinates. Leaders imbue sailors with a sense of honor, share their hardships, and acknowledge their accomplishments. Leaders set the example by ethical behavior and a selflessness that puts duty above all personal concerns.

The human dimension of war will be decisive in the campaigns and battles of the future, just as in the past. In this difficult environment, sailors must have faith in their leaders and fellow sailors. Trust is the basic bond of leadership. Good leaders occupy a position of special trust and confidence in the eyes of their sailors. A motivated sailor in the hands of a competent leader, loyal to and supported by his fellow sailors, can accomplish the most difficult of missions.

Wars are fought and won by sailors, not machines. The human dimension of war will be decisive in the campaigns and battles of the future, just as in the past. Sailors are the heart and soul of the Navy. Leaders mold them, discipline their efforts, supply them resources, and give them direction. But in the end, sailors do the job. Ultimately, sailors make the difference. (Dalton, John H. "The Character of Readiness: The Ethics of Moral Behavior,")

The lesson bridge in: So far in unit 2, we looked at the concepts of what leaders and managers are, the fact that you can learn to be both, and that both skill sets are required to be an effective commanding officer. In lesson 2-2, Capt. Meyer would reinforce the concept of the need to be a transformational leader, to not only lead change, but the importance of being able to recognize a situation in which a different leadership style would be more effective and to apply your dynamic skill base, whether directive or supportive, to deal with it.

We now begin to discuss what most agree is the challenge of leadership, making decisions and managing risk. This is both a challenge and a leadership responsibility. You can't feel strongly both ways. You must make a decision and the decisions you make form a pattern of behavior. A positive pattern of behavior can lead to your operational definition of a successful command and minimize fear, stress and risk while maximizing loyalty, confidence, and commitment.

The rest of the day, we will talk about concepts that play a significant role in shaping leadership patterns of behavior and individual attitudes.

Most sources on leadership agree that the foundation of naval leadership include values, ethics, principles, and personal traits such as integrity (without integrity, the only way people follow leaders is out of idle curiosity).

We will look at values: past and present.

- What they are
- Where they come from
- Why they are important and the role they play from a leadership perspective.

In addition, we will contrast those of the leader with those that they lead. We will look at ethics and how values play a significant role in the decision/risk management process and in how we interact with others. We'll look at some traits like integrity and discuss how a commanding officer's display of it, or its lack, can shape a command, effect command climate, and contribute positively or negatively to combat effectiveness.

In addition to all of this, we will be discussing some of the issues you were exposed to in your readings last night and look at two case studies that illustrates their points.

Issues like the following:

- X generation
- Careerist
- Roles of media, policies, and society, and how they can and do impact values

> I'd like to review last night's readings and briefly discuss the author's key point in each one. These points will need to be kept in the foreground as we try to channel our discussions the rest of the day. Any questions before we get started?

Topic readings are provided at Appendix E, but I wanted to list them here for this lesson because I refer to them so often. Below are the required readings I used for unit 2.3. Each reading tried to highlight a certain point. Collectively the points would conclude that most organizations are a reflection of the leader. A leader that leads from a value based personal foundation seemed to be more successful, based on effectiveness studies, in getting the kind of commitment required to perform well in difficult situations. Those led seem more willing to follow the orders of a leader they felt was an example of integrity.

Required Readings

Dalton, John H. "The Character of Readiness: The Ethics of Moral Behavior," *Vital Speeches of the Day*, January 1994, pages 296–298.

Landenberg, Rear Admiral William H. "1972: The Nadir of the Navy, Professionalism," *Shipmate*, January/February, 1995, Volume 58, No. 1, pages 35–36.

Lynch, Major General J. D. "Nobody Asked Me But…Fish Rot from the Head," *Proceedings*, February 1995, page 73.

Montor, Karel, et al. "Naval Leadership: Voices of Experience." Annapolis, MD: Naval Institute Press, 1987, pages 26–32, Components of Integrity.

Raspberry, William. "Ethics Without Virtue," *The Washington Post*, 16 December 1991, page A23.

Stockdale, James B. *Leadership in Response to Changing Societal Values: What is Today's Skipper of a Destroyer, Submarine or Aircraft Squadron Up Against?* May 25, 1987.

Stockdale, James B. "Taking Stock," *Naval War College Review*, Fall, 1978, "Right and Wrong Changed to Legal and Illegal."

Excerpts from Leadership Jazz by Max Dupree.

Decision-Making and Risk Management

This leadership foundation, which includes values, ethics, principles, and personal traits, such as integrity, is important because

> Historical research and studies show how this personal foundation can be a significant source of strength that can and has often meant the difference in a survival situation. It can provide a bounce-back capability and can create a deep sense of perseverance in you and your command. It is the source of your basic character of leadership. These concepts provide a foundation to assist you in doing the right thing when confronted with a personal or professional dilemma.

Motivating statement: As a commanding officer/leader, you will be asked time and again to make quick command decisions on less-than-perfect information, or in situations surrounded by great stress. Or you will be asked to choose between numerous alternatives perhaps in a no-win situation. A solid leadership foundation can help you make these decisions and, more importantly, deal with the consequences of your decisions.

I hope our discussions will reinforce a foundation that can assist you to do the right thing when confronted with a personal or professional dilemma.

We will provide an information sheet showing how our present core values evolved. But before we discuss that, let's look at the general concept of "values."

The American flag represents key values, truth, justice, and the American way.

We talked about compliance and commitment. Where does the commitment in your people come from? A quote to deliberate:

> A leader who is not passionately committed to the cause will not draw much commitment from others. The world will make way for someone who knows what he or she wants, because there is not much competition when it comes to passionate commitment.
>
> (Laurie Beth Jones, CEO Jesus)

So if you want commitment from others, you need to be committed, you need conviction. But conviction to what? Perhaps to what we value or believe in, so let's define that:

I would then introduce a brainstorming exercise, and a co-facilitator would record student responses on a chart pack.

I'd state, "Let's talk about personal values."

What is one of your personal guiding values? (Have co-facilitator record responses on left side of chart pack). We would record meaningful words I was looking for, but of course not all such words were offered up. Some were given but as synonyms or in phrases, e.g. love of country for patriotism, strength of character for fortitude, kindness for compassion, bravery for courage, loyalty for fidelity, but all in all, a kind of class values foundation.

I would then provide a list credited to their parents: justice, courage, temperance, prudence, fortitude, patriotism, fidelity, charity, hope, compassion, frugality, etc., and some values now considered wimpish, like chivalry. We would briefly discuss the differences in words and compare and contrast the list. Most classes felt the lists were fairly close, just different expressions of the same value. The point that the parents' list comprised more single-word virtues I always found interesting. Those words were somewhat lost even back then.

So this then would be that particular class's value foundation. We would discuss if any of them had changed over time. Some would talk about the birth of their children and how that changed them from an "all about me" carefree individual into one more driven, serious, and concerned about keeping his family provided for and safe.

Next I would ask the question: If this is our value foundation, where did we get them from? *(Again, we would record the answers on right side.)* The answers were usually the same, from parents, grandparents, friends, work, church, school, teachers, mentors, experience, etc We would then talk about the values of the young in comparison to our values and where they get theirs. The impression of the classes was that the value list would be close to theirs, but more self-centered and certainly not close to the list of their parents. The answers as to where they got their values listed videos, movies, chat rooms, computer games, peers, schools, churches, and parents. Always an interesting conversation and that also goes to the heart of where many children may be learning their values today.

Dr. Morris Massey, a behavioral scientist, introduced a theory that events help shape our values.

(Hand out and discuss, talk about significant emotional event.)

The idea presented in the article is that we are a product of who we were when. The idea is that as we go along in life, we are shaped by our surroundings, our decisions, and our experiences. These elements continue to shape us until something happens, which Dr. Massey calls a significant emotional event, or SEE. Such an event changes us, and we get routed down another path. These SEE may be things like the birth or death of a child, the death of a loved one, or perhaps the death of JFK or Martin Luther King.

Having visited Parris Island when I was the aide to the commandant of the Marine Corps, I can tell you that for those young recruits, Marine Corps Parris Island is a significant emotional event!

Likewise, one remembers the moon landing, where you were and the effect that had. How about the Cal Ripken's standing ovation for most consecutive games played, a salute perhaps more for what he represented than the record itself? Some say it was a salute to old values and the importance of old heroes, but in any case that could have been a SEE for some young fan at the game.

And surely the bombings of the Twin Towers and the Pentagon were SEEs? I can tell you, having been in the Pentagon on 9/11, it was a significant emotional event.

Dr. Massey's point is that our values and emotions continue to evolve but are altered when a SEE occurs. To paraphrase, events help shape our values. We are the sum total of those events we have experienced that have shaped our lives.

I would propose that leading men into combat or crisis is certainly one such significant emotional event. I would further argue that because of our responsibilities under the law that military service is a SEE, as proposed in one of the articles, because of what we may be called upon to do. We should not be a mere reflection of society; we should be held to a higher standard.

At that point, I would then lead off the conversation as to why values are important.

I would indicate from the studies that our values are the bedrock foundation to fall back on and live by in times of stress. They are the building blocks of personal character. The way you act and behave is a reflection of what you value. It forms your basic character, but note that character can be positive or negative. The effects of both are significant. The concept of *consistency* is the point to be made here. Values and character are changeless, but leadership styles are not. (As in the four main leadership styles: directing, coaching, delegating, and mentoring that were covered in team building.) Values demonstrate who we are and guide our performance, our conduct, and our decision. To reiterate, *consistency* is the point.

The concept of personal character was then introduced.

Winston Churchill's physician, Lord Moran, published his book, *The Anatomy of Courage* in 1944, the year of the Allied invasion of Europe and the liberation of France. It is a study of men under the stress of war, based on diaries that he kept while serving in the trenches with the first battalion, Royal Fusiliers. Along with *Men in Battle* by S. L. A. Marshall, it is the best I've come across on the relationship between fear and courage. So I would introduce several quotes or slides, and we would then discuss the meaning of them as we continued to build the topic.

A man of character in peace is a man of courage in war. (Lord Moran)

The idea of character is illustrated here. It is who you are. It is what you stand for. We would discuss this quote and settle on the meaning that you cannot turn your value system on and off. Its foundation is built over time and is the same one you take into combat or crisis.

Then we discussed: "No man can climb beyond the limitations of his own character" (General MacArthur).

We already heard MacArthur, during his speech to West Point, talk about the set of values, duty, honor, country, which guided him throughout his life. Those happen to be mine as well.

We then would discuss whether values and character are unchanging. How do values relate to a leadership style? I would remind them of the point of Lawrence Kohlberg's essay on moral development, of the reaction the leader will get when he first attempts to be the SEE. Again, the character of a leader can be positive or negative. The effects of both are significant. Values and character are changeless. Styles are not. You cannot turn on and off your value system.

Okay, let's look at some organizational values, those defined by an organization to which a member of that organization should adapt.

CNO 281945Z OCT 92. In his message, Adm. Kelso states that core values are guideposts for mission accomplishment and readiness. Why did the CNO feel he needed to send this message? We discussed possible answers: Tailhook, family violence, cheating at USNA, sexual harassment, and discrimination. The class had already defined their personal set of values, so we would review them and ask whether the problems would go away if the class stuck to those values. The answer was always in the affirmative.

Next, I introduced our navy's (or our) organizational set of values and linked the two together.

INFORMATION SHEET 2-3-1

A. Introduction:
   This Information Sheet provides two charts depicting US navy core values before and after October 1992.

B. References:
   NAVOP 030/92, <u>Core Values of the United States Navy</u>.
   Navy core values prior to October 1992:

INTEGRITY	PROFESSIONALISM	TRADITION
Honesty	Competence	People
Honor	Teamwork	Patriotism
Responsibility	Loyalty	Courage

Navy core values after October 1992:

HONOR	COMMITMENT	COURAGE
Ethical	Respect chain of command	Professional/Mission:
Honest	Care for personnel safety	Demanding
Truthful	and well-being:	Hazardous
Make	Personal	Difficult
Recommendations	Professional	Sound Decisions
Encourage Ideas	Spiritual	(in spite of
Integrity	Respect for all:	personal consequences)
Responsibility:	Races	Meet Challenges
Legal	Religion	Higher Standards
Ethical	Gender	Personal Standards
Behavior:	Human dignity	Decency
Personal	Positive change	Loyal to USA
Professional	Moral Character	Manage Resources:
Accountable	Technical Excellence	Honestly
	Quality	Carefully
	Competence	Efficiently
	Work as a Team	Strength:
	Improve:	Moral
	Quality at Work	Mental
	Our People	Do Right in Face of:
	Ourselves	Personal or Professional
		Adversity

Navy Core Values: Honor, Courage, and Commitment

<u>Individual values Navy values</u>

—Integrity

- Responsibility Honor
- Honesty

—Competence
- Teamwork Commitment
- Concern for people

—Patriotism
- Loyalty Courage
- Valor

It takes courage to do the right thing regardless of the frustrations or antagonists.

We have looked at this idea that values guide behavior. Based on that behavior, do we as a service have a values problem or not? There are many schools of thought today that are looking at the problem. What do you think?

Are things really that bad, or is it just that the media has us under a microscope, (the power of magnification)?

…Are we held to a higher standard?
…Should we be?

We have been given a life or death responsibility. Perhaps we should be held accountable to a higher standard.

We would discuss the points and most agreed that it does seem that the media is intent on breaking down our precious institutions, almost as if they enjoy bringing down goodness to a lower level. But in the end, we do have a responsibility not equaled in the civilian world. Again a timely reminder of the Title Ten Law, and about responsibility, authority, and accountability.

There is also thinking that postulates what our true value to this country may be:

> A man can be selfish, cowardly, disloyal, false, fleeting, perjured, and morally corrupt in a wide variety of other ways, and still be outstandingly good in pursuits in which other imperatives bear than those upon the fighting man…He can be a superb creative artist, for example, or a scientist in the very top flight, and still be a very bad man. What the bad man cannot be is a good sailor, soldier, or airman. Military institutions thus form a repository of moral resource that should always be source of strength within the state…. The highest service of the military to the state may lie in the moral sphere. (Hackett and Wakin, War, *Morality and military profession*, 123–125)

General Colin Powell said, "First, I want you to believe in yourself. You have to know that you are capable, that you are competent, that you are good… Second, I want you to believe in America…We are still, as Abraham Lincoln said, the last best hope on earth. Finally, Remember the worst kind of poverty is not economic poverty, it is the poverty of values."

We are discussing the importance of a set of values and are introducing the concept that a set of values will be instilled into your command by your day-to-day decisions and actions.

So it is important to know what they are, yet again, this idea of having high standards.

As an example of individual values leading to core values for an organization, in this case, the army, I quoted from General MacArthur's farewell remarks given at West Point. *(Played for the students the first day of class.)*

Idea of Having High Standards

General Douglas MacArthur said. "Duty, honor, country: Those hallowed words reverently dictate what you ought to be, what you can be, what you will be. They are your rallying point to build courage when courage seems to fail, to regain faith when there seems to be little cause for faith, to create hope when hope becomes forlorn."

So what is *your* rallying point? It needs to be something or a series of some things you believe in that can give you strength when life and its decisions and the consequences of those decisions get tough.

Values are often the strength of a leader under stress, what we fall back on.

So then what are ethics? Distinguish between ethics and values and how they relate to navy core values.

Okay, now that I have covered values, we can discuss ethics, for you cannot discuss the latter without understanding the role values play in decision-making and the idea of ethical behavior.

Ethics

    A. Ethics are the moral principles or values held by an individual or group

    B. Ethics are classified by what an individual or group holds important

    Two types of ethics:

1. *Character ethic*. That based on established principles such as integrity, humility, fidelity, temperance, industry, and courage.

2. *Personality ethic*. That based on personality, public image, attitudes and behavior, skills and techniques that lubricate the process of human interaction.

Good advice from Shakespeare: "Speak what we feel, not what we ought to say" (*Shakespeare on Leadership* by Frederick Talbott). Or if you speak the truth, you never have to remember what you said. The difference between saying what may be politically correct but may not necessarily be truthful.

So we are talking about *your personal character*, your ability to walk the walk and talk the talk. This sets up your *pattern of behavior* and your command behavior.

A CO's actions that demonstrate belief and support of ethics impact the ability to lead a command (you will drive the values and ethics environment of your command)

INFORMATION SHEET
HAND OUT "IT'S OK, SON, EVERYBODY DOES IT" AND DISCUSS POSSIBLE IMPACT.

A. Introduction:

- This Information Sheet is provided to support topic discussion.

B. References:

- Griffin, Jack. "It's OK, Son, everybody does it," Chicago Sun-Times.

The following is the text of the article:

When Johnny was 6 years old, he was with his father when they were caught speeding. His father handed the officer a twenty-dollar bill with his driver's license. "It's OK, son," his father said as they drove off. "Everybody does it."

When he was 8, he was present at a family council presided over by Uncle George, on the surest means to shave points off the income tax return. "It's OK, kid," his uncle said. "Everybody does it."

When he was 9, his mother took him to his first theater production. The box-office man couldn't find any seats until his mother discovered an extra $5 in her purse. "It's OK, son," she said. "Everybody does it."

When he was 12, he broke his glasses on the way to school. His aunt Francine persuaded the insurance company that they had been stolen, and they collected $75. "It's OK, kid," she said. "Everybody does it."

When he was 15, he made right guard on the high school football team. His coach showed him how to block and at the same time grab the opposing end by the shirt so the official couldn't see it. "It's OK, kid," the coach said. "Everybody does it."

When he was 16, he took his first summer job at the supermarket. His assignment was to put the overripe strawberries in the bottom of the boxes and the good ones on top where they would show. "It's OK, kid," the manager said. "Everybody does it."

When he was 18, Johnny and a neighbor applied for a college scholarship. Johnny was a marginal student. His neighbor was in the upper 3 percent of his class, but he couldn't play right guard. Johnny got the scholarship. "It's OK, son," his parents said. "Everybody does it."

When he was 19, he was approached by an upperclassman who offered the test answers for $50. "It's OK, kid," he said. "Everybody does it." Johnny was caught and sent home in disgrace. "How could you do this to your mother and me?" His father said. "You never learned anything like this at home." His aunt and uncle were also shocked.

If there's one thing the adult world can't stand, it's a kid who cheats

POINT HERE IS THE IMPORTANCE OF SETTING THE PROPER EXAMPLE

It shows the impact of a negative pattern of behavior or a failure to walk the walk. In the article, fish rot from the head; seniors view the young as having no values and young view seniors as hypocrites. We have all heard the expression, do what I say not what I do.

The above article demonstrates the importance of having credibility, a key element in building bi-directional trust.

In the article **"Ethics without Virtue"** we talk about the difficulty of teaching, learning and practicing values such as decency, honesty, honor, integrity, when we are surrounded by hypocrisy, self-deception, cruelty, selfishness and a careerist mentality.

Admiral Charles R. Larson said, "Good ethical choices do not happen, they are the product of knowledge, wisdom, education, and virtuous habit" (Jeffersonian view which at the time was adopted by the Naval Academy).

What Admiral Larson is implying here is that ethical choices, choosing right from wrong in a situation, are a product of an individual set of values.

Discuss simple everyday examples such as the following:

- Parking space: pulling into a "disabled" spot because you have a short period of time or are just too lazy to walk

- Speed limit: obeying the speed limit? How about with your children in the car? Is there a difference there?
- Lying, half truths
- Backstabbing peers
- Walking by trash in the command
- Being less than kind

Two points:

1. Ethical values must be taught.
2. Ethical values must be practiced.

This is an educational process.

Personal character is what Aristotle referred to as a "habit spawned by years of choosing between right and wrong."

It's the concept of *VIRTUOUS HABIT that I'm introducing here*—that the more you act from an ethical base that is in harmony with your personal values, the more doing the right thing and making the right ethical decisions becomes a habit. It just becomes easier to do the next right thing. It's not easy always doing the right thing. As in the simple examples of parking in a handicap parking space, rolling through a stop sign, speeding with or without your children in the car. While these are simple examples, they say that if you cannot do the simple things, how will you be able to do the more difficult ones.

Main point: If you communicate your set of values consistently and continuously, you will not only make the right decision yourself, you will also lead your people to do the right thing too.

Virtuous habit is the point—and it is not easy.

In your readings, you were introduced to three questions to ask if a decision is ethical or not.

Blanchard/Peale

The "Ethics check" questions:

1. Is it legal?

   Will I be violating either civil law or company policy?

2. Is it balanced?

   Is it fair to all concerned in the short term as well as the long term? Does it promote win-win relationships?

3. How will it make me feel about myself?

   Will it make me proud? Would I feel good if my decision was published in the newspaper? Would I feel good if my family knew about it?

> There is no pillow as soft as a clear conscience. (John Wooden, UCLA basketball coach)

If it's legal does that mean it is ethical or the right thing to do?

If you agree with all this, then how do you go about trying to instill in your people this "do the right thing concept"?

Have groups discuss the following scenarios and be prepared to brief back to the class the key points of their discussion. A couple of very simple examples.

1. A junior officer leaving the ship while moored pier-side passes a third-class petty officer going aboard who does not salute. The JO hesitates momentarily as if to say something but then continues on.

2. A junior officer solicits the assistance of an MM3 who works in his division in the repair of an automobile the JO cannot afford to take in to a repair shop. The MM3 spends several evenings doing repair work on the JO's car. A few weeks later, the MM3 gets a glowing evaluation despite having had public arguments with the divisional LPO.

Q: How does a CO affect a command's value system?

Discussion point: CO serves as role model of ethical behavior and personal values. For example, at a Naval Air Station the current policy (established at a higher level) is that pilots cannot wear flight suits off base. A squadron CO disagrees with the policy and so wears a flight suit off base. This impacts how *other* rules are followed. Again a simple example but one that communicates a message to those you are to lead.

Introduce this concept of tacit approval:

> **Thomas Paine**: "A long habit of not thinking a thing wrong gives it the superficial appearance of being right."
>
> To take no action can translate into acceptable behavior.
>
> There is no right way to do a wrong thing.
>
> Do we know what is the right thing to do and consciously through rationalization decide not to do it?
>
> OR
>
> Have we lost in some respect our right and wrong value system?

ETHICS EXERCISE

TO TAKE NO ACTION IS ACTION BY DEFAULT AND PERHAPS A FAILURE OF LEADERSHIP-TACIT APPROVAL.

-*POINT*: AGAIN THE MORE YOU PRACTICE IT THE STRONGER THE FOUNDATION BECOMES.

TO ILLUSTRATE HOW VALUES CAN FORM YOUR LEADERSHIP FOUNDATION

Stockdale: Prisoner of War, Medal of Honor recipient.

Case Study: Stockdale
CASE STUDY 2-3-1

YEARS OF REFLECTION

Directions: Read the material presented below and engage in small-group discussion to relate the case to the course material.

SCENARIO

In 1965, Vice Admiral (then Commander) James B. Stockdale ejected from his jet over North Vietnam and was taken prisoner. He was released in 1973. During his captivity in Hanoi, he spent a great deal to time thinking about ethics and exercising exceptional leadership, facilitated by extensive covert communications that he and others paid dearly for when caught. He built a command structure, a philosophy, and established regulations appropriate to the circumstances. The following excerpts relating to values and ethics are from a collection of his speeches and writings first published in 1984 as A Vietnam Experience: Ten Years Reflection.

We called our prison Alcatraz...I was the senior officer in confinement there and believe I had the easiest leadership job in the world: to maintain the organization, resistance and spirit of ten of the finest men I have ever known. Each was his own man, with separate senses of purpose and stability, but with a common dedication to the military ethic.

His communications and leadership extended outside Alcatraz, even beyond the Hanoi Hilton as prisoners were moved. Although there were many occasions when under torture he would cry, "I submit," and then write or sign some document for propaganda purposes, he never failed to return to his values when he was physically able. A single failure was not for all time. He looked often to the classics for inspiration:

Aristotle's teacher, Plato, defined courage as "endurance of the soul." Although the Greeks acknowledge the value of the single brave thrust or audacious dash, their hero was more often the man who "hung in there" when the going got tough.

The test of our future leaders' merit may well not lie in hanging in there when the light at the end of the tunnel is expected but rather in their persistence and continued performance of duty when there is no possibility that the light will ever show up.

In "sorting and sifting for a common denominator" that allowed him and other prisoners "to return home with heads held high," he found:

A structured set of values supporting a basic tenet of self-respect was fundamental to the performance of these men.

Looking back, he said he was at first naive about the resources he would need to survive his lengthy captivity:

The system of values I carried with me into this realm was to be tested by my captors. The payoff was my self-respect. I would keep it or it would be torn from me and used as leverage against my senses of purpose and stability. I remembered the basic truth of subjective consciousness as the ability to distinguish what is in my power from that which is not. I recalled that "lameness is an impediment to the leg, but not to the will" and I knew that self-discipline would provide the balance I would need in this contest of high stakes.

The philosopher Durant's said that culture is a thin and fragile veneer that superimposes itself on mankind. For the first time I was on my own, without the veneer. I was to spend years searching through and refining my bag of memories, looking for useful tools, things of value. The values were there, but they were all mixed up with technology, bureaucracy, and expediency and had to be brought up into the open.

Education should take care to illuminate values, not bury them amongst the trivia. Are our students getting the message that without personal integrity intellectual skills are worthless?

Integrity is one of those words which many people keep in that desk drawer labeled "too hard." It's not a topic for the dinner table or the cocktail party. You can't buy or sell it. When supported with education, a person's integrity can give him something to rely on when his perspective seems to blur, when rules and principles seem to waver, and when he's faced with hard choices of right or wrong.

Admiral Stockdale had specific comments about the relationship between legality and values:

"We must realize that laws merely delineate a floor in our behavior, a minimum acceptable level of ethical standards, and that moral standards can and should be set on a higher plane. In the Naval Service we have no place for amoral gnomes lost in narrow orbits; we need to keep our gaze fixed on the high-minded principles standing above the law: Duty, Honor, Country. And on the need for personal leadership and action:

It is certainly convenient to adopt the mores of the bureaucracy and not take on the unpleasant and tedious task of formulating one's own. However, if anything has power to sustain an individual in peace or war, regardless of occupation, it is one's conviction and commitment to define standards of right and wrong.

Self-discipline was vital to self-respect, which in turn is vital to survival and meaningful participation in a POW organization. Self-indulgence is fatal. Daily rituals seems essential to mental and spiritual health. I would do 400 pushups a day, even when I had leg irons on, and would feel guilty when I failed to do them. This ritual paid dividends in self-respect ... (and) it also paid physical dividends. "

Questions:

Relate Admiral Stockdale's comments to specific principles he demonstrated that are important to Navy Leadership.

List the principles identified, and express why they were important in this situation.

POINT: AGAIN THE MORE YOU PRACTICE IT THE STRONGER THE FOUNDATION BECOMES.

Conduct a large group discussion focusing on Stockdale's own personal values.

CDR Stockdale was, by necessity, dishonest with his captors while maintaining the highest integrity.

Main point: It is important to have a personal set of values that you can fall back on to guide you in the actions you take and the decisions you make in your command. Your actions and behaviors will instill a set of values into your command. You have been provided this two weeks to reflect on this and numerous other leadership issues.

"It is by no means enough that an officer of the Navy should be a capable mariner. He must be that, of course, but also a great deal more. He should be as well gentleman of liberal education, refined manners, punctilious courtesy, and the nicest sense of personal honor." (John Paul Jones)

Ask for questions or comments on this quote. Drive home the point the quote is making is the importance of a leader having their own personal values.

John Paul Jones thought personal honor was one of the keys to personal behavior. We will look at this concept of personal honor throughout this course. What is your operational definition of this personal honor?

With that in mind, we then did some case studies, pretty basic ones just to reinforce this pattern of behaviour point.

Montor stated, "Good leaders have an ethical claim to authority. The leader who worries only about the personal gains that he can derive from his position has no such claim. Rather, the ethical claim goes to the officer who only asks where *his duty lies* and then seeks steadfastly to carry it out."

The foundation for the situational leadership model consists of principles, values, and ethics—that was Stockdale's point.

The leadership lesson is the following: While every person may not precisely agree on the definition of values in general, it is *important* that as professionals we agree and support that values are a common basis for ethical leadership decisions.

Why should Navy leadership be founded on ethics, values, and principles?

Ethical behavior and high personal values lead to integrity, which in turn leads to trust. Mutual trust is essential for the leader and follower as both transition through the development stages of leadership.

Do the right thing. Do your duty. Live up to your responsibility under the law.

Read this quote aloud:

> Wrong is wrong even if everyone agrees with it, and right is right even if everyone disagrees with it. (Anonymous)

What do you think this quote is saying?

Discussion points: Terms such as *values*, *ethics*, and *principles* are sometimes confusing and subject to misinterpretation when they ought to illuminate the sometimes-difficult task of "doing the right thing." That is, using sound judgment and applying sound ethical principles to specific situations.

One problem getting in the way of doing the right thing is this idea of careerism.

INFORMATION SHEET

A. Introduction:

This Information Sheet provides excerpts from a 19 December 1994, Navy Times, editorial by Major Michael V. Trujillo, USMC, written while he was stationed at the Pentagon. This excerpt in B. below, presents his views related to core values and ethics.

C. References:

Speaking of men and women who serve our country, Major Trujillo said:

"...they are magnificent young men and women and they continue to serve admirably–in spite of leadership that is all too often unprincipled and self-serving. I know it may come as a shock to many, but there are far too many officers who put their careers first and stepped on the faces of these magnificent young men and women in their "sacred labor" to secure rank.

Sixteen years ago, when I came into the Marine Corps as a second lieutenant, I was idealistic about matters of honor, integrity, courage, those virtues that have been codified as "core values." These days I have come to believe that ethical behavior is all too often situational, based on self-preservation or loyalty to a personality at the expense of integrity. Telling the truth or standing on principle can be tantamount to professional suicide, while complicity in the same situation buys into a larger ascendancy of the same ilk.

We constantly hear how the people in today's military are the best and brightest in history. Yet they are expected to accept with unquestioning obedience behavior from senior officers that clearly wouldn't be tolerated in the lower ranks. Rank does have its privileges; unfortunately, some feel putting themselves above the law without fear of culpability is one of them."

In the same vein, a quote from Roger Nye's The Challenge of Command "It is possible for a captain of average ability to be quite successful in the eyes of higher authorities if he faithfully obeys orders, enforces standards set by others, and does not violate some cardinal rules of leadership and management. This is good follower ship but it is not command."

Theory has it that careerism breeds a "zero defects" mentality:

"All mistakes and crimes become the same mistake, because the punishment is the same. The result is that everyone is fighting to keep an absolutely clean record, they're unwilling to admit mistakes, and you get a lot of "my career" concerns. That's when integrity problems start." Derek Vander Schaaf, DOD Deputy IG

And now the death penalty theory here; meaning that every mistake receives the death penalty, which strikes at the heart and impedes the crucial training concept of intelligent risk-taking. Careerism is not living a life of integrity. It is not living up to your responsibilities under the Law to take "all measures."

By contrast, integrity is conforming those words, "all measures" to reality. Integrity is a firm adherence to a code of espoused values; "walking the talk" of an individual's personal value system.

PERSONAL INTEGRITY LEADS TO PEACE OF MIND, PERSONAL WORTH, AND INTRINSIC SECURITY.

"The integrity of a society or group is approximately equal to the lowest common denominator of its people. When the standards are lowered for an individual, the standards for the group or society to which the individual belongs are lowered." Admiral Burke.

"The leader must always work from an ethical base; the art of leadership depends on value judgments. The leader's personal ability to discriminate between right and wrong may be the only resource at his disposal. Time may not permit him to consult with others. He must stand up for his beliefs, even if he stands alone. The expedient and the right courses of action may coincide; if not, the leader must choose and we must prepare him for his choice by reinforcing, throughout his career, the ethical base as the source of his decisions." Admiral Trost:

What are some examples of when you have seen positive or negative displays of integrity in the fleet or ashore?

Some simple examples:

Positive: A Functional Check Flight (FCF) pilot had multiple check flights to accomplish on a particular day. On the second check flight the #2 engine was tested when it should have been the #1 engine. The aircraft was returned, reported safe for flight, and released on a cross-country flight to a new crew. Upon realizing the error, the FCF pilot interrupted a brief and told the XO who contacted the crew via radio to abort the cross-country flight.

Negative: A seamen went to mast and was fined for using a duty vehicle off base for a personal errand. The next week, the XO reportedly used the CO's sedan to go to lunch at a local fast food restaurant.

DO WE SACRIFICE OUR INTEGRITY BECAUSE OF OUR OWN LEADERSHIP FAILURE?

I think the best piece on integrity was written by Admiral Arleigh Burke in a letter to Professor Karel Montor. This piece was published in the October 1985 issue of *Proceedings*.

Integrity

"First you find yourself overlooking small infractions that you would have corrected on the spot in the past. Soon, you are participating in these infractions. "After all," you say, "everybody's doing it." All too soon you find yourself trapped:

you no longer can stand on a favorite principle because you have strayed from it. Finding no way out, you begin to rationalize and then you are hooked. The important fact is, the men who travel the path outlined above have misused the very basic quality and characteristic expected of a professional military man, or any other professional man for that matter: they have compromised their integrity. "

I took this statement and introduced a concept called "the I box."

The idea is that you start out in life with your personal integrity represented by the letter I, in the middle of a perfect square. We discussed the fact that integrity cannot be taken from you, it must be sacrificed by the individual. Just like in the concept of virtuous habit, the longer you make decisions in line with your values, the longer your integrity square stays intact. But like in the box, if you make a decision against your values, you make a cut in one of the corners of your box, which in turn starts a deforming process. Significant errors make bigger cuts. Each cut creates new corners and so on. The more unethical decisions you make the more your "I" box begins to look like a circle. Once you start sacrificing your own integrity it gets easier to do the wrong thing. The idea introduced that perhaps the true measure of success is to finish your time on earth with as much of your I Box intact as possible.

I know mine has numerous new corners, but it's not a circle yet. How's yours?

Sometimes it's the little things like stop signs and speeding limits. Certainly these things don't count?—Ah! but they do.

TALKING ABOUT THIS TEST OF INTEGRITY

"What you find is that the tough choices are not between good and evil, but between two goods: in this case between loyalty and truth." Adm Larson

The idea of "HIERARCHY OF LOYALTIES" is introduced.

"The naval academy now teaches a hierarchy of loyalties: to the constitution, the country, the navy, the ship, the shipmate and, lastly to self." Adm Larson

If your values were right would loyalty to self take care of this problem?

This Jeffersonian/Thomas Paine idea of living a life of integrity "Where does intrinsic security come from? It doesn't come from what other people think of us or how they treat us. It doesn't come from scripts they've handed us. It doesn't come from our circumstances or our position. It comes from within. It comes from accurate paradigms and correct principles deep in our own mind and heart. It comes from inside-out congruence, from living a life of integrity in which our daily habits reflect our deepest values." Steven Covey

"I believe that a life of integrity is the most fundamental source of personal worth. I do not agree with the popular success literature that says that self-esteem is primarily a matter of mindset, of attitude—that you can psych yourself into peace of mind. Peace of mind comes when your life is in harmony with true principles and values and in no other way." Steven Covey

Short discussion here on Coveys' quote AS A LESSON SUMMARY.

Reference Covey, 1989, pages 195-197 and Covey, 1990, pages 108 and 171.

In this lesson we have covered values (including the navy's core values) and ethics and the need for integrity to live by them, teach them to our commands, and lead in accordance with their tenets. Only in this way can we be true to ourselves and those around us.

This idea of virtuous habit, setting the consistent example concept, bridges the values gap, and is by law your command responsibility and leadership challenge.

For as Roger Nye says in his book—Challenge of Command—for those you are to lead-:

"Their best school is a living one—the men and women around them who have integrity of character to speak and act in a moral manner. Observing and listening to these moral arbiters reveals the roots of their beliefs, the source of their values, and the rationales for their action. Observing and listening also reveals the high value placed on their personal reputations-or, as soldiers have said for centuries, on their personal honor."

Perhaps when we are to "deliver up honor," this is what is meant both in peace and combat or crisis. When in command, what will you deliver up when the time comes? A tough question for all of us and worth a little introspective thought.

In the next lesson, you will look at how your personal values, ethics, and integrity can help create your personal vision and ultimately lead to your command vision and command philosophy.

CHAPTER 7

PERSONAL VISION

The need for a personal vision—based on lesson topic originally written and taught by Captain Mark Purcell.

We've established earlier that leadership is influencing others to accomplish the mission by providing purpose, direction, and motivation. Do we all agree that leadership at least encompasses these requirements?

How does a personal vision contribute to your command leadership task of providing purpose, direction, and motivation? It does so by the concept of "where you want to go?" This forms the foundation from which to articulate the desired end state of the command or organization.

Is this idea of a personal vision a new concept? We are not talking about a vision statement. The idea of a personal vision has been around throughout history.

Is it possible to have a winning organization without some sort of shared vision?

What we are going to be talking about is personal vision, what it is and why it is important, and how you might assess or review your own.

Studies reveal that all successful organizations had a shared vision. So if a shared organizational vision is important to be a winner, then you'll obviously want some of this at your command/organization. If so, then whose responsibility is it to provide this unifying purpose to your command? Do you think you can accomplish it if you haven't settled it for yourself? Why or why not?

It's hard to lead into the future if you don't know where you want to go. This is the reason our navy cares whether you have a personal vision. You need to possess one to effectively build and maintain a winner. Your command will reflect your personal vision.

Then how do we go about examining or developing our own vision?

Let's start at the most elementary level. In his book, "*7 habits of highly effective people*," Covey says all things are created twice. What does he mean? He is talking about the mental process first, followed by the physical creation. Vision is the *mental* creation. So how can we go about developing the mental picture for ourselves? A good way is to figure out how to address all areas of your life. Where you are and where you want to be. Covey provided a very good way to shoe-horn yourself into our "how to think" process introduced earlier.

He talks about imagining yourself at your own funeral. You are this ethereal being hovering in the back row of the church. At the funeral are members from all walks of your life: family, friends, workmates, members of your church, classmates, social contacts, peers, etc. They are all there to eulogize you, and they represent all facets of your life. As each one comes up to speak about you, think about what you would like them to express. In other words, if your brother were to give remarks, what would you like him to say about you as a brother, and so on down the list. What would you like your friends to say, your parents, etc.

This is not a trivial drill, and it takes some time. Once that is completed, then for each aspect write down how you really are. For most of us, there will be a delta between what we would like to be and who we really are. The important part is to then figure out what must be done or changed to achieve what you would like to be in each aspect. A plan to become a better person in all walks of your life is created. You have created a mental vision and a physical plan to become a better person in all walks of your life. The execution of your plan becomes the physical creation of your vision.

In addition, as you do this drill you will also understand more about both your strengths and weakness in your profession. The idea of the plan is to act to take advantage of your strengths and figure out ways to shore up your weakness. As is often said, the first thing needed to correct a problem is to admit you have one. It's a good drill and one that I highly recommend to all. To have an understanding of where you are and where you want to be is an essential leadership decision-making foundation.

So do leaders simply hand out a personal vision statement? No, they do not. So how then do we usually see their vision? Normally it is reflected in their philosophy of actions, in the decisions that they make. It is reflected in the things they hold important, what they hold out that is important for all to see.

Two such examples were assigned for reading. They are provided here for the reader and for discussion.

A. Introduction:

This information sheet provides excerpts from speeches made by Martin Luther King, Jr. and John F. Kennedy. They provide examples of personal vision.

B. References:

1. Martin Luther King's speech of August 28, 1963, given at the Lincoln Memorial in Washington, DC.

2. John F. Kennedy's Democratic Party presidential nomination acceptance speech in Los Angeles, CA, on July 15, 1960.

First MLK's:

"I say to you today, my friends, that in spite of the difficulties and frustrations of the moment, I still have a dream. It is a dream deeply rooted in the American dream.

I have a dream that one day this nation will rise up and live out the true meaning of its creed: "We hold these truths to be self-evident; that all men are created equal."

I have a dream that one day on the red hills of Georgia the sons of former slaves and the sons of former slave owners will be able to sit down together at the table of brotherhood.

I have a dream that one day even in the state of Mississippi, a desert state sweltering with the heat of injustice and oppression, will be transformed into an oasis of freedom and justice.

I have a dream that my four little children will one day live in a nation where they will not be judged by the color of their skin but by the content of their character.

I have a dream today.

I have a dream that one day the state of Alabama, whose governor's lips are presently dripping with the words of interposition and nullification, will be transformed into a situation where little black boys and black girls will be able to join hands with little white boys and white girls and walk together as sisters and brothers.

I have a dream today.

I have a dream that one day every valley shall be exalted, every hill and mountain shall be made low, the rough places will be made plains, and the crooked places will be made straight, and the glory of the Lord shall be revealed, and all flesh shall see it together.

This is our hope. This is the faith with which I return to the South. With this faith we will be able to hew out of the mountain of despair a stone of hope. With this faith we will be able to transform the jangling discords of our nation into a beautiful symphony of brotherhood. With this faith we will be able to work together, to pray together, to struggle together, to go to jail together, to stand up for freedom together, knowing that we will be free one day."

John F. Kennedy's acceptance speech as follows:

"The American people expect more from us than cries of indignation and attack. The times are too grave, the challenge too urgent, and stakes too high to permit the customary passion of political debate. We are not here to curse the darkness, but to light the candle that can guide us through that darkness to a safe and sane future. As Winston Churchill said on taking office some 20 years ago:

'If we open a quarrel between the present and the past, we shall be in danger of losing the future.'

Today our concern must be with that future. For the world is changing. The old era is ending. The old ways will not do.

All over the world, particularly in the newer nations, young men are coming to power–men who are not bound by the traditions of the past–men who are not blinded by the old fears and hates and rivalries–young men who can cast off the old slogans and delusions and suspicions...

... For I stand tonight facing west on what was once the last frontier. From the lands that stretch

3,000 miles behind me, the pioneers of old gave up their safety, their comfort, and sometimes their lives to build a new world here in the West.

They were not the captives of their own doubts, the prisoners of their own price tags. Their motto was not 'every man for himself'–but 'all for the common cause.' They were determined to make that new world strong and free, to overcome its hazards and its hardships, to conquer the enemies that threatened from without and within.

Today some would say that those struggles are all over–that all the horizons have been explored–that all the battles have been won–that there is no longer an American frontier.

But I trust that no one in this assemblage will agree with those sentiments. For the problems are not all solved and the battles are not all won–and we stand today on the edge of a new frontier–the frontier of the 1960s–a frontier of unknown opportunities and perils–a frontier of unfulfilled hopes and threats.

Woodrow Wilson's New Freedom promised our nation a new political and economic framework. Franklin Roosevelt's New Deal promised security and succor to those in need. But the New Frontier of which I speak is not a set of promises–it is a set of challenges. It sums up not what I intend to offer the American people, but what I intend to ask of them. It appeals to their pride, not their pocketbook–it holds out the promise of more sacrifice instead of more security.

But I tell you the New Frontier is here, whether we seek it or not. Beyond that frontier are uncharted areas of science and space, unsolved problems of peace and war, unconquered pockets of ignorance and prejudice, unanswered questions of poverty and surplus.

It would be easier to shrink back from that frontier, to look to the safe mediocrity of the past, to be lulled by good intentions and high rhetoric—and those who prefer that course should not cast their votes for me, regardless of party. But I believe the times demand invention, innovation, imagination, decision. I am asking each of you to be new pioneers on that New Frontier. My call is to the young in heart, regardless of age—to the stout in spirit, regardless of party—to all who respond to the scriptural call:

'Be strong and of good courage; be not afraid, neither be thou dismayed.'

For courage—not complacency—is our need today—leadership—not salesmanship. And the only valid test of leadership is the ability to lead, and lead vigorously..."

It is important to take some time to go through the speeches and underline those things you see that provide insights of their own vision and values in their speech. There are many examples.

We are going to look at two other examples of military leaders creating a vision for their men from their own personal values and goals—their own vision. We will look for key issues, which reveal their ideals and the issues that motivate their followers. After these two videos, we'll compare and contrast some of the differences and similarities between the speeches and videos. *(I will describe the scenes from the two videos and provide the remarks. Most I believe have seen the movies and should remember the scenes.)*

In *Gettysburg*, Colonel Chamberlain is the commander of a Civil War infantry unit from Maine. They are a part of the Army of the Potomac, chasing General Lee and the Army of Virginia into Pennsylvania and ultimately destined to meet at Gettysburg. Colonel Chamberlain is about to address the mutineers of the disbanded Second Maine who have been brought to him under guard. They have refused to fight, saying they only signed up to fight with the Second Maine. Colonel Chamberlain's unit is the only other unit from Maine in the corps and he has been given the authority to shoot these 120 men as deserters, if necessary. Like we covered in topic 1.2, it is a great example of the importance of the leader to be able to explain the reasons "why here?" and "why now?" That is to say, why he is fighting, and why the war is important; why they should fight, and what they are actually fighting for.

As you read his speech, made entirely off the cuff, note his skills at using the word "we," his constant linking of the overall aim of the war with the present choice the men face, and most of all, his repeated use of three points together, as he spoke, one of the most powerful techniques in presentations.

Colonel Chamberlain approached all the deserters just after they arrived and spoke to them as a group:

I've been ordered to take you men with me, I'm told that if you (laughs quietly) don't come I can shoot you. Well, you know I won't do that. Maybe somebody else will, but I won't, so that's that. Here's the situation, the Whole Reb army is up that road aways waiting for us, so this is no time for an argument like this, I tell you. We could surely use you fellahs, we're now well below half strength. Whether you fight or not, that's up to you, whether you come along is is…well, you're coming. You know who we are and what we are doing here, but if you are going to fight alongside us there are a few things I want you to know. This regiment was formed last summer, in Maine. There were a thousand of us then, there are less than 300 of us now. All of us volunteered to fight for the Union, just as you have. Some came mainly because we were bored at home, thought this looked like it might be fun. Some came because we were ashamed not to, many of us came because it was the right thing to do. And all of us have seen men die. This is a different kind of army. If you look back through history you will see men fighting for pay, for women, for some other kind of loot. They fight for land, power, because a king leads them, or just because they like killing. But we are here for something new, this has not happened much, in the history of the world. We are an army out to set other men free. America should be free ground, all of it, not divided by a line between slave states and free – all the way from here to the Pacific Ocean. No man has to bow. No man born to royalty. Here we judge you by what you do, not by who your father was. Here you can be something. Here is the place to build a home. But it's not the land, there's always more land. It's the idea that we all have value – you and me. What we are fighting for, in the end, we're fighting for each other. Sorry, I didn't mean to preach. You go ahead and you talk for awhile. If you choose to join us and you want your muskets back you can have them – nothing more will be said by anyone anywhere. If you choose not to join us well then you can come along under guard and when this is all over I will do what I can to ensure you get a fair trial, but for now we're moving out. Gentlemen, I think if we lose this fight we lose the war, so if you choose to join us I will be personally very grateful.

There were 114 out of 120 deserters joined with the regiment immediately, with another four joining up later.

The next example is in Shakespeare's play, King Henry V. (*Yes, we actually used Shakespeare in the leadership school, to illustrate the "how to think" concept that being introduced to great writers and philosophers, one learns "how to think" versus "what to think."*)

"King Hal" has brought an English Army to France to enforce his territorial claims there. After two weeks of battles and marches through Normandy, the English face a fresh and heavily superior foe as they attempt to withdraw toward Calais. On the morning of the climactic Battle of Agincourt in 1415, King Henry must rally his tired and dispirited troops for a battle against seemingly impossible odds.

St. Crispen's Day Speech *William Shakespeare, 1599*
Enter the KING

WESTMORELAND. O that we now had here
But one ten thousand of those men in England
That do no work to-day!

KING. What's he that wishes so?
My cousin Westmoreland? No, my fair cousin;
If we are mark'd to die, we are enow
To do our country loss; and if to live,
The fewer men, the greater share of honour.
God's will! I pray thee, wish not one man more.
By Jove, I am not covetous for gold,
Nor care I who doth feed upon my cost;
It yearns me not if men my garments wear;
Such outward things dwell not in my desires.
But if it be a sin to covet honour,
I am the most offending soul alive.
No, faith, my coz, wish not a man from England.
God's peace! I would not lose so great an honour
As one man more methinks would share from me
For the best hope I have. O, do not wish one more!
Rather proclaim it, Westmoreland, through my host,
That he which hath no stomach to this fight,
Let him depart; his passport shall be made,
And crowns for convoy put into his purse;
We would not die in that man's company
That fears his fellowship to die with us.
This day is call'd the feast of Crispian.
He that outlives this day, and comes safe home,

Will stand a tip-toe when this day is nam'd,
And rouse him at the name of Crispian.
He that shall live this day, and see old age,
Will yearly on the vigil feast his neighbours,
And say 'To-morrow is Saint Crispian.'
Then will he strip his sleeve and show his scars,
And say 'These wounds I had on Crispian's day.'
Old men forget; yet all shall be forgot,
But he'll remember, with advantages,
What feats he did that day. Then shall our names,
Familiar in his mouth as household words—
Harry the King, Bedford and Exeter,
Warwick and Talbot, Salisbury and Gloucester—
Be in their flowing cups freshly rememb'red.
This story shall the good man teach his son;
And Crispin Crispian shall ne'er go by,
From this day to the ending of the world,
But we in it shall be remembered—
We few, we happy few, we band of brothers;
For he to-day that sheds his blood with me
Shall be my brother; be he ne'er so vile,
This day shall gentle his condition;
And gentlemen in England now-a-bed
Shall think themselves accurs'd they were not here,
And hold their manhoods cheap whiles any speaks
That fought with us upon Saint Crispin's day.

What a great play to read or view in its entirety, because it has great lessons in leadership throughout. Rallying men, mental and physical endurance, the sustaining strength of values in times of doubt, fear, and defeat, the need for second and third efforts in combat, and the value of humility and mercy in victory.

So we have provided some examples of "vision." Now let's have a discussion on some common threads between these visions.

How are they different? Could the principal characters adhere to one another's vision statements and be credible? Did each leader understand his men well enough to translate his own values into an appeal that pushed the right buttons? Would Henry's vision have worked for Chamberlain's troops? Chamberlain reveals his own deep moral convictions to his country and to the justness of its cause. He appeals to his men's values and the unique contribution each can make. He reveals his personal values when he says–"most joined because it was *the right thing to do.*" Would the men have followed him without a belief in his personal commitment to those values/vision?

Henry conveys to his bedraggled troops his own exhilaration and appeals to their patriotism and honor. He creates a vision of glory and brotherhood. Not sure that would have worked in the case of Chamberlain's deserters.

There are some common threads here: challenge to a worthy cause, a higher mission or purpose, shared values and the idea of being special or unique, the notion that the effort is worth the struggle.

All resonate with who we are as individuals, and this is precisely why your personal vision must be more than just "my success" in career terms. Otherwise, your people will not share that vision! Nor will you be able to articulate a different vision that you can actually live out for several years and be credible.

Whose speech seems most similar to which video? And why?

Kennedy or Henry V:

JFK: "Should not cast their votes for me regardless of party."

Hal: "Let his passport be made and coins for convoy—we would not die…"

The challenge: call to courage, conflict, struggle, leadership, "glory"—the idea that the world can be made better.

Col. Chamberlain or Dr. King:

Both dream of struggle and the value in freeing men. All created equal under the Constitution, God's image of man, struggle is for our own ennoblement too! Call to values, inner principles. Man can be better!

In *The Fifth Discipline* by Peter Senge, he uses the example from the movie *Spartacus* to illustrate the power of a *shared* vision:

> You may remember the movie Spartacus, an adaptation of the story of a Roman gladiator/slave who led an army of slaves in an uprising in 71 B.C. They defeated the Roman legions twice, but were finally conquered by the general Marcus Crassus after a long siege and battle.

In the movie, Crassus tells the thousand survivors in Spartacus's army, "You have been slaves. You will be slaves again, but you will be spared your rightful punishment of crucifixion by the mercy of the Roman legions. All you need to do is turn over to me the slave Spartacus, because we do not know him by sight.

After a long pause, Spartacus (played by Kirk Douglas) stands up and says, "I am Spartacus." Then the man next to him stands up and claims he too is Spartacus; then the next; then the next, etc.... Within a minute, everyone in the army is on his feet.

It does not matter whether this story is apocryphal or not. It demonstrates a deep truth. Every man, by standing up, chose death. But the loyalty of Spartacus's army was not to Spartacus the man. Their loyalty was to the shared vision which Spartacus had inspired, the idea that they could be free men. This vision was so compelling that no man could bear to give it up and return to slavery.

A shared vision is not an idea. It is not even an important idea, such as freedom; it is, rather, a force in people's hearts, a force of impressive power. It may be inspired by an idea, but once it goes further—if it is compelling enough to acquire the support of more than one person—then it is no longer an abstraction. It is palpable. People begin to see it as shared vision.

At its simplest level, a shared vision is the answer to the question, "What do we want to create?" Just as personal visions are pictures or images people carry in their heads and hearts, so too are shared visions pictures that people throughout an organization carry.

They create a sense of commonality that permeates the organization and gives coherence to diverse activities.

A vision is truly shared when you and I have a similar picture and are committed to one another having it, not just to each of us, individually, having it. When people truly share a vision they are connected, bound together by a common aspiration. Personal visions derive their power from an individual's deep caring for the vision. Shared visions derive their power from a common caring. In fact, we have to come to believe that one of the reasons people seek to build shared visions is their desire to be connected in an important undertaking.

Shared vision is vital for the learning organization because it provides the focus and energy for learning. While adaptive learning is possible without visions, generative learning occurs only when people are striving to accomplish something that matters deeply to them. In fact, the whole idea of generative learning— "expanding your ability to create"—will seem abstract and meaningless *until* people become excited about some vision they truly want to accomplish.

Today, "vision" is a familiar concept in corporate leadership. But when you look carefully you find that most "visions" are one person's (or one group's) vision imposed on an organization. Such visions, at best, command compliance—not commitment. A shared vision is a vision that many people are truly committed to, because it reflects their own personal vision. (*The Fifth Discipline* by Peter Senge)

One of the great examples we used as an effective vision was the story about the reporter who toured NASA in the sixties and got to talk to all the important folks, etc. Near the end of the day, the reporter saw a cleaning lady working and asked her what she did. The woman replied she was helping to put a man on the moon. That's an effective institutional vision and an example we used often.

We put together an assignment sheet to assist the students in writing their vision:

ASSIGNMENT SHEET 2-4-1

A. Introduction:

This Assignment Sheet is designed to assist the student in the development of a draft vision statement.

B. References:

Covey, Stephen R. The 7 Habits of Highly Effective People. New York: Fireside Edition, Simon & Schuster, 1989, pages 96-144.

Develop a personal vision statement. This statement is to be your personal vision, not a command vision statement, and should address those issues and concerns of most importance to you. Your statement may address all areas of your life, for example family, civic, and spiritual, etc., though it need not do so for this exercise. However, your statement must address the professional aspects of your personal vision.

Recognize that this assignment is not something that can usually be done quickly, but rather usually requires some introspection and personal evaluation. Developing a valid personal vision statement will force you to come to terms with those things that you personally value most or perhaps even recognition of areas where you desire to change. Think back to the funeral example as one way to start.

This statement is not designed to be disseminated, as a command philosophy would be, it is for your use only. Within this course, no copies will be made and no grade assigned to your paper. Your original will be held in strict confidence by the staff and will be returned to you personally.

As an aide in developing this statement the following approach may be helpful. Draw up a list of values, which are most important to you, and the characteristics you would like to see reflected in your command. Include in this list your own personal ideas of what success is for you. Ask yourself how you will know or measure whether you have had a successful command tour. Then review these items and consider how they might be reflected in your tour. Now you can begin to assess what it is that you really want to envision for yourself and your command.

For example, if you believe in the innate value of all people then your vision would probably encompass a desire to build an equal opportunity mind set in your command, perhaps combining respect for individual differences with individual responsibility to the organization. Or, if you believe that a strong spiritual foundation is important to your command, your vision might drive you to attend weekly religious services as a personal example, which might encourage others, and to ensure time is available for the religious observations of your crew.

Your personal statement should be about a page in length, but may go longer if you desire.

If you have any questions please feel free to talk with your mentor concerning this assignment.

(Students were required to turn them in to their assigned mentor. I have provided an example in the back, appendix C, one that I particularly liked from all the ones I received while an instructor. I asked the CO if I could keep it as an example—he said I could. I always wanted to follow up and see if this CO was able to instill his vision in his command. A command that was like his vision would have been a thing to see. I sincerely hope he achieved it.)

Personal vision not only provides the well-spring for your command philosophy. It also will serve to animate and inspire you, helping transform purpose into action, perhaps pushing you to that higher level, when "good enough" might otherwise have been tempting.

If you think back to MacArthur's or Chamberlain's speeches, you can clearly see what it is that keeps them going. Intentions and ideas are great (and a necessary first step), but ultimately, it is what we *do* that counts. Surely we live what we truly value in our hearts?

Know yourself well enough to be secure in what you really value and really want. Only then you will be able to live it consistently, and it *will* ring true for your subordinates.

For the purpose of the book, I have presented two topics from unit 2, "Foundation of Personal Leadership," "Ethics and Core Values and Personal Vision."

Unit 2 was intended to examine the personal and ethical aspects of leadership, including our own leadership styles and their application to the leadership model; and the valuable role of personal vision in building and sustaining command vision and ultimately your command philosophy and command climate.

Unit 3, "Command Leadership," was designed to take this foundation and begin applying your personal abilities and strengths to interactions with other people, in an optimal way. I will present three topics from unit 3: 3.1 The Command Leadership Framework, 3.7 Developing Subordinates, and 3.8 communicating with superiors and other COs.

CHAPTER 8

....

3.1 COMMAND LEADERSHIP FRAMEWORK

THE ART OF PLANNING

Where we are

So far we have talked about your personal values and the importance they play in leadership decision-making. You have been provided an opportunity to sort through your values, leading to a personal vision, who you are and what you want to be. That "how to think" exercise, should lead you to your personal philosophy of how you want to live your life. To accomplish this change, you should have developed personal goals designed to become a better person in all facets of your life. Then we discussed the next step, which is to develop a command or organizational vision, a drill to define what your command is to be like and, what you want it to value. To accomplish this, you will need to have a plan that is based on realistic goals, goals that will lead to unity and achieve the right side of your successful command or organizational leadership equation.

We have talked about creating things twice, the *mental* followed by *the physical*. In Unit 3 we focus on your command and the importance of your positive and values-based leadership in making it a successful command, as personally defined. To achieve this you must formulate a plan. In this topic, I will briefly talk about the importance of planning. We'll discuss a tool used in the old Command Leadership School that, if applied, should lead to a well thought out execution plan to achieve your command vision, and instill your personal and command philosophy. The command leadership framework allows you, if you so choose, to logically incorporate the information and concepts you will be exposed to in Units 3, 4 and 5.

PLANNING

Enhanced command effectiveness is the purpose of planning. Planning is a tool that enables CO's to incorporate their visions and goals throughout the command.

In topic 1.2, I introduced three main responsibilities of leaders, to provide *purpose, direction and motivation*. Along with previously mentioned topics, IE 2.4, personal goals, plans and vision. This lesson topic introduces, the second of these three, namely **direction.**

Definitions serve no purpose unless they are useful in pointing out that some simply do not lend themselves to any argument or in-depth intellectual discussion. These are usually a blinding flash of the obvious, so here is my definition of planning. Post slide.

Planning is the process of deciding in advance what to accomplish and how to accomplish it.

It takes a lot of effort and energy to prepare for the tasks and missions we are asked to perform. You are currently in the planning phase to assume command. How well you are prepared to take command, and what both you and your command will accomplish, has a lot to do with the planning you are or are not doing right now. Without effective planning you will not reach your operational definition of a successful command.

Throughout most military history, at least all the history I read in strategy and policy, most things did not just happen. Most victories and defeats were a result of planning, obviously some good, and some bad. The successful execution of a plan that was the result of an evolution or process of planning made the Admiral or General to appear endowed with genius. Napoleon was asked 'how come you're so smart? His reply was:

(Post Napoleon slide.)

> If I always appear prepared, it is because before embarking on an undertaking, I have meditated for long and have foreseen what may occur. It is not genius, which reveals to me suddenly and secretly what

> I should do in circumstances unexpected by others; it
> is thought and meditation. (Napoleon, 1769–1821)

The point here is it takes a lot of work to be successful.
The difference between good and genius is a lot of hard work.

The purpose of planning are the following:

- Builds teamwork
- Develops a shared understanding
- Facilitates decision making
- Established control and measurement

Can you think of any additional advantages planning
offers the leader of a command or organization?

Superior commands:

The importance of effective planning was pointed out in the
command excellence study. Planning was singled out as the
significant reason differentiating those commands that were
superior and those that were only average. (Twenty-one
commands air, surface and subsurface, shore, twelve superior,
nine average). In superior commands, these points were
common with regard to *planning*.

(Post planning slide.)

- Planning is a regularly scheduled activity.

- Planning occurs at all levels.

- Planning is long-range.

- Plans are specific.

- Plans are publicized.

- Systems are put in place to implement plans.

- Command tries to stick to the plan.

We will talk more about the difference between inadequate planning and effective planning. It has a lot to do with outlining goals to achieve objectives that are *smart*. I hate acronyms, but this is a good way to remember this important concept, and when you are studying the framework, you will need to know what this means.

SMART

S–Specific
M–Measurable
A–Achievable
R–Results-oriented
T–Time determined

Long-Range Planning

I can tell you from my experience as a commanding officer, that as the CO, you are the long-range planner and big picture guy. This is not by design but rather by default, because no one else is preoccupied with the future, they are wrapped up in the slings and arrows of the here and now. The point is that you as the CO either control your destiny and schedule, or someone will control it for you. In our business, all situations demand that you lead, follow, or get out of the way. You all have to be in the *first* category, the point being that you must not let someone outside the command drive your command, because if you let them, they will.

Why use the framework?

All of us plan and control events important to the organizations we direct. In smaller, reasonably well-structured organizations, planning may be a combination of working with subordinates, memory, and back of the envelope notes. This method works reasonable well until the size and complexity of the organization/command involves a stream of events that are beyond your cognitive limits. When this happens, resorting to memory or a "one thing at a time" approach to events, will inevitably result in a negative impact on your organization's effectiveness. Instead, you must adopt some sort of formal planning and control system in order to grasp and then guide organizational and personal purpose.

Command Leadership Framework
Phase I: Where Are We?

1. Determine the mission.

2. Personal responsibilities, leadership style.

3. Analyze the external and internal environment.

Comments/Questions to Ask:

Command's mission?

Do you agree with the mission?

What must I do? Who am I? Do my values fit the command? What leadership style is appropriate? My strengths and weaknesses?

External: Opportunities, threats, risks, expectations, superiors, resources, constraints, mission?

Internal: Strengths/competencies, structure, process, trends, uncertainties, commitment, officers/crew, culture, morale, command climate?

Phase II: Where Do We Want to Go?

4. Develop the vision and command values.

5. Define the key processes.

6. Identify the gap(s).

7. Develop objectives.

Comments/Questions to Ask

Formulate and constantly communicate the "future" command.

Tasks with greatest effect on command mission success.

Difference between real (as is) and ideal (vision) command end state.

Long-range (strategic) and short—range (operational) objectives. Goals developed to achieve Objectives. Think smart (*s*pecific, *m*easurable, *a*chievable, *r*esults-oriented, *t*ime determined). What key variables to track and measure? What do they tell about efficiency and effectiveness? Do they improve combat readiness?

Phase III: How Do We Get There?

8. Develop implementation plan.

Phase IV: Are We Getting There?

9. Monitor performance/feedback analysis.

Comments/Questions to Ask:

What, how, who, when? Priorities? Planning/control system support? Output measures appropriate? Delegation? Culture/socialization?

Quality in daily work emphasized.

10. Review and evaluation.

Comments/Questions to Ask:

Planning/control system with appropriate measures. Efficiency and/or effectiveness? Formal? Informal? Goal displacement?

Changes inserted as SOPs (standard operating procedures). Reprioritize. Continuous improvement.

WHERE DID IT COME FROM?

The command leadership framework was introduced to me at the Naval War College during a strategic planning phase of NSDM, (National Security Decision Making) I took the basic idea, modified and expanded it to apply to an operational command. The concepts apply to a large or small ship, fleet, or to a shore command or organization.

The command leadership framework reflections memo should be the starting point to begin to get a better understanding of what we are trying to provide to you.

REFLECTIONS ON THE COMMAND LEADERSHIP FRAMEWORK

Units 3, 4, and 5 of the course focused on you as the leader, and on the process of leading your command. Each of you has had considerable leadership experience in getting to this point in your careers. However, this part of the course is concerned with commands that you are not expert in everything that happens. These commands are too large to be led by reaching out and personally touching each and every function and task.

Taking over this type of command requires a well thought out and balanced plan. The concepts and the framework are intended to serve as tools for you to use in constructing and implementing such a strategy. You will benefit by carefully considering the framework and the concepts before attempting to orchestrate a significant change, or establishing a planning process to achieve success in your command.

BREAKING DOWN THE FRAMEWORK.

The natural tendency in the military is to jump right into the fray by listing problems and developing solutions. As understandable as this approach is to those of us who are action-and results-oriented, it could turn out to be a mistake. If insufficient attention is paid to the front-end of the process, the command might miss valuable opportunities, and its priorities may end up being established by others through the tyranny of the in-box. (If you as the CO are not controlling your command's destiny, some staffer will). Your command could be in a crisis mode, and fixing things that **are symptoms of a problem**, when instead, the **root cause** could have been discovered and fixed which get you out in front of the power curve.

It is worth noting that the process involved in formulating a command plan can be extremely beneficial even if all the specific elements of the plan are never precisely implemented. For example, thinking about a vision and about how it might become genuinely energizing, or about how to make sure that your plans become more than just another piece of paper, will be constructive whether or not you decide to use the framework.

Below are some observations that you may wish to consider if you see a benefit in a systematic approach to balancing long term priorities with the demands of the here and now. Taking a systems planning look at your command might be the difference between a superior and an average command.

OBSERVATIONS:

Where are we? The first step, mission, can be interpreted in a number of ways. For those of you familiar with five-paragraph OP orders, mission could imply a specific set of tasks. In using our framework, it would be better to consider the broader and implied missions of the organization. The mission describes the present situation, what the organization does, the purpose for which it was established and that it is funded by the taxpayer

Similarly, when considering personal responsibilities, leadership style and values (step 2), and the internal and external environments (step 3), it's usually better to keep a general command focus. Some of the things you'll want to consider as part of this step are: your own personality, with its strengths and weaknesses; the capabilities and competence of subordinate internal staff/organizations; the expectations, threats and opportunities that exist in the external environment.

Opportunities are more than just the identification of supporters or friends who may be able to help. Opportunities should also be thought of as objective conditions, changes that can be anticipated or niches that can be created. Such opportunities may be difficult to identify during a short period of time; but looking for them may be time well spent.

Where do we want to go? Some argue that "vision" is the most important element in any leadership effort, because it can put purpose into the group effort. Whether you agree that it is the most important or not, the fact is that a vision can be powerful in at least two ways. First, a vision can be a source of energy of creative tension that stimulates innovation and leads to command unity. Second, it can be a source of guidance that helps members orient their behavior. Don't forget, you are trying to influence future decisions by others who are your subordinates.

Vision is deceptively difficult. It's easy to say: "Best squadron in the Navy." But what does that really mean? "Best" in what respects? A vision should convey the key contributions that the command hopes to make and the means by which it will deliver them. Vision necessarily looks toward a *future* state, whereas mission describes the here and now.

Steps five and six are the place where the general (mission and vision) should begin to narrow to the specific. Key processes identify the most important functions that the command performs. The point here is to identify the command functions that deserve priority when resources are being allocated. Arguably, precise identification of key processes may be less important when budgets are flush; but flush budgets are not likely to be an issue for some time. "Gaps" are the important shortfalls in key processes as well as the areas of "creative tension" where improvements or innovations must be made if the command is to realize its vision of combat readiness.

The next step is to identify end states that must be attained if the vision is to be realized. Some refer to these end states as "objectives," others as "goals." Either way, the point is that end states should be identified because they quantify, or express in concrete terms, the vision. Interim steps or milestones flow from the end states. They should be SMART, (specific, measurable, achievable, results-oriented, time determined), but not all desired outcomes are strictly quantifiable. However, a major problem in a significant process should not be swept under the rug just because it is hard to measure. Even when the outcome is not strictly quantifiable, thinking about how you might state a "SMART" goal usually improves the goal statement. It may also improve the measuring process that you employ to monitor progress and provide feedback.

Below is an example on a carrier to illustrate the relationship between end states, interim steps, and key variables:

An end state could be "A SAFER COMMAND ENVI-RONMENT"

An interim step would be "A 10% REDUCTION IN ACCIDENTS IN THE WORKPLACE WITHIN 30 DAYS"

The key variable for measuring progress toward the interim step would be the NUMBER OF ACCIDENTS

How are we going to get there? Step eight of the framework may be usefully displayed as a matrix. Most of us are familiar with the term "plan of action and milestones," and that is essentially what you are developing here. Your plan should identify: WHAT is to be done, HOW it will be done, WHO will do it, and WHEN it will be completed. This is not intended to be an exhaustive plan. That will be completed by the officer assigned responsibility for the action. Rather, this is a skeletal outline of the actions to be completed, who is responsible, and when action is due/completed.

Are we getting there? This phase is often treated lightly, but is the one you may spend the most time with in real life. You should think about how you'd really determine progress toward your goals, and perhaps even set criteria in advance for what would cause you to change your approach. Again, some of the other concepts we will introduce (difficulty of measurement, e.g., efficiency vs. effectiveness) will be helpful in this phase.

We have introduced the framework and believe it could be useful in approaching the challenge of command. That said, it is not our position that leadership is a task, which is in any way amenable to a "cookbook" or "checklist" approach. However, any opportunity to reflect on the incredibly important task of command leadership is time well spent. We further believe that a considered, organized approach, coupled with the widest possible "bag of tools," is an improvement over an unstructured approach to the task.

You are strongly encouraged to refer often to the framework throughout Units 3, 4, and 5. We hope you will recognize the application as more background of its framework is provided. The usefulness and application of the framework can be discussed at any time during the course, but will be specifically addressed at the conclusion of Unit 5.

I will discuss the applications of this at any time, but the more study you put into it, the more sense it will make, at least we hope so. You should approach this framework by seeing if it may or may not be useful for you to plan for THE ASSUMPTION OF your command. Your feedback in this area will be important to the course. We want you to go through the personal drill of studying the framework. This drill we believe will be useful regardless whether you use the framework or not. The more you think about it as we proceed through Units 3, 4 and 5, the more you will benefit from it.

SET OF PRINCIPLES

The set of principles is illustrated in various topics throughout the course. It is put together from various sources and highlights agreed upon leadership concepts. For instance, we have already discussed pts. 2, 3, 1, 6, and accountability.

A SET OF PRINCIPLES FOR THE APPLICATION OF THE COMMAND LEADERSHIP FRAMEWORK
(this also applies to any civilian organization).

1. First, get in touch, and then stay in touch, with what is really going on and what people are thinking about.

2. Spend time (continuously) articulating the vision and clarifying the goals and priorities, making it easy for individuals and teams to question whether or not a particular policy is out of line with command values.

3. Develop a clear plan for creating and sustaining a climate that is routinely supportive, trusting, and in every respect integrated. (Drafting this plan must be a team effort).

4. Always explain the intent of directives and rules so that subordinates can use initiative and independent action to achieve the desired objectives.

5. Focus organizational energy on priority matters; identify and attack non-productive policies and meaningless routines; and keep some energy free for adaptation and innovation.

6. Insist that key leaders set the example in representing the organization's values and priorities. (Take prompt action when key leaders do not reinforce the values and support the vision).

7. Ensure that the staff acts to reinforce the leader's intent and the organization's vision and priorities through coordination and integration of programs and policies, and establish and maintain communication channels for uncovering disconnects and dysfunctions.

8. Ensure that leaders at a given level do not routinely handle actions that could be done as well by subordinate leaders, and that latitude to act is described for each level. Explain and draw attention to the model of an empowered leader, the authority, the boundaries, and the patterns of mutual trust.

9. Assume good intent and, when something goes wrong, check first for flaws in the system. (Trust people, but be suspicious of systems).

10. Test, measure and transmit evaluation data carefully and openly, with clear intent and flexible format, so that the vision, goals, and priorities are clarified and supported by the overall measurement scheme.

11. Reinforce outstanding individual and team accomplishments with an appraisal and reward system whose rules are straightforward and open to discussion, and that is consistent with organizational goals, values, priorities and quality standards. (Encourage risk-taking and trust-building while simultaneously focusing on quality output.)

12. Ensure that policy changes are always explained first to leaders, so that they may in turn explain to their subordinates the rationale for those changes before the changes are announced and implemented.

13. Eliminate any competition that hampers idea-sharing across the organization.

Attend to personnel selection and assignment so that the organization identifies and educates potential leaders who want responsibility consistent with the values of the organization. Plan carefully for succession and transition of key leaders.

Okay, one last look, some specific questions, but more important, an easy way to apply the framework. The approach taken here in the lesson is to introduce the framework at the beginning in a data block discussion and description, and then repeat points trying to build from data to info to knowledge to wisdom—you are not in the wisdom block—you'll need to actually work it to reach that block.

Here's how to get started:

1. Mission

   - **Why do we exist?**

     Is the mission clearly stated in policy documents?

     Are their implied missions?

2. Personal responsibilities and leadership style

- **What few functions am I personally responsible for?**

  What can be decentralized?

- **Who am I?**

  What "types" do I have working for me?

  Where do I need to "improve"?

- **What leadership style is required?**

  Should I be more or less directive?

  How much time is available?

  Is the organization already in good shape?

3. External and internal environments

- **What threats and opportunities face the command?**

  What changes should we anticipate?

  Are we already in a crisis mode?

  What are the short-term obstacles?

  What power centers in other organizations do I need to cultivate?

- **What are the organization's weaknesses?**

  What should be divested?

> Is the need for change widely accepted in the organization?
>
> Whom should I exclude?

- **What are its strengths?**

  What internal standards can we build on?

  What is our organizational essence?

4. Vision and values

   - **Where do we want to be in 3 years? In 5 years?**

     What is our vision?

     Is it consistent with the mission?

     Is it realistic?

     Is it ambitious enough to spur innovation through creative tension?

     How can the vision become more shared?

     Who are the informal leaders in the command that could become the critical mass for innovation?

   - **How do we want to treat each other?**

     Are we oriented towards our mission and those we serve?

     Are values consistent with the vision? With the command essence?

5. Key processes

- **What are the tasks that have the greatest effect on mission accomplish?**

    What tasks deserve the highest priority in resources support and institutional strategies?

    What areas deserve highest priority throughout steps 6-10 of this plan?

6. Identify the gap

- **What are the differences between the "as is" and the vision?**

    What areas require attention if we are to achieve the vision?

    What are the problems?

    Where has the vision raised the standards?

7. Objectives and goals

- **What end-states or performance targets must be attained if the vision is to be realized?**

    Have we translated the vision into concrete targets that can be used to orient performance and support appropriate innovation?

    What roles have my key players played in the formulation of targets?

- **What steps should be taken to attain the end-states/targets?**

  Are the steps SMART: **s**pecific, **m**easurable, **a**chievable, **r**esults oriented, **ti**me-determined?

  What key variables will we use to tell whether we are making genuine progress?

  Are the goals appropriate for anticipatory, reactive or crisis change?

8. Implementation plan

   - **What means are we using to achieve the steps and through them, the desired end-states/targets?**

     How will we overcome resistance to change?

     Are the roadblocks cultural?

     Localized in a particular component?

     Have I really delegated responsibility consistent with step 2?

9. Performance monitoring and feedback analysis

   - **Are we making enough progress?**

     How we will identify better key variables?
     Do the trends we are watching reflect efficiency, or effectiveness?

Are we really measuring mission effectiveness and readiness?

How will we know if there are unintended consequences to our control systems?

10. Review and evaluation

Has our mission changed? Do we need to redefine or adjust our vision, objectives and goals?

Has the organization become more receptive to innovation?

Are we really more committed?

What have we done to institutionalize the essential elements?

How much of the plan will survive after I leave?

Have we really stopped focusing exclusively on the short term?

Are we really on the road to continuous improvement?

End Points

Application of framework allows looking at planning at the beginning of your command.

Allows a way to communicate the plan, which incorporates your vision into action. Helps get your people on board and aligned quickly. Provides an assessment tool, a way to track and measure your progress toward achieving your successful command.

You never know if your boss might want to see your approach to taking over command and how you intend to get things quickly running smoothly. You must use something—if not the framework we have introduced what will *you* use?

CHAPTER 9

3.6 DEVELOPING SUBORDINATES

Introduction: Measure of success of a leader.

We believe that the real success of a leader can be measured by the ensuing success of those he has led. Developing subordinates is a significant responsibility and leadership challenge. To develop them, they must first be challenged. They must accept authority and accountability, and you must accept something as well. We will get to that shortly. *(Accept risk and less than perfect performance.)*

START

We will talk now about the leadership responsibility for developing subordinates—*(this responsibility to provide them purpose, direction and motivation)*

CO's are responsible for assisting their subordinates in their personal and professional development. This topic examines some methods to development subordinates.

"The higher an individual goes in the service, the more important his ability to delegate becomes." Admiral David L. McDonald.

Facilitate a discussion: As a CO do you have more or less control over your own destiny?

(Sphere of influence span of control discussion)

Power and authority to a person to act as his/her representative: as a CO, this delegation takes on a different feeling. WHY? Recall the lessons of responsibility, authority, and accountability. While the person to whom the CO assigns the task is accountable for the completion of the task, the *CO is still ultimately responsible.* Whatever subordinates do, you are held accountable. *This is a big change, and you have to recognize it up front.*

Delegation is an action:

Facilitate a discussion of the actions involved in delegation. Ensure the following are discussed:

- Leader assigns the tasks.
- Person to whom a task is delegated receives the authority necessary to complete the assignment.
- Involves very definitive supervisor/subordinate relationships

"One of the first signs of truly strong leaders is that he is comfortable delegating authority." Admiral Thomas B. Hayward.

In last night's homework, you read the thoughts of three former CNOs who discussed delegation. Was there a common theme?

INFORMATION SHEET

A. Introduction:

This information sheet provides three naval leaders' thoughts on delegation.

B. References:

Montor, Karel, et al. Naval Leadership: Voices of Experience. Annapolis, MD: Naval Institute Press, 1987:

"A leader may justifiably be reluctant to delegate under certain limited conditions. There are times when tasks that normally would be appropriate for a junior should not be delegated to him. Exceptions of this type are driven by one or a combination of these three constraints:

- Mission criticality
- Available time
- Experience level of the subordinate

Under normal peacetime conditions, a senior should fail to delegate only rarely, and only for these reasons."

Admiral Elmo Russell Zumwalt, USN, on seniors' reluctance to delegate:

"An officer's reluctance to delegate, in over 90 percent of the cases, indicates an absolute *lack of self-confidence by the officer who does not delegate.* In the other cases, it is the officer saying 'I know so well what to do and nobody else knows nearly so well, that I'm going to try to do it all'. Unfortunately, no one person has the time to do all his subordinates' jobs."

Admiral David Lamar McDonald, USN, points out that:

"The higher an individual goes in the service, the more important his ability to delegate becomes. Many officers as lieutenants, lieutenant commanders, commanders, are outstanding, but as they go a little bit higher, their job performance suffers because they are either unable or unwilling to delegate. And when he delegates, the officer must be willing to accept a less-than-perfect performance from the individual doing the job. The lieutenant commander who, say, has always done the job perfectly, tells Ensign Smith to do it; but although he might be doing it satisfactorily, Smith is not doing it as well as the lieutenant commander thinks he himself can do it, so the lieutenant commander pitches in and does it. This ruins the confidence of Smith, to whom he delegated the authority; furthermore, the lieutenant commander can step in and do it himself just so many times. He must learn to accept performance that is short of perfection-although, of course, an unsatisfactory performance is not acceptable.

One reason officers are reluctant to delegate is that they are afraid someone else's mistake will reflect badly on them. But juniors cannot learn unless they are given the opportunity to do things on their own. When I took command of the carrier Coral Sea after having the little Mendora for a year, people asked me whether I would practice putting the ship alongside a tanker. I said no, because when I was executive officer of the Essex during the war my skipper let me do practically all the refueling and all the replenishing, so even though I hadn't done it with that particular type, I'd done it many times. Furthermore, the commanding officer must be willing to delegate various things like that. Otherwise, how are these fellows going to learn? When he delegates, the officer should tell someone what to do, being careful most of the time not to tell him how to do it. There will be times when the officer must tell the individual how to do a job, and the officer should say, "I would prefer if you do it this way this time."

Admiral Thomas Bib Hayward, USN, notes that:

"While responsibility cannot be delegated, it is necessary at times for authority to be delegated to subordinates to ensure that a job is done in the absence of the senior or because the senior cannot possibly supervise everything himself. One of the first signs of a truly strong leader is that he is comfortable delegating authority. The good leaders have developed the ability to permit others to make mistakes, to give people more leash than they would have expected to get, and to show confidence in those people, to let them know that they expect them to be able to perform. Most people will respond affirmatively to that authority, to that delegation. In almost all cases the individuals will be surprised at how much they enjoy having the authority, and they will do better than the leaders might have anticipated.

The errant leader is the one who is uncomfortable taking a chance with his troops because of how it might reflect on his or her performance. There are times when close supervision is essential—while a unit is developing its team approach, for example—but almost everyone has talent, and leaders need to recognize and use other people's talent.

When there is one junior in a squadron made up of senior officers, the skipper and the exec are offered a challenge. They must delegate down into the organization far enough to bring out the junior officer and make sure that he is identified and that his talents are not overlooked. Effective leaders build their team around the talented people.

The skipper can never give up his basic responsibility for the whole unit. Nor can a division officer delegate his responsibility for the conduct of anyone in his or her division or the quality of performance of that combat information team. But how can the leader develop a capability in his unit to deal with combat damage when his top supervisor is either dead or immobile? Someone must have the experience to step forward into that spot. The supervisor can only be replaced in an emergency if someone has been given the opportunity to perform some of his duties prior to the emergency.

Most people wait for the opportunity to take on a challenge, and the leader ought to let them try. After he has successfully delegated authority on several occasions, the leader will develop confidence in his people's ability and will be less concerned about them making a mistake. In any echelon in the chain of command, the supervisor must grant authority and delegate to the maximum, so that he knows that when the chips are down he has a team that can perform, he has more than one person who can carry the load."

What is an acceptable risk? Basically it's the willingness to accept an end result of an assigned task that may not be completed exactly correctly.

The delegator must be willing to accept less than perfect performance, i.e., take some risk to allow for training opportunities. You cannot do all the assigned tasks yourself.

Facilitate a discussion on CO's perceptions of the pros and cons of delegation. Are the risks worth the gains? What are the advantages?

- CO time efficiency.

- Subordinate development strengthens the team

- Delegating is essential to effective mission accomplishment

Facilitate a discussion of the importance trust plays in delegation.

- Trust is bi-directional: CO cannot do everything

- CO must trust subordinates and subordinates must trust the CO to stand by the authority given to complete the task.

- A CO must prepare to properly delegate authority

Research boils down to four things to consider prior to delegating:

Display TRANSPARENCY T-3-6-3 Preparing to Delegate.

- Task complexity and scope

- Individual capability

- Risk, authority, and support

- Monitoring methods.

Delegation requires the CO to trust his/her subordinates to some degree.

Above talks about four things to consider. Karel Montor indicates the leader must consider the points below to really do delegation correctly:

Full complexity and scope of the task to be delegated

- Capabilities and capacity of the individual to whom authority is to be delegated

- Authority and support the individual needs to complete the project

- Degree of risk the CO is willing to accept if the subordinate fails in carrying out the authority

- The method of monitoring project performance, which can be accomplished without interfering with or diluting the individual's authority

- A feedback/evaluation system that allows the individual to learn and improve.

Display TRANSPARENCY T-3-6-4 Responsibility.

"To determine a young officer's ability to act decisively and effectively, they must be handed increased responsibility at every opportunity. In other words, if you're going to bring a youngster around you've got to throw responsibility at them and as fast as they can take it." Vice Admiral L.P. Ramage

OK, so let's break down the four main bullets of delegation.

1. <u>Task complexity and scope:</u>

Facilitate a discussion of which tasks a CO might readily delegate, and which might require greater evaluation of the situation. Evaluate an example of a delegated task based on its importance and the individual's readiness for the task (e.g., the bridge team during underway replenishment, versus independent steaming). Consider the following tasks:

- Routine operations

- Recurring tasks (monthly reports)

- Information collection (research)
- Meeting representation
- Future responsibilities the subordinate may have
- Tasks that through cost effectiveness are better accomplished at a lower level
- Signing performance evaluations
- Disciplinary actions
- Morale problems
- Sensitive situations

DECISIONS AS TO WHAT TO DELEGATE IS BASED ON:

- Time
- Trust
- Training
- Risk

How do they know what you expect?

- By your personal example based on your personal vision.
- By your promulgated command philosophy.
- By the way you instill what is important in the command.
- By your demonstrated set of values.

The Point.

Unless you have trained your people properly and provided them your expectations, you may very well end up delegating something you did not want to delegate.

2. Individual Capabilities:

As you walk aboard, where is your XO? Where are you? Where does your Commodore think you are? Where do you want to be?

Mission accomplishment depends in large measure on the proper application of subordinates' strengths. You have to learn the skill of combining task complexity with individual capability.

CO must assess subordinates to understand their experience, maturity, and self-reliance in order to appropriately assign tasks and responsibilities. Studies reveal that in any organization there will be only 18% that will be go to people. Those individuals that are the backbone of any organization.

Facilitate a discussion on the importance of properly assessing subordinates' strengths and weaknesses and relate that discussion to mission accomplishment. Ensure the following elements are discussed:

Task requirements are different throughout the command.

Different development levels can accept varying degrees of responsibility.

Different subordinates have varied capabilities and may be better suited to some particular type of tasks. Ensure students understand the correlation between assessing subordinates' capabilities and situational leadership. Failure to properly assess readiness levels could result in assignments that are either overwhelming or not challenging to the subordinate.

<u>POINT</u>—NEED TO FIGURE OUT WHO YOUR PLAYERS REALLY ARE—HOW WILL YOU DO THAT?

<u>Studies Show:</u>

"To determine a young officer's ability to act decisively and effectively, they must be handed increased responsibility at every opportunity. In other words, if you're going to bring a youngster around you've got to throw responsibility at him, and as fast as they can take it. "Admiral Ramage.

Identifying subordinates' strengths and weaknesses is accomplished through direct and indirect observation.

HOW WILL YOU DO THIS ASSESSMENT?

A self-evaluation form of some kind.

Facilitate a discussion of methods a CO could use to identify a subordinate's strengths and weaknesses. Examples include:

Direct:

In work environment, bridge flight deck, intensive care unit, submarine control room, quality improvement teams, liberty, social situations, wardroom interaction, and intramural sports. PQS system, PMS evaluations, inspections.

Other than direct:

Service records or evaluations, inspection of results, counseling records.

Will you look at these on your officers? How will you get to know them? How will you learn what you need to teach them? How will **you** prepare them for their next job? How will you assess their readiness?

Idea is that you can evaluate your people based on competence and commitment levels.

Capabilities Assessment

Readiness levels	4	3	2	1
COMPETENCE	HIGH	MODERATE	SOME	LOW
COMMITMENT	HIGH	MODERATE	SOME	LOW

POINT

Competence—
—Need to understand this is an art.
Commitment—

COMMITMENT IS A COMBINATION OF MOTIVATION AND CONFIDENCE. So what tasks would you assign an individual with a high commitment but low competence? What tasks could be assigned to an individual with a high competence and high commitment? That's the 18% go to people we have talked about. You could go through each combination.

With this concept in mind we did an identifying a subordinate's capabilities' exercise case study.

CASE STUDY
SECOND CRUISE

Directions: Read the case, and in small groups, discuss proposed responses to all study questions. Be prepared to brief and facilitate class-wide discussion on an area of the case selected by the instructor.

SCENARIO

The CO of an aviation squadron is preparing for deployment. One of the junior pilots in the command has recurring problems in the carrier-landing environment. The problems occur in the final landing phase, causing the pilot to have a difficult time making an arrested landing. The pilot has not done anything that has been blatantly unsafe, but sometimes requires more than one attempt to land safely on board.

The pilot has been in the squadron for one year and has made one cruise. Toward the end of the last cruise, the landing deficiency developed, requiring that the Human Factors Board (HFB) be convened to determine the cause of this substandard performance. The board recommended that the pilot continue flying and the pilot's performance improved over the last three weeks of the cruise.

During the turn-around training period for the second cruise, the pilot has continued to advance in the squadron, attaining Mission Commander and Division Lead qualifications. The pilot's airborne leadership is above average, and the CO feels comfortable that the pilot would excel in a combat situation.

As work-ups continue, the pilot still struggles with the final approach phase of landing the aircraft. The cruise is several months in the offing, and the pilot's performance is acceptable in every flight regime except the arrested landing phase.

If the CO opts not to take this pilot on cruise, his replacement will be another category one pilot with unknown flight deficiencies and will require corrective training prior to the cruise. This squadron had eight category one (first operational squadron tour in their aircraft) pilots out of a total of 15 pilots. The training and special handling required to increase initial proficiency reaches a point where it places inordinate burdens on the available training opportunities.

Some additional factors to consider are that the pilot is a good officer and has only that single weakness to overcome. The pilot has received special treatment in terms of an HFB and additional time to work on flight landing problems. The trend, however, is established. There is no consistent improvement at the ship, and it is expected that the pilot will continue to require special handling in terms of flight scheduling.

Questions:

What are the strengths and weaknesses of this subordinate, and how were they identified?

How do the qualifications for Division Lead and Mission Commander figure in?

What is this pilot's potential?

What is the risk of taking the pilot on cruise versus taking an unknown pilot?

What should the CO do?

There was a particular slide I used here. It showed the bow of a carrier and the "meatball" light configuration. I would explain to those other than pilots how pilots use a scan technique to land on a CV. The scan (MB-LU-AOA) starts with the *meatball* which determines his position high or low and left or right; then *Line Up* relative to the center of the landing deck of the CV; then the airplane *angle of attack* meaning nose up, hook down and correct approaching speed. The pilot just keeps that scan going until touchdown. Sounds simple but it is not, especially in bad weather or at night.

Point of case study:

You must give them what they need to get them to the next level of development. How you do that is not always easy, nor is determining what they need. Or that they cannot get there and to continue to allow them the opportunity becomes counterproductive. It also does not allow others the opportunity they need for advancement.

It is always tough to have to give up on someone, but not all can be led. In this case the individual may have a *high commitment* but only *some competence*. As he becomes more senior that may not be enough for his career progression. Not all decisions have such heavy consequences.

3. Risk, Authority, and Support:

Delegation and Risk Management.

"Taking calculated risks. That is quite different from being rash." George S. Patton.

"First recon, then risk"—(Helmuth Von Moltke –the "elder," 1800-1891.

(Moltke lived a long time. Let's give him a little credit here). So you need to have a good idea of the strengths and weaknesses of your people before you delegate.

"A CO must determine when to make command decisions and when to delegate command authority. CO's responsibility is to manage risk rather than merely avoid risk." Vadm Bowman on intelligent Risk Taking.

It is a leadership issue. There are lots of models out there that try to put this mental drill into perspective. I like the Air Force model:

RISK MANAGEMENT MODEL				
	Very Capable	LEVEL 1 Totally Delegated	LEVEL 2 Post-Approval	LEVEL 3 Guidelines
	Capable	LEVEL 2 Post-approval	LEVEL 3 Guidelines	LEVEL 4 Pre-Approval
	Not Capable	LEVEL 3 Guidelines	LEVEL 4 Pre-Approval	LEVEL 5 No Delegation
		Not Serious	Serious	Very Serious
		Consequences		

Level 1: Totally Delegated: "Take charge. Handle it on your own."

Level 2: Post-Approval: "Go ahead and handle it on your own. Tell me what you did later."

Level 3: Guidelines: "Help the customer, but follow guidance."

Level 4: Pre-Approval: "Check with me before doing this or that."

Level 5: No Delegation: "You aren't allowed to handle this situation."

In this model the individual is placed in three levels of competency: very capable, capable, and not capable. It then describes that a failure to perform the task assigned correctly could result in three categories of consequences: not serious, serious, and very serious. It then provides delegation and monitoring levels based on matching the individual's capability with the seriousness of the assigned task failure. It is a good delegating process to provide to those in leadership positions.

Challenge of Leadership: Making Decisions and Managing Risk

Facilitate a discussion of how delegating implies a degree of risk for the CO and the need for risk management in command.

The level of trust in the subordinate and individual capabilities may best determine the level of risk associated with delegating a particular task. COs balance the amount of risk they are willing to manage against the amount of freedom they want to allow the subordinates.

Now a mental drill.

Facilitate a discussion on how a CO manages risk while encouraging subordinate development.

Lower risk tasks: Easier for the CO to allow personnel to make their own decisions.

Risk policy: Subordinates do tasks then advise CO.

Higher-risk tasks: As risk increases, so does the need for CO involvement.

Risk policy: Subordinates recommend actions and then proceed upon approval.

You should be doing this drill all the time to minimize mistakes and ensure your people have not been set up to fail. As discussed, the amount of delegation has a lot to do with your own confidence and competency. To enhance any subordinate's sense of empowerment, a CO has to practice hands-off management as much as possible, and hands-on management as much as necessary. It's a delicate balance.

Examples of delegating tasks at the very capable/very serious consequences level:

> I neither ask nor desire to know anything of your plans. Take the responsibility and act, and call on me for assistance. (Abraham Lincoln to US Grant on his appointment to command the union armies, 1864)

COMSOPAC's message, 240552 Nov 1943, to Adm. Burke during the engagement off Cape St. George:

> Thirty-one knot Burke get athwart the Buka-Rabaul evacuation line about 35 miles west of Buka. If no enemy contacts by 0300 love, 25th, come south to refuel. Same place. If enemy contacted you know what to do.

I doubt most of you will enjoy that kind of delegation from your superior at the start of your command tour. But in these cases, these leaders had already proven their leadership.

Grant had already taken Vicksburg and Adm. Burke was already called thirty-one knot Burke. But you need to remember that your reporting senior is *also* evaluating *you*.

Another example:

In the movie *Yellow Ribbon* starring John Wayne, "We all have to hold our own river crossings at some point in our life."

He sent the lieutenant out in the morning because he was not ready to do it at night.

Delegating to the appropriate level of authority enhances a subordinate's feeling of empowerment. It sets him up to succeed and builds confidence rather than failure.

Facilitate a discussion of the guidelines a CO must follow to ensure proper delegation. Ensure the following are discussed:

Who will be tasked?

Select the people who have the ability to do the job. Train those who do not. Clearly explain what is expected of them (standards/guidelines). Set a deadline for completion of the task. Provide latitude for them to use their own imaginations and initiative. Let them know you will be following up, and then follow up. Reward them appropriately for the results they obtain. Do not do the job for them.

4. Monitoring Methods:
    FOLLOW UP (USMC *sixth troop leading step***)**—set them up for success—DON'T LET THEM FAIL

Guidelines for proper delegation monitoring based on individual readiness level:

Proper delegation requires monitoring of the task.

CO must determine how well personnel are meeting standards agreed upon and communicate this to the subordinates.

Methods to assist subordinates after tasks have been delegated depend on level of subordinate development. (D4 is highest level of readiness).

FollowerReadines Development Levels	Appropriate Monitoring Level
D1	Assign task but control and supervise process
D2	Available for direction and support
D3	Report at regular intervals
D4	Self-sufficient, exception reporting

Question: Should you delegate to subordinates at every level of development? Yes of course, but again gets at the importance of a program or process that provides an accurate readiness assessment of your people.

TRANSPARENCY T-3-6-8 Monitoring Progress
Important characteristics of a monitoring system:

- Predetermined Standards
- Open Communications

- Tailored Controls
- Accurate Measurement
- Adequate Frequency
- Correction Capabilities
- Internal Consistency

Monitoring is something we are not very good at.

DISCUSSION HERE ABOUT DELEGATION VS ABANDONMENT. To assign a task and not provide yourself an opportunity to jump in prior to a failure is both abandonment and poor leadership.

Methods for monitoring:

Facilitate a brainstorming session of the methods a CO uses to monitor for risk management. For example:

- Effective organizational reporting structure
- Personal follow-up
- Sampling techniques
- Progress reports
- Management by exception
- Statistical controls
- Historical comparisons
- Self-monitoring

Key to successful monitoring is to maintain appropriate control of the delegated task without making subordinates feel a lack of trust in their ability to complete the project. A leadership fine line.

Again the importance of understanding the four main points to consider prior to delegation:

- Task complexity and scope
- Individual capability
- Risk, authority, and support
- Monitoring methods

SUMMARY: NOW COVERED ALL FOUR BULLETS:

SO YOU HAVE DELEGATED TASKS—NOW LETS TALK ABOUT HOW YOU DEAL WITH THE RESULTS.

Dealing with Results.

"Responsibility is the test of a Man's courage." (Lord St. Vincent, 1735-1833)

Evaluating the results of delegated tasks requires analysis of the factors influencing the outcome. Performance is the result of both the system and the individual. A determination of poor performance by an individual cannot be made without identifying the cause(s).

Solicit examples students have seen of a CO censuring subordinates, only to learn that the problem was a failure of a system or method. Important to understand the root cause of the failure. Again, a determination of poor performance by an individual cannot be made without identifying the cause(s).

Facilitate a discussion of how a CO can address poor performance without creating fear or distrust.

He/She Counsels subordinates. Holds subordinates accountable. Points out deficiencies. Can rescind some of the authority. He/She can ask subordinates to report on all aspects of the task. The activity or task can be reassigned to a more experienced person. Have clear understanding of the situational leadership readiness level.

Facilitate a discussion of how a CO evaluates and encourages exceptional performance by an individual.

Counsel subordinate on fine performance. Encourage same level of effort on future projects. Provide opportunity to build self-esteem and a feeling of accomplishment by additional tasking and authority.

Reference Montor, 1991, page 167.

Dealing with results exercise:

Facilitate a discussion on how Lt. Jones' poor airmanship during formation flying reflects either a complacent attitude or is the result of insufficient practice due to budget cuts.

Questions: If the problem is attitude, what is the cause?

How can it be corrected? If the problem is training, given fuel constraints, how can Lt. Jones improve his performance?

Aviation Community: has two different actions: one to find the root cause to eliminate the safety hazard, and another to fix blame and satisfy the accountability requirement of the chain of command.

It is important to identify causes rather than attack symptoms.

We just talked about attitude. That leads us nicely into the end result of proper delegation and subordinate development. There is this idea that beyond proper delegation is a dimension called empowerment.

Empowerment defined: the establishment of an attitude among members of a command that their contribution is valuable to the organization and that they can make a difference in outcomes, plans, and programs.

<u>So empowerment is an outcome.</u>

Facilitate a discussion on how empowerment is the result of leadership actions to create an environment of trust and mutual respect.

HOW DO YOU KNOW WHEN YOUR PEOPLE ARE EMPOWERED?

Individuals are empowered when:

They take responsibility for their jobs.

They feel they have the authority to make decisions.

They take appropriate action to accomplish their jobs.

They have access to the CO.

They get action when they bring up a problem.

Their mistakes are treated properly.

They feel they are trusted and respected.

Reference Scott, 1991, page 80.

Let's talk about the relationship between delegation and empowerment

Delegation is a precursor to empowerment. Delegation, by itself, will not create empowerment. It requires a different level of bi-directional trust, which extends beyond a specific tasking.

Facilitate a discussion of the benefits of empowerment to both leaders and subordinates.

Is having your people empowered a good thing and why?

Studies point out following benefits of empowerment:

- Encourages ownership

- Improves morale

- Builds teamwork

- Adds clarity to the decision-making process for the subordinate

- Enhances communication

- Promotes the flow of new ideas

- Allows seniors to move away from the patriarchal role of taking care of personnel

- Gives personnel the ability to take care of themselves

- Fosters a sense of trust and cooperation

Delegation/empowerment exercise:

So how do you build this empowerment?

"I built trust among my commanders because I trusted them" (General Norman Schwartzkopf). A flash of the obvious, but trust starts at the top.

Empowerment has three essential factors:

- Proper mind set
- Proper relationships
- Proper structure.

Facilitate a discussion of how a sense of empowerment develops from the individual.

Proper mind set:

Personnel must feel a sense of ownership and responsibility for helping make the organization run better. Personnel must feel responsible for their own career paths. A proper relationship of mutual trust must exist.

You need to start building trust the very first day.

Proper relationships:

1. Trust: defined as total confidence in the integrity, ability, and good character of another, is one of the most important ingredients in building strong teams.

2. Teamwork: work centers/divisions/ departments co-operate to improve performance.

3. Supervisors assume the role of team leader and facilitate team activities.

<u>Proper structure:</u>

Organization/command structure allows personnel to achieve successful results and they are recognized or rewarded appropriately.

Facilitate a discussion of what the command structure provides that contributes to empowerment.

Direction: specific guidelines and standards, key result areas, goals, and measurements

Resources: provide adequate tools, materials, facilities and money

Support: personal approval, coaching, feedback and encouragement

An empowering environment requires three things:

VALIDATION—INFORMATION— PARTICIPATION POINTS HERE ARE:

1. Validation–Personnel are respected as people. They have flexibility to meet personal needs. Leadership encourages learning, growing, and developing new skills

2. Information–Personnel know why things are being done. They get current information about the organization, its missions, and its goals

3. Participation—Personnel have control over how they do their work. Personnel are involved in decisions that affect them.

    So to repeat the question I asked at the beginning of this lesson: As a CO, do you have more or less control over your own destiny?

    A lot depends on how well your command understands the art of delegation and subordinate development. Again, it takes a lot of effort and energy to develop subordinates correctly so that they feel empowered. *It takes inspirational leadership.*

Summary:

To develop your people you must delegate and when you delegate you accept risk.

You must be willing to accept less than perfect performance. You must delegate so as to not set your people up for failure. You must trust them once you have trained them. You need to monitor and provide feedback. You need to build bidirectional trust that leads to empowerment. This trust and empowerment will be required by your command in unit 8. This should be your philosophy.

Again, it sounds simple but is difficult to achieve.

CHAPTER 10

··

3.8 COMMUNICATION
WITH SUPERIORS AND OTHER COs

Based on a lesson written by Captain John Meyer.

Purpose of the Lesson:

<u>Where it fits into the flow of the course.</u>

Throughout Unit 3, there has been an underlying theme of communication within the command, in all command relationships, and in subordinate development and team building. Effective communication is the key that makes the command run efficiently. It can also be considered an art that requires constant attention. Many of the problems that occur within a command are the result of poor communication. There are times when you think you are communicating well when in fact you are not getting your message through to your people. The reasons can vary between inattention, listening to refute, selective listening, or misunderstood operational definitions.

These same issues pertain to your communication with those outside the command, specifically your immediate superior in the chain of command. Your ability to effectively communicate up the chain of command and with other COs will enhance significantly those critical relationships.

How it connects to previous and future lessons

Effective communication both internally and externally is crucial to mission readiness. Communications is accomplished verbally, in writing, and by your pattern of behaviors. Issues of trust, loyalty, consistency, professional competence, integrity, decisiveness, courage, etc. are all impacted by how you communicate. This is equally true with your communication outside the command. Your ability to keep the chain of command informed, know what is expected of you and your command, providing feedback up the chain of command, all have an impact on mission effectiveness.

What the students are supposed to get out of the lesson

The students should come away with an appreciation of the critical importance of open and honest communication up the chain of command, what factors can potentially make those communications difficult to accomplish, and methods and techniques to improve those communications.

As we have discussed thus far in the course, adequate communication is a critical aspect in the effectiveness of a command. Frequently, good two-way communication is listed on the attributes of a successful organization. It is an equally important factor in the success you will have with your immediate superior in your chain of command. Communicating your vision, command philosophy, intentions, orders, etc. must be done effectively and in a confident and calm manner, whether you are communicating with your sailors or with the boss. The impact of how you communicate will be felt in your ability to carry out your command's mission.

There is one fundamental aspect of this communication up and down the chain of command that is crucial to your success. If you take nothing else away from this lesson, remember this fundamental tenet. In developing a relationship and communicating with the boss, open and honest communication is critical. This is a blinding flash of the obvious, but there are many factors that can get in the way of your ability or even desire to carry this out. If your boss has just a perception that you are not being open and honest, your effectiveness as a commanding officer will be significantly diminished. It will also have an impact on your sailors and their faith, trust in and loyalty to you. Let me give you an example of what I mean. The following story comes from feedback received from a commanding officer, and I quote:

"I had a tough situation within days of taking command. It involved a potential hazing case. On closer review I determined it was not hazing but that it could have been viewed as such without all the details. This was on the heels of a rather forceful anti-hazing message from my ISIC. The XO, department head and CMC recommended squelching it – not to report it or it would be taken out of my hands. I sent my ISIC a "Personal For" describing the incident, the action I was taking to address the incident and then claimed personal responsibility for what happened. The outcome surprised me (and my XO, department head, and CMC). My ISIC called me at sea and concurred with my actions and said it was my command – he would not interfere. Bonus – the sailors involved couldn't believe that a CO who didn't even know them would put himself up for blame for something they did. These sailors each came up to me unsolicited and told me how sorry they were to have put me in such a position. They said I could count on them to be the best sailors I've ever known. Indeed, they've been doing great."

Roadmap for the lesson:

During this lesson we will examine how to develop a relationship and communicate with your boss and other CO's orally, in writing, and in many other ways. This is mainly an experience-based discussion, drawing on the post-command facilitators and your experiences. If any of you have served on a staff, please feel free to contribute your observations of how communication coming up the chain of command is handled. Everything we discuss will be in the context of open and honest communications. We will explore both situations and personality types of bosses and the impact that has on your ability to maintain open and honest communication. We will finish the lesson with a discussion of the benefits of developing a good rapport with other CO's.

RELATIONSHIPS WITH SUPERIORS

Learning points:

Mutual dependence for mission accomplishment
Power and leverage
Feedback to the CO
Personal development

Mutual dependence for mission accomplishment is self-explanatory. The other bullets require some explanation.

Power and leverage. There will be a few times when you will need the power and leverage of the boss to accomplish your goals. The point is that you will not need it often, but when you do, do not hesitate to use it. It is not a sign of weakness to ask for help in a matter that is beyond your capability to resolve. These matters will obviously be fairly substantial and critical to mission readiness. For example, you may need to make significant changes to your schedule to better sequence significant milestones during your work-up cycle. There may be some personnel issues that require assistance even beyond the level of your immediate boss. This power and leverage of the boss are among the reasons for having a boss.

<u>Feedback to the CO</u>. This is another area where there will be a handful of times when you need some feedback from the boss on what you are trying to accomplish. This is not asking for feedback on how you are doing in command. This is feedback on a significant issue or problem that you are working on to resolve. It may involve several different options with no one option standing out as the best one to employ. This is a time to take the issue to the boss, outline the situation and the solutions as you see them, and highlighting the solution you think is the best. Your boss may have had to address a similar situation in the past or may have additional information or insight that can assist you in making your decision.

<u>Personal Development</u>. Like it or not, your boss is going to be interested in your development as a commanding officer from the beginning of your tour. This can manifest itself in a variety of ways depending on the personality of your boss, where your command is in its cycle, your service reputation, your first impression on the boss and his/her sense of your character. Your boss is also interested in your professional development as well. You need mentorship as much as anyone else and it's your boss's responsibility to provide that mentorship. Take advantage of it.

Let's talk about developing a relationship with your boss. Although you may pay a courtesy call you on boss prior to the change of command, the most important meeting will be the first one after the change of command. That's when you get to establish the climate of open and honest communication. This is you opportunity to provide an accurate assessment of the command, and lay out your plan and goals. Your boss will compare what you say with his/her own knowledge and perception of your command.

The most important aspect in the development of this relationship is for you to determine what your boss needs to know from you. He/she may tell you, but if not, it's your obligation to find out that information. It is often a common assumption that the routine reports and messages you send up the chain of command will tell the whole story. That is not a good assumption. The following is an example:

At a Seventh Fleet daily OPINTEL briefing, the admiral was briefed on the C-3 and C-4 CASREPS in Seventh Fleet. He inquired about one of the C-4 CASREPS. The staff did not have the answer to the admiral's question. They passed it down to the battle group for answer. That staff did not have the answer, so they tacked on a few more questions due to the interest expressed by Seventh Fleet, and sent them down to the Destroyer Squadron. That staff also did not have the answers so they tacked on a few of their own questions and passed it all down to the ship. When the ship received these questions it was late in the day and a response was required by COB. The CO of the ship felt imposed upon by the chain of command for asking a series of questions he thought were explained by his CASREP. The problem was his failure to provide amplifying information over and above what was included in the CASREP. You will know what issues, both good and bad, will generate interest up the chain of command. Take the initiative to provide the amplifying information that will preclude you having to respond to short notice tasking.

You will need to determine the form and frequency of communication desired by your boss. Keep this in mind when you have a change in bosses. The new boss will have different expectations and requirements and once again, it's your responsibility to find that out if he/she does not provide you with that guidance. Communication can take a variety of forms from how-goes-it messages on a periodic basis, to letters, phone calls, or office visits. The proximity of your boss to your command can also determine the type and frequency of communication.

Private communication between you and your boss requires some forethought. Almost any form of personal written communication with your boss will be shared with other members of the staff. That is simply a fact of life. The reason for this is that your boss is not an action officer, and any significant issue you bring to the boss will most likely need to be worked by the staff. E-mails and "Personal For" messages do not guarantee privacy, in fact, just the opposite is true. Therefore, the following tips are offered for that type of communication:

Stick to the issue that is the subject of the message. Outline what the issue is and your solution or input on a solution in the first paragraph, then provide amplifying information in subsequent paragraphs as appropriate.

Don't try to be funny. You are not.

Keep emotion out of your message. It may be a very emotional issue for you, but you will lose the battle, regardless how right you are, if you put emotion in your message.

Write the message knowing it may be forwarded up the chain of command. Your boss will frequently quote your message to the next level in the chain of command. He/she will do this for a couple of reasons. First, everyone wants to hear from the commander. The best way to do that is to simply quote your message. Second, it gives your boss the opportunity to give you exposure up the chain of command.

Write your message knowing the boss's staff will be reading it and working the issue you raise.

Knowing what to bring forward to the boss can be a challenge. If in doubt bring it up to the boss, but first, you may want to broach the subject with the Chief Staff Officer/Chief of Staff first to determine if it really is a worthwhile issue to bring forward to the boss. Recognize however that the CSO will tell the boss about your conversation in either case.

Another factor that can arise is an issue that tests your loyalty. If you let it, this can have a serious impact on your willingness to provide open and honest communication both up and down the chain of command. Are you willing to "tell the emperor he has no clothes?" A major part of loyalty to the boss is in your responsibility to tell him/her that what they are doing, saying, or asking you to do, is wrong. There may also be times when your command is tasked to do something that, for very good reasons, you do not want to do. This doesn't have to be something major or illegal, it can be a part of everyday operations. You have a couple of options. One is to simply do as you are told, but to your disadvantage, or take on the boss and provide either a reason why you do not want to carry out the assigned task, or provide an alternative option.

One of the most challenging aspects of open and honest communication up the chain of command is how information is disseminated in fast breaking operations. Decisions are held very close, almost up to the time of execution, before those tasked with the mission find out about what they are tasked to perform. This can happen in almost any command and is not limited to operational scenarios. The operational scenarios potentially offer the most challenge not only for the commanding officer and his boss, but also your sailors.

Another challenge you will face is in providing purpose, direction and motivation to your sailors when you do not know what is going on. Changing from a peacetime to wartime mindset is difficult, and even more so when you do not know what your role is or when/if you will be tasked to perform your mission. From your standpoint, you are trying to be a team player and provide information up the chain of command, but it is difficult to determine what the boss needs. This is when open and honest communication is severely tested.

Facilitator can provide a personal story to help illustrate how this works. A humorous story follows:

In the preparation for Operation Urgent Fury, Admiral Train, CINCLANTFLT, was walking out of his house on Dillingham Street in Norfolk one Saturday morning, and noticed his neighbor, Admiral Metcalf leaving his house with his golf clubs. Admiral Train marveled at the confidence being displayed by Admiral Metcalf to leave the planning for such an important operation in the hands of his staff. Here was the JTF, (Joint Task Force) commander actually going off to play golf as his staff was conducting planning. All of a sudden Admiral Train remembered that he had neglected to tell Admiral Metcalf that he had been assigned as the JTF commander.

The next section of the lesson is devoted to examining how different personality types can impact the concept of open and honest communication.

Suppose your boss turns out to be a "screamer." How do you deal with him/her in this spirit of open and honest communication?

First, your requirement and obligation still exists to provide open and honest communication, even if you do not want to.

Must find a way to communicate, and you need to find some common ground.

As with any boss, you must bring a solution along with any problem.

Screaming back will not work. If there is a personality conflict it is important to remember that the boss has the personality and you have the conflict.

Suppose your boss is a "micro-manager." How do you deal with him/her in this spirit of open and honest communications?

One option is to provide more information than you would normally care to under other circumstances. This is a two-edged sword. While it may satisfy this type of personality, it could become a problem if the boss dislikes having all of this information.

Must determine the cause for the micro-management. Make sure you are not the cause by failing to properly keep the boss informed, or failing to plan properly, etc.

Suppose your boss says to you that it's your command, run it as you see fit. How do you deal with him/her in this spirit of open and honest communication?

While this is clearly the best of all possible situations, it does have its drawbacks. It may be difficult to determine what the boss wants or needs to hear from you, and with what frequency. You will have the tendency to keep things from the boss unintentionally because of this guidance. That is an easy trap to fall into rather rapidly.

You are still required to provide open and honest communication and bring forward issues and solutions as you would with any personality type.

This is a good time to talk about the boss's staff and your relationship with them. You must set the tone for how your people interact with the boss's staff. The following is an example of a CO who did not take the time to explain the relationship he desired with the staff, and the consequences that had on the ship. The CO's philosophy was to make his people self-sufficient as much as possible, clearly a well-intentioned plan. Unfortunately, his people turned that philosophy into an antagonistic relationship with the staff that made them feel unwelcome on the ship.

Another example of how your relationship with the boss can impact the staff's perception of your command. Let's say that the staff never hears from you, because your boss has a hands off policy. What will likely develop as a perception about your command on the staff?

Your command is self-sufficient (that's the impression you hope they develop)

They may start to believe that you are hiding something because of the lack of communication.

Now let's say your boss is the "micro-manager" and you are providing a lot of communication to the boss and staff. What will likely develop as a perception about your command on the staff?

They may start to feel that your command cannot do anything without the staff's involvement.

The may start to believe that you are hiding something because you are telling them everything.

The last personality type to examine is the boss who simply cannot take bad news. This can be a real challenge to providing open and honest communication. How do you do it?

Ensure you provide the solution with the problem.

You may want to feel out the Chief Staff Officer first before bluntly bringing an issue forward.

I showed the film clip from Robin Hood Men in Tights as a humorous way of providing bad news to a boss who can't take bad news.

In this clip the actor, playing the sheriff of Nottingham is relaxing on his throne. His henchman burst in and says he has news. The Sheriff asks what kind of news? He states it's not bad news is it? I cannot take bad news. The sheriff says, perhaps if he were told bad news in a good way that might work. So the henchman, in a laughing style, told the fact that the king's men had just got the "crap beat out of them" by Robin Hood. As you can imagine that did not work very well. There is no really good way to deliver bad news except straight out.

Throughout this lesson we have focused on the importance of open and honest communication with the boss, some of the pitfalls associated with maintaining that type of communication, and some ideas and things to consider when establishing and maintaining good communication up the chain of command.

It is important to remember that you will have some difficult times and situations arise during your command tour. Everyone has them and you will not be the exception. Your boss understands and expects those things to occur. He/she is more interested in how you deal with adverse situations more than the event itself. The following true story illustrates this point.

Two ships in the same squadron had almost identical mishaps occur with small boats within a month of each other. Fortunately no one was injured in either incident, but there was damage to both boats and their handling equipment. Clearly the potential for physical injury to personnel was present. In the first case, the CO quickly investigated the incident and reported to the commodore the facts of the incident, the cause, and took responsibility for the incident due to a failure in properly training personnel in lowering the boat into the water. The commodore, satisfied with the report, closed out the incident with no further action. In the second case, the CO was not as forthcoming with his report. In fact, the commodore's staff had to repeatedly prod the CO to submit his report. When the report was finally received, it was a long and convoluted. Responsibility for the incident was spread around to the people involved despite the fact that it was clearly a training issue. Upon receiving the report, the commodore immediately directed an Article 32 investigation into the incident. After the investigation was concluded, the commodore had a talk with the CO regarding his handling of the incident, and although the CO is now doing a better job, he will never fully regain the trust he lost with the commodore.

Open and honest communication is the key. That point was made clear in Command Excellence Study.

Learning point: *Benefits of developing good relationships and communication with fellow CO's and CO's that support your command.*

This may be an area you have not given a great deal of thought to in your preparation for command. There may be a tendency to think that relationships with other commanding officers, particularly with ones you will compete with for FITREPS, will be somewhat adversarial. That not only does not have to happen, the inverse is probably going to be true.

Remember that it is lonely at the top. You will have your XO, CMC, and perhaps your spouse to talk to about many things, but no one knows how you feel except another CO. You are entering a unique fraternity that can end up being one of the most rewarding aspects of your entire command tour.

There are many benefits from cultivating a good working and social relationship with other CO's:

You set a good example for your officers and sailors to emulate with respect to their relationships with their counterparts in other commands.

A spirit of teamwork and camaraderie will develop.

A great social relationship can ease the stress and strain that sometimes is attendant to command.

You have resources to turn to when you need assistance, besides the boss.

Getting to know the CO's that support your command can foster a spirit of cooperation that will benefit your people.

Lesson Summary and Bridge to the Next Lesson

This lesson was designed to provide you with some food for thought in the importance of developing open and honest communication with superiors in your chain of command and other CO's. Hopefully, you also picked up some ideas on the do's and don'ts of effective communications.

This lesson brings Unit 3 to a close. We have devoted this Unit to the development of relationships within your command, based on our discussion in the course thus far in units 1 and 2. We have emphasized the application of leadership in developing your people and their commitment to the command. Now we are going to turn our attention to the application of leadership to enhancing mission readiness.

CHAPTER 11

....

6.3 COMMAND SAFETY

Tie In

In 6.2, "Developing Command Unity," we had several great discussions about some tough emotional leadership challenges. Much of what you must deal with in command are perceptions and mind-sets. Changing mind-sets, like any change, requires energy and effort. This mind-set refocus problem can be solved by providing a sense of purpose or unity that will relegate personal bias and beliefs to a position of secondary importance.

What will *you* use to build this unity and cohesion? How will *you* develop the proper mind-set?

This morning, we will talk about the safety mind-set of those we are to lead.

All of you are and will be concerned about the safety of your people. This personal concern builds trust, which is essential if you are to build command unity and cohesion. These will in turn facilitate achieving your definition of a successful command.

Safety is always on the top of all our lists of things to be concerned about, yet many poor leadership and safety examples still persist in the fleet.

Excerpt from recent COMNAVSAFECEN NORFOLK VA—R 211936Z AUG 95

> RMKS/1. RECENT AFLOAT SAFETY SUR-
> VEYS AND OTHER SHIP VISITS REVEALED
> THE SAFETY CONDITION OF OPERAT-
> ING UNITS WAS NOT WHAT YOU AND I
> EXPECT. I AM TROUBLED PARTICULARLY
> ABOUT WHAT WAS TAKING PLACE IN THE
> DECK SEAMANSHIP. THERE IS A FORCE
> TAKING HOLD OF SOME PARTS OF OUR
> SHIPS AND IT'S COSTING US THE LIVES
> OF OUR YOUNG SAILORS. THIS FORCE
> IS COMPLACENCY. THIS COMPLACENT
> ATTITUDE HAS ME WORRIED. IT WASN'T
> RESTRICTED TO JUNIOR SAILORS, IT
> ALSO CAME FROM OLDER, MORE SENIOR
> LEADERSHIP (OFFICERS AND CHIEFS). WE
> SAW AND HEARD IT THROUGHOUT THE
> SHIPS WE VISITED. SOME OBSERVATIONS
> INCLUDE:
>
> A. A VISIBLE EXAMPLE IS AS CLOSE AS
>   THE COVER OF "ALL HANDS" (JUNE
>   1995). "THE MAGAZINE OF THE U.S.
>   NAVY," SHOWS AN OFFICER OR CPO

WEARING AN UNZIPPED AND UNAU-
THORIZED LIFE JACKET. (STEARNS
LIFE JACKETS ARE FOR BOARD-
ING OPERATIONS ONLY AND THE
WORKING LIFE JACKET IS AUTHOR-
IZED FOR OTHER TASKS. THE PIC-
TURED BOAT CREW WAS ENGAGED
IN NEITHER.) THE OTHER KHAKI
IN THE PHOTO IS WEARING A MK
5 LIFE PRESERVER, BUT HE ONLY
ZIPPED IT UP PART WAY.

B. THIS SAME COMPLACENT ATTI-
TUDE AFFECTS THE WAY we ATTACK
SOME OF OUR MORE HAZARDOUS
EVOLUTIONS. DURING AN UNREP
AND RHIB DAVIT OPERATIONS
(BOTH EVOLUTIONS ARE FULL OF
RISKS), THE IMPRESSION GIVEN BY
SOME OF THE SHIP'S MORE SENIOR
LEADERS (DEPARTMENT HEADS
AND BELOW) AND SAFETY OBSERV-
ERS WAS THAT THESE TASKS HAD
BECOME ROUTINE.

The message goes on to provide additional observations and answers to questions posed, all of which indicated bad attitudes and more complacency. So it's the same old story, talking the talk, but not walking the walk. The article summed up the waterfront environment, as it existed in 1995 and addressed the following:

- Complacency in both senior and junior ranks
- Unsafe boat operations
- Lack of attention to detail
- Cutting corners for expediency
- Overall deck seamanship performance unsatisfactory
- Numerous poor engineering practices.

Overall, the article catalogued the lack of a safety mind-set.

Understanding the safety mind-set can be difficult. Just as in all unity issues, we must ask ourselves, "What message are we communicating day in and day out?"

So just what is a safety mind-set? Why is it important and how can we develop it in our people? We all listed it close to the top in our command philosophy, high amongst the main objectives we wanted to achieve in our command.

What is it that we really want? (Discussion here.)

Let's begin with a safety mind-set that we do *not* want:

Read Darwin Award.

1995 Darwin Award Winner.

You all know about the Darwin Award. It's an annual honor given to the person who did the gene pool the biggest service by inadvertently killing themselves in the most extraordinarily stupid way.

Last year's winner was the fellow who was killed by a Coke machine, which toppled over on top of him as he was attempting to tip a free soda out of it.

And this year's winner is:

The Arizona Highway Patrol came upon smoldering metal imbedded into the side of a cliff rising above the road, at the apex of a curve. The debris resembled the site of an airplane crash, but was in fact a car-wreck. The type of car was unidentifiable at the scene, but the folks back at the lab finally figured out what it was and what had happened.

It seems that a guy had somehow got hold of a JATO unit (jet-assisted takeoff unit, actually a solid-fuel rocket) that is used to give heavy military transport planes an extra "push" for taking off from short airfields. He had driven his Chevy Impala out into the desert and found a long, straight stretch of road. Then he attached the JATO unit to his car, jumped in, got up some speed, and fired off the JATO!

Best as they could determine, he was doing somewhere between 250 and 300 MPH when he came to that curve. The brakes were completely burned away in a vain attempt to slow the car down. Guess the guy didn't figure that solid-fuel rockets don't have an off switch. Once started, they burn at full thrust till the fuel is all gone….

That is not the safety mind-set we are looking for…

I often had the visualization of the guy bolting that JATO unit onto his Impala. Always wondered what was going through his mind. How did he determine that stretch of road was straight enough and long enough? It was no doubt a wild ride, his foot doubtless pounding on the brake in sheer panic.

The leadership challenge is, how can you influence people to take safety seriously into consideration prior to taking any action?

Let me repeat the same question I asked before the Developing Subordinates lesson. As a CO/leader, do you have more or less control over your own destiny?

> The time for taking all measures for a ship's safety is while still able to do so. (Fleet Admiral Chester W. Nimitz, 1945)

Taking all measures here means you must prepare the crew mentally. You must develop their safety mind-set.

How will you do that? Again, a leadership challenge. How can you weave this safety mind set into your command?

Simple. Just walk the walk and talk the talk. As with most anything else, your actions dictate your safety philosophy.

We have talked a little about a safety mind-set. In reality, is it compatible with what every-day naval jobs are all about, whether in peace or at war? Of course, *optimizing* safety must remain a major focus, but at the same time our navy has to get underway.

The point is to accomplish that which is inherently unsafe as safely as possible. Getting to that point is not a trivial effort.

Facilitate a discussion of the value of safety standards in relationship to military goals. Are they compatible in an inherently dangerous environment?

As CO, what will *you* do? What messages should *you* communicate?

- The importance of cleanliness and its simple relationship to safety
- The critical importance of discipline
- Adhering to high standards and following procedures
- Your exhibited pattern of behavior
- The trust you have built based on your actions and decisions
- Caring for your subordinates and their families
- Keep subordinates focused on the tasks, day in and day out.

Reference: U.S. Navy Regulations, 1973. This underscores the importance of communicating the right message:

> The commanding officer shall require that persons concerned are instructed and drilled in all applicable safety precautions and procedures, that they are complied with, and that applicable safety precautions, or extracts there from, are posted in appropriate places.

In any instance where safety precautions have not been issued or are incomplete, he or she shall issue or augment such safety precautions as deemed necessary, when appropriate, notifying higher authorities concerned.

So that is a safety mind-set. How will you know that your command has it?

What will *you* use to measure it?

Case Study
WHERE'S THE FOREIGN OBJECT DAMAGE (FOD)?

Directions: Read the case. Engage in class-wide discussion using the case study questions to ascertain appropriate CO action.

SCENARIO

A squadron deployed with their air wing aboard a CV that was conducting high-visibility Battle Group (BG) air operations in support of UN relief efforts ashore.

There were only two aircraft available for the next two-plane launch cycle. The Maintenance Officer informed the CO that his maintenance detachment discovered that a small knob was missing from a gauge in the cockpit of one of the aircraft.

No one could say for certain when the knob came off or whether it was inside or outside the cockpit. The CO was aware that debris in the cockpit can sometimes migrate into the flight control linkages and create a safety-of-flight issue. He was informed that a sweep of the area around the aircraft and a thorough search of the cockpit had not located the knob.

The Maintenance Officer recommended that the aircraft be authorized as safe-for-flight because the knob could not be located, and was too small to cause significant damage. The aircraft's availability was important for meeting the BG's support commitments.

The launch was scheduled to occur in 60 minutes and the CO was scheduled to fly in the other aircraft in the same two-plane launch. Time was of the essence as crews needed to begin pre-flight checks. The CO questioned whether he should approve the flight, or perhaps fly that aircraft himself.

On the flight deck, the search for the knob was intensified. As the CO climbed into his aircraft, he realized that if the questionable aircraft did not start as soon as possible, it would not be ready for the scheduled launch. By radio, the Maintenance Officer again asked for authorization to fly the aircraft. The plane had been searched by several maintenance crews, with no success in locating the missing knob. The choices boiled down to authorizing the aircraft as safe to fly, or removing the ejection seats to complete a time-consuming and labor-intensive search for the knob. Launch was scheduled to occur in 25 minutes. A decision was needed immediately. What should the CO decide?

Questions:

As the CO, do you approve the flight?

Do you fly the aircraft yourself?

Do you require that the ejection seats be removed to facilitate the search?

What do a CO's actions say about his priorities and accountability?

Case study highlights:

Pattern of behavior/command climate/high standards/concern for well-being/acceptable risk/personal commitment/the right thing to do/importance of professionalism.

As CO, you will have numerous opportunities to reinforce your operational definition of a safety mind-set. How well you do that will impact the tenor of your command.

Ways to communicate the importance of safety in your command or organization: your subordinates must see you making decisions which support a safety mind-set. Simple things like:

- Appoint a safety officer to implement safety policies and procedures
- Authorize delays in equipment repair due to safety issues.
- Reduce mission capability due to safety.
- Allow additional resource expenditure for safety.

LEAD IN:

Historical studies indicate there are likely two aspects of this safety mind set.

Perhaps the best way to ensure your people are safe is to train realistically so they are ready to fight.

In command you must keep asking yourself, what have I prepared them to do?

Discussion here about realistic training vs. peacetime conservatism. Why take risks?

Remember that "The Law" states:

"All CO's...are required to show in themselves a good example of virtue, patriotism and subordination; to be vigilant in inspecting the conduct of all persons who are placed under their command; to guard against and suppress all dissolute and immoral practices, and to correct...all persons who are guilty of them; and to take all necessary and proper measures, under the laws, regulations and customs of naval service, to promote and safeguard the morale, the physical well-being and the general welfare of the officers and enlisted persons under their command."

(*Show clip from* Glory *here.*)

> *The movie is a story about the Fighting 54 Regiment of Massachusetts. It was the first black regiment to fight in the Civil War. Matthew Broderick plays the leader. In an earlier scene he was involved in combat and when faced*

with battle and the fog of war, proved himself a coward. He did not cross the line between fear and courage. He hides and was separated from his regiment. No one knew of his cowardice, and when he returned with a slight wound, he was considered a hero. Through family influence, he attained the rank of colonel and was placed in charge of the fifty-four. It was supposed to be a political appointment until a significant emotional event provided the catalyst needed to unite the regiment as one. He was then faced with the true challenge of leadership, responsibility toward those he has to lead. He is forced to deal with the challenge as to what he has prepared his men to do.

The scene begins with Broderick selecting one of his men, a man known for being a good shot. When asked what he has hunted, the man indicates "squirrels and such." Broderick asks him to fire his rifle and the man hits his target. The other men applaud. Broderick then asks him to reload quickly and fire again. The man begins, with Broderick yelling at him to hurry. Stressed and fumbling, the man manages to load and fire. Broderick yells to reload again and pulls out his revolver, firing rounds near him while the man attempts to reload. With Broderick's yelling and firing, the man finally panics, flusters, and drops his rifle. He just stares at Broderick. The point was made. In battle a complexity of issues abound, and for that very reason, training must be realistic.

So if realistic training is what you decided to do, how will you do it? What are the challenges involved?

<u>Instinct/Training:</u>

"In the heat of the battle you don't remember very much, you don't think very fast, you act by instinct, which is actually training. So that you've got to be trained for battle and you will react just exactly the way you do in training." (Admiral Arleigh A. Burke)

Why do realistic training in peacetime?

Transition from peace to war is often sudden. The difference between peacetime and combat training should be as small as possible. For us, the issue is bringing your people to the dance ready, and bringing them back safe. You can feel that when you get back from deployment. The relief is indescribable. I for one really did not understand that until we finished our deployment and all returned safe.

Note however, that to train realistically means you must accept risk.

<u>Realism in training:</u>

"Thus, it appears that in the war of the future we will again be required to make decisions without satisfactory knowledge of the enemy. It is therefore important to practice this in peace for in war we will do well only that which we have learned to do in peace. "(Capt. Adolph Von Schell, <u>Battle of Leadership,</u> <u>1933)</u>

What risk is acceptable?

Realistic training versus unacceptable casualties. Why take risks in peacetime?

The theory is that because we are not committed to real training, i.e. the way we fight, we make mistakes when pressure or realism is added. The more our mistakes, the more our seniors dictate conservatism. This can continue until being tied to the pier and taking no risks seems to be the best way to keep mistakes from happening. That is not a safety mind-set. That is a failure of leadership.

"It is my perception that the only thing some of you appear to lack is the self-discipline to apply your skill and experience consistently." (Air Commodore D.T. Bryant Commander, 1st Wing, RAF)

Do you think this is true? Are we training realistically? The important question is, will you? That answer depends a lot on *your* own commitment and competency.

How can you know if your command is both safe and combat ready?

What will you use to measure this? What direction do sailors need?

They want to do what they are supposed to do. They want to operate like it was for real. They want to know what is expected from them. They want to feel ready, but they don't know if they are or not. Realistic training attacks the heart of the maximizing part of the leadership flow diagram, namely, to maximize loyalty, confidence and commitment in peacetime, and to minimize fear, stress and risk in crisis and combat.

If you are combat ready, are you safe? Are you prepared to give and take hard knocks and win/survive? What is the mindset of a combat ready organization? What does such an organization look like and feel like?

Would we know it if we saw it?

How will your command compare to that vision at your one year in command point? What will you do to get there? What's your plan?

I would say that if you are combat-ready, then you are safe and have lived up to your responsibilities under "The Law."

Obviously, "hands on" CO commitment is a must here.

The CO needs to blend a safety mind-set with combat readiness.

Vice-Adm. Laplant, who led Amphib. Group One in Desert Storm, said that the biggest safety threat *is combat*, and the best way to deal with this threat is realistic training. You have to fight for it regardless of the environment. He also said that there is a, "difference between dangerous and unsafe."

The leadership challenge is that you must understand where your command's mind-set is at. Maintain risk at the same level, but through realistic and increased difficulty, keep raising the level of training complexity until you get to the level desired.

Yet again, the critical importance of your being confident and competent.

You have to put your effort and energy into cohesion building. This is an essential element of unity. It builds the critical mindset that the actions of each of us affects the lives of all of us; that we are all in this together; that our safety rest in the hands of the person next to us knowing and doing his/her job well.

It is really that simple, but hard to achieve.

Summary:

At the beginning of this topic, we talked about the problem of complacency. To any extent to which it may exist, that level of complacency is set by you. Your command safety attitude and professionalism are reflections of your training level of commitment. You cannot maintain a positive command climate and not show high concern and personal interest in your subordinates' safety and well-being. They are loyal to you because they trust you. They trust that you always have their best interest at heart. That is the essence of the leader-follower relationship. *Break that trust and you lose your ability to lead.*

So perhaps the only way to really ensure your people are safe is to provide them a mind—set that is based on realistic combat-readiness training. Everything must be ready to be used in combat. Their very lives may depend on it. They must be mentally ready. Their equipment must be ready. Their procedures and tactics must be ready. Their attitudes must be ready. Above all, *your leadership* must be ready.

So again the question, as CO/leader, do you have *more* or *less* control over your own destiny?

CHAPTER 12

....

LEADERSHIP IN COMBAT/CRISIS SITUATIONS

I have tried to put into this book the major lessons and points of the old Command Leadership Course. It is simply not possible to duplicate here the experience of the whole two weeks' worth of readings and lessons. A necessarily important part of the course was the interchange that daily occurred amongst the students. Our goal was to facilitate actual learning, not simply teach the points of every lesson, a "how to think" approach in contrast to "what to think." The in-class discussions were indeed critical elements of the entire course.

Recommended course readings and many of the important quotes or points have been provided at the end of this topic. The intent is to move the reader towards "the wisdom block," the desired pinnacle with respect to an appreciation of the course's flow and its key leadership building blocks. I believe it all comes together in this topic.

The focus here is that in combat/crisis, the leader must deal with the element of *risk*, risk for yourself, risk for your people, risk for your command and risk for your country. As the CO you must weigh many factors and make decisions under great stress, often based on less than perfect information. Your leadership foundation, values, ethics and strength of character all play a large role in how confident you are when faced with tough decisions in difficult situations. History bears witness that your command will react based on how well prepared they are, both physically and mentally. Are they a united team? Have you provided them unity of effort and purpose? The whole two-week course flow and framework comes into play in this topic and we trust it ties in all the leadership variables discussed over the last two weeks.

- Research and studies used (listed as additional references)
  - Persian Gulf Study, 1991-1992 (Navy) now finished
  - Davenport Study, 1919 (Navy)
  - Harsfield Book 'The Art of Leadership in War"
  - Royal Navy Study, 1980
  - Naval Academy Leadership Conference 1987
  - World War Two Combat Leadership Effectiveness Studies
  - U.S. Army Infantry Squad Field Exercise leadership Effectiveness Studies
  - Korean War U.S. Air Force Study
  - Vietnam War U.S. Army Study
  - U.S. Army National Training Center Study
  - Navy Peacetime Effectiveness Study—1985

This topic will address the following questions:

1. Can combat/crisis leaders be developed in peacetime?
2. What are some personality traits common to combat-effective naval leaders?

3. Is there a difference between combat leadership and non-combat leadership?

4. Is leadership an integral element of combat power?

5. What is the role of vision, empowerment and communication in a combat/stress—filled environment?

6. Risk taking and realistic training in peacetime, a dilemma or a necessity?

7. Can I prepare myself and my crew/command to respond well in combat/crisis?

Lead in.

Everything you have done or not done impacts how your command will react in a combat or crisis situation. We have discussed basic things like:

- Have you developed your subordinates?

- Did you surf the leadership model?

- Is your technical, political, and cultural (TPC) environment, balanced both inside and outside your command organization?

- Have you stabilized your key and essential processes?

- Is Quality in daily work, (QIDW) an adopted and implemented command mindset?

- Have you trained realistically?

- Have you played the "what if" game?

- Are you mentally and physically prepared, confident, competent, dynamic and effective?

Set-up

In this last topic we are going to focus on what is considered the primary difference between our military leadership challenge and that of our civilian counterparts. We will focus on those elements and variables that come into play for our people and ourselves as we lead and prepare them to deal both physically and mentally with combat or crisis.

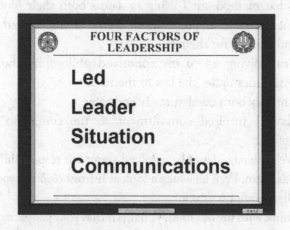

FOUR FACTORS OF LEADERSHIP

Led

Leader

Situation

Communications

THE FOUR FACTORS:

Throughout the course we have discussed the four main factors of leadership. We have put you in a lot of different situations with those you are to lead, and talked about different ways to communicate in those situations. We will now focus on these four elements again, but specifically as they relate to leadership in combat or crisis situations.

I will tie in the readings and points to ponder quotes as we go.

Those you are to lead:

Studies discussed illustrate that as far as those we are to lead are concerned, our primary challenge is again the constant mental drill of answering questions like:

What have I prepared them to do?

What is my measure of readiness?

What method am I using to assess both their physical and mental state of preparation? What is my desired end state of training for them?

Am I living up to my command philosophy and my responsibilities under the law to them?

Are they both combat ready and safe?

Have I inspired commitment to the command and its mission?

We understand and have talked about our responsibilities towards them. Well let's take a look at it from *their* viewpoint.

Discussion question.

Think with me out loud. What is it that your people expect from you, another words what kind of leadership and skills are they looking for from you in a combat/crisis situation?

Studies indicate they are looking for a determination to take it to the end, a resolution, calmness, steadiness and commitment.

Here is what Roger Nye says about it:

The Challenges of the Commander – "To command is to direct with authority. To command a military organization is to think and make judgments, employing specialized knowledge and deciding what those commanded will and will not do. To command in wartime is to assume responsibility for taking and saving human lives. To command in peace and war is to direct how human beings will conduct themselves toward each other. As such, the commander sets moral standards and sees that they are obeyed. To command, therefore, is to think and decide to feel and moralize, to act and wield power."

Or, as we have said throughout this course, when in command, command!

TO ACT AND TO WIELD POWER

Power is the responsibility to exercise your authority, to act when the time comes. Studies suggest this is what is required from the leader: *to step forward and make the decision,—that is what your command wants, and that is what they expect.*

If stepping forward is what they *want* from you, studies also say that what they *need* from you is a plan that will address some fundamental questions:

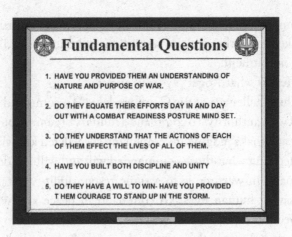

1. Have you provided them an understanding of the purpose and nature of war? John Keegan, Lord Moran, Victory at Sea, S.L.A Marshal, what will you use?)

2. Do they equate their efforts day in and day out with a combat-readiness posture mindset?

3. Do they understand that the actions of each of them affect the lives of all of them? (Sense of purpose/cohesion)

4. Have you built both discipline and camaraderie?

5. Do they have a will to win, or as Vadm. Stockdale indicates, courage to stand up in the storm?

We have already discussed these points, but in this lesson the last two points will be discussed in greater detail.

We have looked at those you are to lead. Let's look at you as:

The Leader

As the leader, what concerns do you or should you have about your leadership abilities/skills in this situation of combat/crisis?

Points to facilitate in the discussion: Have I covered all the 'what ifs' in my own mind? Have I translated the 'what ifs' into the training program? Do I have the big picture? Am I making decisions based on the best available data? Do I understand the threat we are facing? Do I know how best to address it? Am I mentally and physically prepared? Can I, or how can I maintain situational awareness? How do I know they will they follow me?

Do I have the strength? (Courage and stamina).

We have already talked about key foundational leadership strengths: the strength that comes from a leader who knows who he is; a leader that understands his strengths and personal foundation; a leader that takes advantages of his command's strengths and shores up their weaknesses; a leader who knows he/she can make these decisions.

Your people have a right to expect a leader who is mentally and physically prepared to lead the command, a leader who is committed, competent and confident.

In effectiveness studies, there is persistent reference to the mental toughness of the leader. This again brings us back to the idea as to what those we lead expect from us in this situation. All the studies agree and I think Adm. Stockdale answers it best when he says:

"I call the center of gravity of the naval officer corps those 40-year old destroyer, submarine, and aircraft squadron skippers. I think a case can be made that the success of our whole naval enterprise rests heavily on the shoulders of this elite group of three-stripers who have run and won the race of all-around, mid-career competence–particularly operational, that is, flying, steaming, deep-diving competence–and who are at last where they want to be, where they must stand up and be counted and take the heat or praise as the chips fall. In business idiom, they have arrived where they "have to meet a payroll.""

But "meeting the payroll," in the final analysis, is not just to be prepared to deliver up cash on demand, it is to deliver up the manifestation of efficiency. Their payroll objective, in the final analysis, is to *deliver up honor.*

Honor is a strong word, heavy with emotional overtones, sometimes embarrassing to articulate. Its very mention gets lost in everyday life. It even gets lost in the daily life of the average military officer. (I'm sure "efficiency" appears more frequently in DOD publications than "honor"). But most of those skippers, whether on destroyers, submarines or carrier squadrons, maybe as they ponder their new responsibilities during one of their first nights at sea, come to realize that above all else, it is personal and unit honor that their countrymen and their crew ask them to be prepared to deliver up when the crunch comes."

Leadership in Response to Changing Societal Values, James Bond Stockdale, May 1987:

Last night you had some time to reflect on this concept: What is this "honor" we are expected to deliver up?

All that you hold sacred:

- Provide the determination and desire to win the day.

- Overcome the fears and things that must be overcome so you can do what must be done.

- Do the right thing regardless of the consequences.

- Don't give up the ship, persevere, inspire, and continue to lead until the challenges are overcome.

We have talked about the leadership responsibility to provide purpose, direction and motivation. That must, indeed cannot change in this situation. There are some added variables and elements that must be dealt with, but you must still, as Adm. Stockdale remarked, "do your duty."

Do your duty:

Studies say: Here is where we combine the internal strength or commitment of the leader, and the honor we are expected to deliver up.

So what are these elements that must be overcome in order to deliver up honor and continue to provide purpose, direction and motivation? What has changed or is there a change from peacetime leadership?

Risk, Fear, the Unknown, Stress in decision-making, Consequences, Life, Death and Fatigue: these are the main elements now added to the leader's decision-making.

We will discuss these elements further today, but let's try and define operationally as a class what is this honor we are expected to deliver up?

Studies suggest it boils down to:

- We must continue to provide purpose, direction and motivation.

- We are held accountable to be able to do this and make decisions, decisions based on less than perfect information, under great stress, where the consequences are significant for yourself, your command, your service and your country.

The luxury of time is not there. You can't wait any longer. You must decide now with what you have or what your gut says. To delay in these cases may result in an even worse outcome.

And guess what? Even when you make this decision, it is not over, it's not "Miller time."

You make these decisions knowing that the results may not be good and you will have to deal with that, make another decision and another decision, until one way or another it's over, regardless whether it turns out alright or not.

(Most classes, having sat in the school for two weeks, would arrive at about the same operational definition—but knowing it and doing it are two different things.)

In order for *you* to be able to do that, you must first be able to step over the line between fear and courage.

You have to be able to deal with what is happening, all the situational elements, internalize them, get yourself under control and provide continued purpose, direction and motivation. Why? Because what *will* happen is this: when the situation is stressful and the potential consequences great, the eyes *will* turn to you. Your command's collective IQ, and you will see it, has suddenly gone to zero. If yours also goes to zero, if you cannot deal with the fear, stress and risk, you *will lose your command*. It's as simple as that.

At that time when they turn to you, they are looking for direction and inspiration. They are not looking for a discussion of options. They are not looking to provide input. *They want direction.*

There are numerous examples of this, and the impact on those that are led, when the leader fails to make that crucial step over the line.

QUOTES HERE

To emphasize the significant role of leadership, its duty to those led, and its ability to reduce panic, there was an excellent example in the Yom Kippur War of 1973.

Major Dov, intelligence officer of the Barak Brigade, one of the formations holding the Golan Heights, encountered vehicles, guns and tanks withdrawing along the road from Nafekh to the Bnet Ya'akov Bridge: "All signs pointed to a withdrawal motivated by panic." He halted the retreat and sent the forces back, having discovered that "many of the units were only too happy finally to receive orders, cut off as they had been as a result of the fighting from their chain of command."

The war correspondent, Alan Moorhead, caught up in a panic in the Western Desert, felt that the absence of firm instructions played a large part in causing it. "In ourselves, we did not know what to do," he wrote. "Had there been someone in authority to say, 'Stand here. Do this and that,' then half our fear would have vanished. I badly wanted to receive orders. And so, I think, did the others."

A Civil War story during the capture of Fort Donelson from the book Mask of Command, by John Keegan. He writes,

"Grant tells a story that he rode to where the attack had occurred—it had been fought at night-on the right side of a three mile battle line the enemy was concentrated and trying to push through and escape—the Union soldiers of Smith and Wallace forces stood up gallantly until their ammo in their cartridge boxes ran out."

Grant states:

"I saw the men standing in knots talking in the most excited fashion. No officer seemed to be giving any directions. The soldiers had their muskets but no ammunition, while there was tons of it at hand…I directed Colonel Webster to ride with me and call out to the men as we passed…

Fill your cartridge boxes quick and get into line; the enemy is trying to escape and must not be permitted to do so." This acted like a charm. The men only wanted someone to give them an order.'

As a result the Confederates were left with the choice of surrender or be captured the next day.

So, just giving orders can be enough in and of itself!

Maybe if you have done what we have talked about these two weeks, you may only need to do what King Henry did when the eyes turned to him, "stow yourself with speed my lord." The eyes turned and he said "all is well if our minds be so, you all know your places."

Just giving orders, or stepping forward and providing direction when needed….

The XO of the Constellation related a story that happened during their massive conflagration. The XO was below when he came upon a hose team that had been effective in fighting the fire. He noticed that although the hose team was comprised of mostly ensigns and LTJG's, it was being led and directed by a Third Class Petty Officer. The XO asked the young PO how it happened that he came to be in charge. The PO replied, "I said follow me, and they did."

Follow me!!

Maybe that's all you need, or maybe more, but you must do *something*. You must step over that crucial line.

What are we considering here? What will or can give both you and your people the capability to step over the line?

Stockdale and Macarthur discussed what helped them. They indicated what was their source of inspiration, strength and mental toughness. In any event that is the expectation. It will likely be in the mind of your command that *in you* lies their safety and their lives. It could be as simple as that.

Has anyone been in this situation when the eyes have turned to you, and would you like to share *your* thoughts?

How long did you feel they would have waited? *(Many had such stories and confirmed the feeling that they only had precious seconds to react before their people might panic, or turn to someone else for direction.)*

Tough feeling! A significant leadership test of character. There is no place to go. You have no one to turn to. You must deliver up honor and live up to your responsibility, *or lose your ability to lead.*

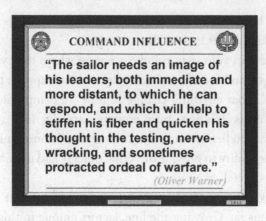

COMMAND INFLUENCE

"The sailor needs an image of his leaders, both immediate and more distant, to which he can respond, and which will help to stiffen his fiber and quicken his thought in the testing, nerve-wracking, and sometimes protracted ordeal of warfare."

(Oliver Warner)

That point and the relationship between the leader and those we are to lead is stated above in this quote from Great Fighting Admirals, from Hawk to Nimitz.

This is your responsibility under the law, and it is *absolute*.

Again, backed up by numerous combat veteran discussions, this is your responsibility as far as your subordinates are concerned. No different than setting the example, same as we have been talking about all along. You must be prepared and you must mentally and physically prepare your command by actions and deeds to cross that line as well.

In aviation, you may not be there to get them to cross the line. You must have prepared and led them in a manner that gets them ready to execute without additional guidance. This thought brings into discussion the importance of communication in this combat/ crisis situation.

We have already discussed how communication is an art. Let's take a closer look at that concept.

Create in your own mind a scenario where the eyes will turn to you and focus on what we say here as it applies to your scenario. Does anything change in how we communicate in combat/crisis situations from how we normally do?

Many studies confirm that calmness and communication skills, the ability to provide direction quickly and understandably, are crucial.

Now a video which combines several key points introduced thus far. Crossing the line, factors unique to this combat/stress situation, looks at the question of what should I prepare my command to do, and introduces the question of command centralization. How much is too much? After you see this, we will discuss these and some additional points,

1. What was your impression of their readiness?

2. Could they have been better prepared, and if so, how?

Introduction of the video from the script.

Tough to recreate a video, but I will cover the main points.

It was a Desert Storm cockpit communications tape of an F-16's Surface-to-Air Missile (SAM) evasion in Jan 1991. The missiles being fired were SA-2's and SA-6's. The pilot's call sign was Stroke 3. He ends up successfully evading 5 SAMs. He had just completed a bombing run when he detected a SAM launch. The video has two cockpit presentations. One is from an F-16 pilot not engaged in the evasions, which as a result of the mission commander being shot down realizes he is now in charge. The second cockpit presentation is Stroke 3, who is doing the evasions. The video plays the same communications sequence but from the two different cockpits. The students were asked to listen closely to the communications of all, but especially call sign Stroke 3. There were two hits by the SAM's, on Stroke 1 and Stroke 4. Observations indicated, "Stroke 4 hit, no chute, meaning no sign of an ejection.

There was lots of jargon used:

Defending means evading SAMs. Two methods back then:

(GLIB MANEUVER/ OVERSHOOT MANEUVER) turn in place SAM on the beam and keep it there.

SAM Lock, meaning a surface to air missile had locked on. A missile lock would cause a loud audible alert in cockpit.

I would have the students look for the trails of the missiles in this clip and asked them to try and place themselves in this clip if possible. I asked them to listen to the emotions of the various players and their positive or negative contribution to the event.

The video starts on the routine mission. Then comes the first indication of a launch. The leader of the strike was shot down. The mission leader tries to contact Stroke 1 then realizes he is now in charge and quickly changes his tone and steps across the line and directs the remaining aircraft. He states he was also hit and has "lost everything up here guys." So he dealt with his own safety issue and assumed leadership in spite of his concerns for his own well-being. Meanwhile he listens to Stroke 3 communications as he evades five SAM's. The video goes from cockpit to cockpit showing the difference. In the confusion there are many communications from those not involved trying to ask questions and input what they think is important. The leader's cockpit is very quiet and flying steady, while Stroke 3's heads up display shows incredible motion and G forces as he continues to turn to evade. All you can hear is his "hooking" and the loud audible alert of a missile launch. Hooking is a procedure which is a breathing requirement done by pilots during significant G's to keep the blood flowing to extremities and prevent them from passing out. It is a traumatic and draining event. The video goes back and forth. Just when Stroke 3 gets one evaded, he remarks 'here comes another one', then back into his hooking drill, over and over, 2-3-4-5 times, until finally it is over.

POST VIDEO DISCUSSION POINTS

We talked about getting beaten down in the envelope. The pilot in Stroke 3 used his breathing to calm himself. He just focused on that while he did his maneuvering. He could not really process anything else, except what he *had* to do.

So what was transpiring throughout this crisis situation?

Pace of operations increases along with complexity and personal anxiety, all tending to contribute to a break-down of communications over a wide spectrum.

There is a big change in the tone of the communication when the first person is hit. It becomes a very personal connection. The reality that someone is really "shooting at me, at me," and maybe for the first time! How do you deal with that?

- People to people communication increases in scope and volume. Those in direct touch feel they need to say something, as it helps cope with anxiety. Priorities have to be developed *ad hoc*, unless previously anticipated, discussed and trained for.

- Adequate communication between seniors and juniors can sometimes deteriorate, due to the volume of information the senior has to process and act on in a timely manner. The irony here is that time sometimes seems to stand still, but that can have the effect of spacing out communication intervals.

- Poorly trained and inadequately self-disciplined staff can be disastrous for communication (as heard in the video, talkers merely stepping on one another). The need to instill discipline in action and communications through practice and drill is crucial to crisp communication in combat/crisis.

- Judging your subordinates' communication skills under stress is probably the easiest test to evaluate prior to actual combat/crisis. An excellent example of adequate training is that the bridge maintains minimal chatter, even during stressful situations.

The video makes some great points:

- Importance of stamina.

- Endurance, never over until it is over.

- Step over the line again and again. As Stroke 3 said, "defending" again and again.

- Going to the well, digging down and gutting it out. What gives you that capability? That will to win?

- Importance of the leader to build and keep situational awareness. Stroke 3 went hot mike to control his emotions by concentrating on the sound of his breathing.

This brings to bear another important point. We have said in this course that command is not about you. For how can you really keep command of situational awareness if you are too much concerned as to your own safety?

The video also points out the need to maintain a mission mindset. There had been assigned SEAD (suppression of enemy air defenses) ea-6's, wild weasels in this case. They ran out of fuel and had to turn back. The decision was made to do the mission without them. As they proceeded, they lost situational awareness and went too low. That's when the SAM's got a lock. Nothing can prepare you to be shot at for the first time. Stroke 3 could only say, "defending" and try to control his breathing to get himself under control.

We then showed a communications example from the Israelis. It was very succinct, no non-essential info, no stepping on one another, just short descriptive words or actions.

The point is that there should not be such a big difference in the quality of communication during combat/crisis, compared to that during everyday training.

There are two *key* leadership issues to think about here, seeing and knowing, plus the concept of centralization.

The Mask of Command, Seeing and Knowing by John Keegan. This quote is centered on Hitler's desire to micromanage his armies:

"For the radio did not bring to the Fuhrer's headquarters all the other information of an "immaterial" but much more important kind—as opposed to equipment and unit positions etc.—the look of the battlefield, the degree of heat and cold, the variation in intensity of the enemy pressure, the level of noise, the flow of wounded backward, the flow of supply forward, the mood of the soldiers, to be judged by the expression of their faces and the tone of the answers to questions—which only a man on the spot would gather. Without recourse to such essential impressions—he was skimming the surface of generalship…"

The substance of this quotation goes to the heart of the argument about today's communication ability and control. *How much is too much?*

In the video the controller in the CV told Stroke 3 (who is evading) to gain altitude. It is of course understandable that he is concerned and helpless, but his comments were not helpful. It is tough to sit on your hands as a leader sometimes, but ask first if you are being additive and is what you are saying important and helpful. Again, the "not about you" concept.

"Without the stress and strain and the limit on time, nobody can actually duplicate the strain that a commander is under in making a decision. Consequently, it's a brave man, or an incautious one, who criticizes another man for the action he took in battle unless it is obviously an error caused by a lack of character." Adm. Burke.

This is such a great point and one often not understood by those "cold timid souls who neither know victory or defeat." Teddy Roosevelt

There was a break at this point after an hour and a half of the lesson. When the students returned I showed a clip from the movie Glory. *I have discussed the movie before in the "Safety" topic.*

The movie is a story about the Fighting 54th Regiment of Massachusetts. It was the first black regiment to fight in the civil war. Matthew Broderick plays the leader. Prior to assuming command of the 54th he was involved in combat for the first time, and when faced with battle and the fog of war, proved himself a coward. He did not cross the line between fear and courage. He hid, crawled along to safety and was separated from his regiment. No one knew of his cowardice and when he returned with a slight wound he was considered a hero. Through family influence he attained the rank of colonel and was placed in charge of the 54th. It was supposed to be political appointment until a significant emotional event provided the catalyst needed to unite the regiment as one. He was then faced with the true challenge of leadership, responsibility towards those he has to lead. Knowing from his previous experience he is forced to deal with the challenge as to what he has prepared his men to do. And what he now is prepared to do.

We have already introduced this concept of crossing the line between fear and courage. I had not heard that expression anywhere else before, and my best definition of it is two-fold:

- The mental and physical preparedness required to maintain situational awareness, and to take the necessary action.
- The gap between perception and reality of combat which can be devastating and difficult to overcome.

We have just discussed the relationship between the leader and those they lead as it pertains to a combat/crisis situation. The following quotation of Patton brings out what we will focus on for the rest of the day.

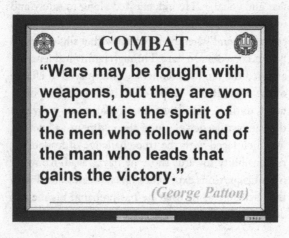

COMBAT

"Wars may be fought with weapons, but they are won by men. It is the spirit of the men who follow and of the man who leads that gains the victory."

(George Patton)

S.L.A. Marshal said "Winning of battles is the product of winning men"

Let's look at these two points:

We will see if we can operationally define this idea of "spirit" that Patton is talking about.

In the Pursuit of Excellence was discussed the "born leader" concept. What are your views on this theory?

Facilitate a discussion about the capacity to retain information, the inherent ability to synthesize data. Some simply can do it better. Some can maintain focus while numerous things are going on around them. Some have the ability to absorb information and not get overloaded. Some simply shut down quickly. We all have seen these kinds of differences.

Studies indicate there is a certain potential inherent in each individual. The point is to know where *you* are on this scale, and where each of your people are. With some people, you know that if the bus breaks down on the way to the game, they can carry the bus the rest of the way. Some people just have an innate sense of awareness. Some people have an ability to slow things down and maintain situational awareness, they just stay calm. If you have been in a car accident, how did you handle that? Did things slow down for you and you remained in control? You need to learn about yourself. You need to know how you have handled stress-related situations before.

Can you keep the big picture?

USMC STUDY ARTICLE

The USMC decided to create the Commandants Warfighting Laboratory. On the first Monday in December 1995, a dozen Marine Corps Generals and Colonels, led by General Richard D. Hearne, assistant Commandant of the Marine Corps, stormed the New York Mercantile Exchange to take a few lessons in information management from commodity traders. This unique exercise was the first war game conducted by the CWL since its inception three months earlier. They participated in simulated commodities trading designed to teach participating senior Marine officers the way traders make rapid decisions in an information-loaded environment.

The USMC realized the crucial importance of the leader's ability to be able to make decisions in the fog of war. Trying to come up with ways to develop those traits in peacetime is difficult, but not impossible.

So it is very important to be able to handle information and maintain situational awareness.

We have all seen this many times, the sponge vice the one who can never get or keep the big picture. We have seen IQ's go to zero. We have seen people shut down. Some are better than others. We talked earlier about subordinate development. The Command Excellence Study indicated successful CO's staff adequately to optimize performance.

So let's discuss here the art of leadership to identify who your players are, who are the men/women to carry the broken bus. How can you identify them, and who needs to do what, then place your people where they can help you the most in critical situations. What percent of your people will fit into this category? Studies indicate the average is *less than 18 percent*, not a big number.

Lord Moran's Anatomy of Courage: "A few men had the stuff of leadership in them, they were like rafts to which all the rest of humanity clung for support and for hope."

If that is true, and based on his experience I have no reason to doubt him, all the more reason to figure out who such leaders are in your command or organization.

Let's discuss this "born leader" concept. Are they indeed just born that way, or is there a formula to create them? For example, on the Constellation, the Third-class PO's "follow me." What would make him say that? What would make him stand up and take charge?

General S.L.A. Marshal indicated that there is no set formula for combat leaders. Studies however do reveal certain factors. What do *you* think are some common personality traits found in all combat-effective naval leaders?

Let's look at them:

The Davenport and Harsfield Study lists 3 basic traits:

- Shared a common understanding of past battle experiences. (Unit 1.2)

- They had a harmonious working relationship with those junior and senior. (Units 3-7 and 8)

- And most importantly, they shared a breadth of vision in both the military and political arena, (again the importance of lesson 1.2)

The Persian Gulf study stipulates:

- Vision
- Communication
- Empowerment

Other studies all agree on:

- Courage
- Boldness

- Initiative
- Instinct

We will talk about a couple of these in more depth. But we are now beyond the scope of the leader/manager and into the Combat Leader arena. As we have stressed from the outset, it all boils down to leader and the led.

S.L.A. Marshal says: "while there are no perfect men, there are those who become relatively perfect leaders of men because something in their makeup brings out in strength the highest virtues of all who follow them"

Let me repeat, "something in their makeup brings out in strength the highest virtues of all who follow them."

We will focus on these aspects for the rest of the day.

The spirit of the man and those who follow—and the *intangibles* that bring out in strength the highest virtue of all who follow them....

Let's look at what this "something in their makeup" might be.

We have talked about leadership roles, responsibilities and skills of the leader as we focus on combat and crisis leadership. Let's discuss a fundamental leadership question:

Does the CO's leadership role and/or skill-set differ when in a combat rather than a routine situation?

Discussion:

Navy's position is there is no change in leadership skills between combat and routine. This is backed up through many discussions with combat leaders. There are additional factors added, but the leadership skills remain the same. Everything just gets speeded up...

The leader still must apply purpose, direction and motivation to get his people to cross the line. That is to say *you still have to get the glaze out of their eyes.*

OK, so what causes the eyes to glaze and the IQ to go to zero?

Studies boil them down to four most significant elements that affect everyone's performance during combat/crisis. These are additive elements as well, meaning they impact and can cause one another. Let's define them operationally at this point

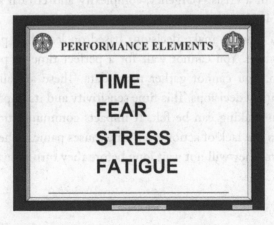

PERFORMANCE ELEMENTS

TIME

FEAR

STRESS

FATIGUE

- Time: we showed the impact in decision-making.

- Fear: an unpleasant, often strong emotion caused by anticipation or awareness of danger; anxious concern.

- Stress: a physical, chemical or emotional factor that causes bodily or mental tension that tends to alter an existing equilibrium.

- Fatigue

You need a plan to get yourself and your people ready to deal both mentally and physically with all these elements. Let's break these factors down a bit.

Time:

How does time sensitivity weigh in the decision-making process in a crisis? (Urgency, complexity and critical action are involved).

You have to make decisions based on less than perfect information. You cannot wait for a perfect time or perfect solution. You cannot gather more data. These are all now time critical decisions. This time sensitivity and its impact on decision-making can be felt. It impacts communication. In addition the lack of action over time causes panic. When the eyes turn, they will not wait long before they turn away.

Fear:

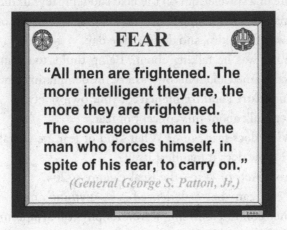

FEAR

"All men are frightened. The more intelligent they are, the more they are frightened. The courageous man is the man who forces himself, in spite of his fear, to carry on."

(General George S. Patton, Jr.)

Discussion here about the quote. What are your fears as they pertain to this type of situation? What can be done about them? (*Always a great discussion as we have now actually put them, many for the first time, mentally into this situation. I always enjoyed this point in the lesson*).

General S.L.A. Marshall says something is added in the leader's role in combat or crisis.

Let's look at that:

"For when it comes to combat, something new is added. Even if they have previously looked on him as a father and believed absolutely that being with him is in their best assurance of successful survival, should he then show himself to be timid and too cautious about his own safety, he will lose hold of them no less absolutely. His lieutenant, who up till then, under training conditions, has been regarded as a mean creature or a sniveler, but on the field suddenly reveals himself as a man of high courage, can take moral leadership of the unit away from him, and do it in one day."

What was he talking about? Being timid, too cautious, more concerned about his own safety, the debilitating emotion of being scarred and frightened for your own safety.

Let's talk about this concept of fear.

What does fear cause? What kind of fear are we talking about? How does it manifest itself?

From Acts of War—the Real Enemy, p. 204.

"Fear can be experienced as anything from mild apprehension to paralyzing terror. Its physical symptoms are well documented, and one does not have to survive battle to have experienced at least the most moderate of them. A violent pounding of the heart is the most common: at least 68 percent of the soldiers questioned by Stouffer acknowledged this symptom, as did 69 per cent of John Dollard's veterans. A sinking feeling in the stomach, uncontrollable trembling, a cold sweat, a feeling of weakness or stiffness and vomiting were also reported, in more or less that order of frequency. Six percent of Dollard's sample admitted to involuntary urination and five percent to involuntary defecation. In one of the divisions examined by Stouffer, these symptoms were reported by 21 percent and 10 percent of those questioned."

Can you create this kind of fear in peacetime? Can you prepare yourself and people to cope with this fear?

One theory says stress-related training, realistic training, training that puts these factors in play allows the individual to understand his/her own reaction.

Again, consult the studies:
Persian Gulf 1991-92
Davenport 1919
Harsfield's book Royal Navy study-in-depth 1980
Naval Academy study 1987

These studies show stress-related training, as Sec. Webb states "continue to place yourself in stress related situations and learn as much as you can and make adjustments."

In the movie Crimson Tide, there was a galley fire. The crew reacted swiftly, with no indication of indecision or panic. Even though there was a real fire, they simply thought it was a drill and reacted according to how they had been trained over and over again. In Glory, we talked about the scene where Broderick was showing the difficulty of doing routine things when the elements of pressure and criticality are introduced. We have talked about the importance of realistic training.

We have already discussed the connection between combat readiness and safety. If you are combat-ready then perhaps you are safe, by definition,

So what is your plan for accepting the responsibilities under Title Ten, The Law?

The leadership question is: What is your measure of effectiveness here? What is your plan to build this battle-mindedness mindset in yourself and your people?

I played a clip from Hunt for Red October:

There is a great scene in The Hunt for Red October. You may remember it. Sean Connery was the CO and they were underway. He knew they would soon be faced with adversity, as his plan was to defect. He needed to test himself and his crew and prepare them. They were coming on a difficult navigational leg, one that in any normal circumstance would test even the best-trained crew. He purposely delayed the normal turn, requiring his team to recompute the recommended turn time and time again. He injected stress, and concern for personal safety. He learned who could be counted on and who could not, and relieved his navigator. He tested himself and his crew. He introduced time-fear-stress into his training.

The point here is the need to take *intelligent* risk. As stated earlier: *There is a difference between dangerous and unsafe.*

With these three elements already discussed, time, fear, stress, let's do a readiness-for-combat case study.

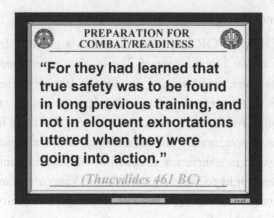

> **PREPARATION FOR COMBAT/READINESS**
>
> **"For they had learned that true safety was to be found in long previous training, and not in eloquent exhortations uttered when they were going into action."**
>
> *(Thucydides 461 BC)*

Last night you read about the Vincennes incident, when they shot down a commercial Airbus. For the purposes of our discussion it is not important whether you feel Capt. Rogers was right or wrong. As said earlier, we were not there. It's easy to criticize and say what you might have done or not done.

And as covered earlier in this lesson:

"Without the stress and strain and the limit on time, nobody can actually duplicate the strain that a commander is under in making a decision. Consequently, it's a brave man, or an incautious one, who criticizes another man for the action he took in battle unless it is obviously an error caused by a lack of character." Adm. Burke.

I am sure the decision was not based on lack of character.

So, having said that: let's talk about some of the leadership lessons and concepts.

Vincennes Background:

USMIDEASTFOR had been alerted to a possible Iranian air attack over July 4 weekend. The Iranian government was under pressure to show some response to Iraqi victories, and the U.S. was perceived as supporting Iraq. Increased tactical air (Iranian F-14) activity was observed. A potentially hostile P-3 was approximately 40 miles distant and the Vincennes was engaged in a surface action with small Iranian gunboats.

After Flight 655 was shot down, the Vincennes faced an emergence SAR during which they searched for survivors and recovered bodies.

Break up into groups

What did you get out of this reading? What pertinent leadership issues did you see unfold during the incident? What were the significant leadership challenges in this scenario?

Debrief concepts introduced here:

- Running out of time
- What have you prepared them to do
- Level of thinking
- Stress training
- Crossing the line
- Then the eyes turned
- Need to explain the why

We are talking about the concept here known as the fog of war, looking again at the relationship between safety and combat readiness.

We are introducing what the studies say is a tendency to accept data that fit into a pre-conceived picture. Your mind is building a scenario, and you tend to accept data that reinforces that and reject data that does not add to it. All the more reason to have put people around you already directed by you to guard against group-think.

Mark Purcell had a great story about rolling down the path tending to accept data that fit into his preconceived picture. Many in each class had similar stories.

Now for another leadership responsibility, one not often mentioned or trained for:

Picking up the pieces after a mistake.

This is a significant leadership challenge, how to get it back and keep it together? You have to:

- Explain to your crew the why
- Rebuild morale
- Keep focus
- Rebound

Still provide: Purpose, direction and motivation. You don't get to go into your stateroom, close the door and put your head in your hands.

It is important to maintain a big picture looking for different operational patterns. It is also important to develop your firing criteria. You need to have thought about how you want information to flow to you and in what order. You need to establish your triggers. Which way will you lean? There is an image many of us have used. It is a green table in a Court Marshall proceeding. The vision is to determine whom would you rather have sitting around the table, seniors to judge your reasons for firing, or parents of your sailors asking why you did not. A true and difficult test of the authority, responsibility and accountability triad.

(A difficult situation presented in Vincennes—the above comment was always followed by a sparked discussion. Most students were really into the topic mindset at this point.)

Let's re-iterate the several concepts introduced in this study:

- Invincibility
- Inherent morality
- Lack of critical evaluation
- Group think
- Reaction to stress
- Importance of establishing an environment that generates different interpretations of collected data. Encourage a dissenting viewpoint.

More questions:

Will you train the way you intend to fight?

Who will train your watch teams?

How will you match up responsibility and accountability?

What do you believe are some significant leadership challenges?

We already discussed realistic training in the safety lesson. Let's take a closer look.

Realistic training implies risk-taking. Perhaps the answer as to why to take risk in peacetime is contained in this quote.

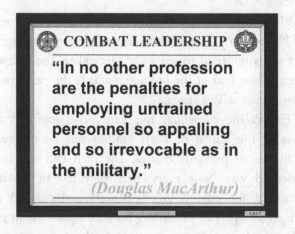

COMBAT LEADERSHIP

"In no other profession are the penalties for employing untrained personnel so appalling and so irrevocable as in the military."

(Douglas MacArthur)

So we do have to train the way we fight.

Why do I keep saying this? Because that is what all the studies and personal interviews with combat veterans stated.

Given today's environment of operations other than war, you will not have time to train specifically for every mission. You may only have time to react, and sailors react the way they have been previously trained.

Now let's look at the importance of discipline.

FEAR OF THE UNKNOWN AFFECTS THE PERFORMANCE OF UNSEASONED SAILORS

"Halsey believed firmly in the old leadership rule, tell your man what to do but not how to do it; if you have to tell him how to do it, you have picked the wrong man for the job." Page 7.

With Halsey embarked, the USS Enterprise returned to Pearl Harbor on 8 December to re-provision. The carrier and escort ships returned to sea on 9 December. The following illustrates how fear of the unknown affects the performance of unseasoned sailors at sea.

"The Pacific to which the Enterprise returned after witnessing the horror of Pearl Harbor was no longer the friendly sea of previous cruises. The men had not before experienced war. Now everywhere they felt the invisible presence of the enemy. Green officers and enlisted men imagined snoopers or oncoming bomber squadrons in every low-hanging cloud, submarines beneath every wave. The nerves of the aviators were frayed by the sight in wardroom and ready rooms of the empty seats of their comrades lost over Oahu. All hands were startled out of their sleep by the nightmare screams of new men on board, survivors of the sunken and burned ships at Pearl Harbor, who had been redistributed among the undamaged vessels.

Admiral Halsey, sensing that his aviators were jittery, came to the Big E's wardroom before lunch on the 10th and bucked them up with a short talk. The words are not recorded, but the effect is summarized by an entry in the Fighting 6 diary:

'Those Japs had better look out for that man.'

Meanwhile the raw nerves of the task force produced a spate of spurious contact reports. Sonar operators identified whales as submarines, a deck swab lost overboard and floating vertically was likely to be reported as a periscope, a playful porpoise heading at night for the bow of ship while streaming phosphorescent bubbles might be mistaken for a torpedo. False identifications sent the ten thousand men of the task force hurrying night and day to battle stations, caused the destroyers to expend dozens of depth charges, and sent the other ships maneuvering at high speed, which wasted hundreds of barrels of fuel oil. Once, when the destroyer Benham was running down a supposed contact, a young officer on the Big E's bridge suddenly shouted, 'Look! She's sinking! There she goes!'

Halsey quickly put his glasses on the Benham. She was hull down in a trough but rose up on the crest of the next swell. The admiral turned wrathfully upon the young man. 'If you ever make another report like that,' he shouted, 'I'll have you thrown over the side!'

When the lookouts continued to report non-existent submarines, Halsey, his patience exhausted, signaled the task force: 'If all the torpedo wakes reported are factual, Japanese submarines will soon have to return to base for a reload, and we will have nothing to fear. In addition, we are wasting too many depth charges on neutral fish. Take action accordingly."

Pages 15-16. Potter, E. B., Bull Halsey, Naval Institute Press, Annapolis, Maryland, 1985.

Let's now put together these elements, class discussions and study conclusions and operationally define leadership in combat or crisis as a class.

We have discussed the difference between decisions in combat/crisis and routine operations; in short, the additive effect of stress + fear + fatigue + less time for decisions + decisions based on less than perfect information combined with the knowledge that when you make them, you understand full well that these decisions can have significant consequences for your command and your sailors.

So can you prepare yourself and your command to deal with this situation and these elements we have introduced?

What will *not* work is talking about being a hero prior to combat, and unrealistic training.

Marc told a humorous true story about the difference in what you think you will do and what you actually do once in a combat or crisis situation. Many in the various classes had similar experiences, but they learned from them.

What *does* work, studies say, is stress training. But they also say that no peacetime training can adequately prepare for or predict success.

The Lt. Col. Hamburger study recounts that 200 foreign and domestic combat leaders maintain that no amount of stressful non-combat assessment can predict battlefield performance. *But it greatly helps!*

So what has gotten many combat leaders through these episodes of stress, fear and tough times?

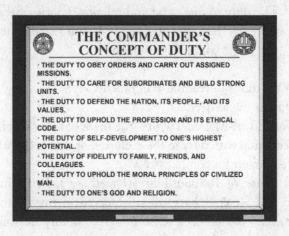

THE COMMANDER'S CONCEPT OF DUTY

· THE DUTY TO OBEY ORDERS AND CARRY OUT ASSIGNED MISSIONS.

· THE DUTY TO CARE FOR SUBORDINATES AND BUILD STRONG UNITS.

· THE DUTY TO DEFEND THE NATION, ITS PEOPLE, AND ITS VALUES.

· THE DUTY TO UPHOLD THE PROFESSION AND ITS ETHICAL CODE.

· THE DUTY OF SELF-DEVELOPMENT TO ONE'S HIGHEST POTENTIAL.

· THE DUTY OF FIDELITY TO FAMILY, FRIENDS, AND COLLEAGUES.

· THE DUTY TO UPHOLD THE MORAL PRINCIPLES OF CIVILIZED MAN.

· THE DUTY TO ONE'S GOD AND RELIGION.

Studies and combat leaders say that what can get you through is the Commander's Concept of Duty, as defined by these eight points. Having one is good, having them all is better.

1. The duty to obey orders and carry out assigned missions

2. The duty to care for subordinates and build strong units.

3. The duty to defend the nation, its people, and its values.

4. The duty to uphold the profession and its ethical code.

5. The duty to self-development to one's highest potential

6. The duty of fidelity to family, friends, and colleagues.

7. The duty to uphold the moral principles of civilized man.

8. The duty to one's god and religion. (Ecclesiastes x12 verse 13 "fear god and keep his commandments for this is the whole duty of man."

What did your reading assignments say?

Duty is the answer.

Gen. S.L.A Marshall wrote "the mark of the warrior, this preoccupation with duty to the exclusion of worry. There is no other easement for combat stress"

In Sense of Responsibility (Israeli war), Ernst Junger shared this view: "I have often observed in myself and in others, that and officer's sense of responsibility drowns his personal fears."

The Fact of being in Command, Shai: An Israeli infantry officer in the Six-Day War, Shai thought: "One of the things that solves all officers' problems is simply the fact of being in command. The need to set the example, the very fact that you are responsible for the men and their lives. It relieves you completely of the need to pretend."

The sheer fact of being responsible for the lives of the men and women of your crew or organization indeed does exactly that, *it gives you incredible strength!*

Barbara Tuchman in her book written after many years of researching commanders from the middle Ages through WWII concluded their primary quality was RESOLUTION.

That is "the determination to win through, whether in the worst of circumstances merely to survive, or in a limited situation to complete the mission: but whatever the situation, to prevail."

She praised Gen. Joseph Stilwell's command presence in WW11 as having, "The absolute, unbreakable, unbending determination to fulfill the mission no matter what the obstacles, the antagonists, or frustrations."

Gen. Marshall in his talk to a West Point graduation class said the same thing:

"This sense of duty and responsibility relegates your fears to a position of secondary importance and assists in maintaining situational awareness."

All the studies and research indicate, as we have mentioned, that this heightened sense of duty can lead to the one significant personal trait needed by a leader, as seen by those that are being led, *personal courage.*

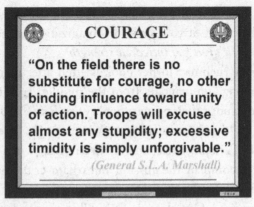

COURAGE

"On the field there is no substitute for courage, no other binding influence toward unity of action. Troops will excuse almost any stupidity; excessive timidity is simply unforgivable."

(General S.L.A. Marshall)

Delivering up honor can readily be put in the category of courage.

How about *your* crew? How will *you* give *them* courage to be prepared for times of stress or combat?

Earlier we discussed who succeeds in these environments. Studies also show who fails as a combat leader:

- The coward, already discussed.

- The one man show, doing everything by himself. Someone who cannot and does not delegate. Discussion?

- The driven man. Going down the wrong path, commits to an end state too early. Discussion?

- The too great, or too many risk takers. The risk factor again and its relationship to building bi-directional trust. The leadership challenge of making decisions and managing risks.

So, by discussing this responsibility to deliver up honor and courage, you can prepare yourself and your people by building a positive command climate.

To illustrate that point, let's do the Cdr. Evans case study Ernest E. Evans, USS Johnston (DD-557) In Harm's Way.

- First to fire, last to fall
- Put ship in peril on purpose
- Look at questions again

Discussion here about Risk (Refer back and look at "Initiative and Instinct").

Vision: he told his crew from the very beginning. "This is a fighting ship I intend to go into Harm's Way"

- He was sailor's sailor
- He reacted instantly
- Showed instinct and initiative:
- Smoke screen to cover Sprague's carrier force
- Did not need orders, knew what he must do and steered into the fleet
- He sank Kumano, a 12,000 ton cruiser
- He had failures but bounced back, a very important concept of leadership

Cdr. Evans lost his shirt, helmet and took lots of shrapnel. He told his corpsmen "don't bother me now, help some guys who are hurt."

When he lost his bridge he shifted to the fantail yelling orders through a hatch.

Discussion:

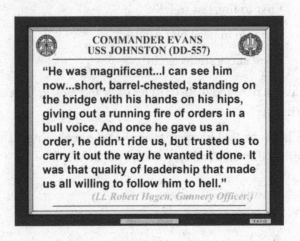

COMMANDER EVANS
USS JOHNSTON (DD-557)

"He was magnificent...I can see him now...short, barrel-chested, standing on the bridge with his hands on his hips, giving out a running fire of orders in a bull voice. And once he gave us an order, he didn't ride us, but trusted us to carry it out the way he wanted it done. It was that quality of leadership that made us all willing to follow him to hell."

(Lt. Robert Hagen, Gunnery Officer.)

I would point to the slide and say "*Not a bad vision to keep in mind*"

Yet again, the spirit of the man and its impact on those who follow. Again, from topic 2.3, the idea of a man of character in peace leads to courage in war. Perhaps deliver up honor is clarified by Cdr. Evans' example.

We all know that it's great when everything goes well. Awards are written up and received. But sometimes the dragon wins. It's easy when things go right, but how do you bounce back when things go wrong? How good are you at re-grouping, or, as in Stockdale's point of showing courage and hanging in there, knowing that the light at the end of the tunnel might never show up?

How many of you have a mental image of Cdr. Evans?

And, please don't raise your hands here, how many of you think you would react like Cdr. Evans?

The Evans story is a good example of mental toughness and of the right leadership combination. A clear connection between vision, philosophy and a plan of action. He created an environment that minimized fear, stress and risk, but maximized loyalty, confidence and commitment. He did it right. *He had a plan.*

He simply had mentally and physically prepared his command and himself to deal with the situation. His is a classic example of the relationship between fear, courage and honor. Studies show the importance of building courage through discipline, delegation, decentralization and empowerment.

What are additional ways to prepare your team? Point out again that what has been rehearsed ahead of time is a significant factor in terms of the performance of every individual, unit and team.

One approach to discussing this is this idea of empowerment.

See the article Empowerment versus Authoritarian:

Recent research in Israel and the U.S. in the Persian Gulf suggests trusting and empowering subordinates, those led, are more likely to lead to success in combat than the traditional authoritarian mode of structuring relationships within a military hierarchy.

Cdr. Evans built on this premise, as did Broderick with the 54th in the movie "Glory." One was reality and the other merely a movie, but the points are the same.

More on Empowerment:

Gen. Powell, CJCS: "Someone once said that men of genius are admired, men of wealth are envied, men of power are feared, but only men of character are trusted. Without trust you cannot lead. I have never seen a good unit where the leaders weren't trusted. It's just that simple.

What they see you do is the key, not what you say. If you want them to work hard and endure hardship, you must work even harder and endure even greater hardship. They must see you sacrifice for them. They must see you do the hard things, they must see you giving credit to the platoon for something good you did, and they must see you take the blame for something they hadn't gotten just right.——Words won't get you through there, either. If you don't feel it in your heart, if you don't love your soldiers in your heart, they will know it. "

We have talked about the qualities of leadership that have been common to every good leader, character, love for soldiers and professional competence. These things can lead to a positive command climate. They can build the will to win.

Cohesion: studies identify this as building a combination of physical and mental commitment.

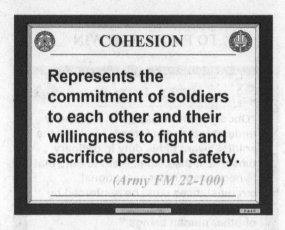

> ### COHESION
>
> **Represents the commitment of soldiers to each other and their willingness to fight and sacrifice personal safety.**
>
> *(Army FM 22-100)*

Cohesive units function smoothly and perform missions well under stress. Battle data in WWII show fatigue rates are much lower in cohesive units.

What does cohesion build?

Possible responses:

- Confidence
- Morale
- Courage
- Will to fight and win

This idea of unity and its importance was discussed in Unit 6.2 "Build for your team a feeling of oneness, of dependence on one another and of strength to be derived of unity." Vince Lombardi

IMPORTANCE OF THE WILL TO FIGHT AND WIN

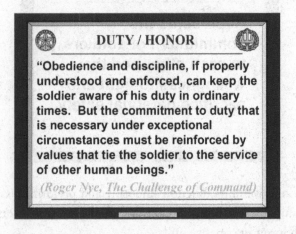

DUTY / HONOR

"Obedience and discipline, if properly understood and enforced, can keep the soldier aware of his duty in ordinary times. But the commitment to duty that is necessary under exceptional circumstances must be reinforced by values that tie the soldier to the service of other human beings."

(Roger Nye, The Challenge of Command)

All studies show this, as Patton said in earlier slide, Spirit of the Men and Leader.

What is the fundamental reason why men fight?

Two main reasons:

1. Belief in cause (sense of purpose, the importance of explaining the "why," as Chamberlain did to the mutineers, and Henry V did just before battle began).

2. Because they do not want to let their comrades down.

"Men who have been in battle know from first-hand experience that when the chips are down, a man fights to help the man next to him, just as a company fights to keep pace with its flanks. Things have to be that simple. An ideal does not become tangible at that moment of firing a volley or charging a hill. When the hard and momentary choice is life or death, the words once heard at an orientation lecture are clean forgot, but the presence of a well-loved comrade is unforgettable. In battle the most valued thing at hand is that which becomes stoutly defended."

Men against Fire, the problem of Battle Command in Future War, S.L.A Marshall.

Without cohesion and leadership comes panic, as cohesion reduces stress and fear.

Freud said that panic arises either owing to an increase of the common danger or owing to the disappearance of the emotional ties which hold the group together, the absence of leadership or cohesion.

Here's an illustration of the impact of the disappearance of leadership and cohesion:

The WWII Normandy invasion: during the Omaha beach assault a unit got separated into two locations. One made it across the sand and reached a berm, a narrow ledge or shelf along a slope. The other was at a shoulder in the road, a ledge between a parapet and a moat in a fortification. Both groups essentially were intact, in terms of few casualties and senior leadership. In one unit, after the troops caught their breath and looked around, no direction came from the officers and NCO's. Over a short period, its members wandered off, intermixed with other units, and stalled there for the rest of the day. The other unit, after catching their breath at the berm, got immediate direction from its leaders to push up the ravine. By the end of the day, that unit had spearheaded one of the deepest penetrations inland from Omaha beach Yet again, the example of stepping over and stepping up.

Wilfred Rotter's Instincts of the Herd in Peace and War: "The peace of mind, happiness, and energy of the soldier come from his feeling himself to be a member in a body solidly united for a single purpose."

Discusses the importance of a sense of purpose.

If you have built cohesion, commitment, loyalty and a sense of purpose in your organization, studies show you will reduce the effects of fear, stress and the uncertainty of war.

So how do you build cohesion? Focus on these four major concerns:

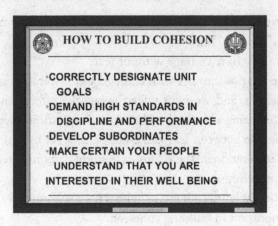

HOW TO BUILD COHESION

- CORRECTLY DESIGNATE UNIT GOALS
- DEMAND HIGH STANDARDS IN DISCIPLINE AND PERFORMANCE
- DEVELOP SUBORDINATES
- MAKE CERTAIN YOUR PEOPLE UNDERSTAND THAT YOU ARE INTERESTED IN THEIR WELL BEING

We have already discussed the importance of each one of these:

- Command Philosophy
- Attitude
- Purpose
- Values

"Cohesion can overcome fear and bring about courage," Richard Holmes, Acts of War, the Behavior of Men in Battle, p.300.

"Comradeship was stronger than the fear of death, numberless soldiers have died, more or less willingly, not for country or honor or religious faith or for any other abstract good, but because they realize that by fleeing their posts and rescuing themselves, they would expose their companions to greater danger. Such loyalty to group is the essence of the fighting morale." Ibid.

Can you have courage without fear?

The relationship between courage and inspiration is well documented, and we have talked about the effects on your people of being a coward or being an inspiration. Stepping over the line between fear and courage, that act by you alone can be inspirational. The Evans case study demonstrates that effect on a command.

Your display of courage, or at least no display of cowardice, is so important in building cohesion.

Can you show fear or must hide it from your mess or wardroom?

Studies say yes, just don't let it get in the way of your leadership duties. Followers must have confidence in their leaders. Conversely, loss of trust in a leader devastates morale, reduces performance on the battlefield and further increases stress.

Per Arleigh Burke, "sailors watch their leaders closely for signs of panic or loss of confidence. You must look and sound as calm as possible."

The relationship between courage and fear is also conveyed by this quote from Lord Moran's The Anatomy of Courage:

"There seems to be four degrees of courage and four orders of men measured by that standard. Men who did not feel fear; men who felt fear but did not show it; men who felt fear, showed it but did their job; men who felt fear, showed it and shirked...the story of modern war is concerned with the striving of men, eroded by fear, to maintain a precarious footing on the upper rungs of that ladder."

You are trying to provide your people with the leadership and climate that get them to the upper rungs. It is in the end an internal choice, a mindset decision. You must prepare them for that decision and provide them the intangibles that will help them chose correctly.

More from R. Holmes Acts of War "Cohesion follows as a matter of course, and this is the root of it. Men are inclined to do what their comrades expect them to do, or, more accurately, because nobody actually wants to fight, they do what they imagine their comrades expect them to do. In the good unit, trust and cohesion both grow from and create a good unit. The assumption is, of course, that actions will be governed by those never-mentioned concepts, duty and honor."

How to build courage leading to honor?

There are many different levels of courage. I know I tend to think that you either step over the line or you don't. That may be true for us, but it's not so clear-cut for your people.

The theory about courage seems to be that it is achieved by the constant struggle against fear. Just like the concept of virtuous habit, doing the right thing continuously, makes it easier not to compromise your integrity. Some of these struggles against fear can be difficult and gut-wrenching.

My favorite quote that illustrates the difficulty of the majority of those you will lead, the other 82 %, not those strong players you have identified, but good people, and how they cope, comes again from Holmes's Acts of War....

"The middle man, the man who wants to try but has already died more than once, squirming under bullets, going through the act of death and coming out embarrassingly alive. The bullets stop. As if in slow motion, physical things gleam. Noise dissolves. You tentatively peek up, wondering if it is the end. Then you look at the other men, reading your own caved-in belly deep in their eyes. The fright dies in the same way Novocain wears off in the dentist's chair. You promise, almost moving your lips, to do better next time; that by itself is a kind of courage."

As Lord Moran said, "striving to maintain a precarious footing on the upper rungs of that ladder."

Gen. C.C. Krulak, USMC states: "courage is not the absence of fear, but is our personal assessment that something else is more important than the fear which confronts us." Let's name a few of those things the studies indicated are in the category of "something else":

- Duty
- Patriotism
- Honor
- The responsibility to each other

- The fact of being in command
- The importance of the mission
- Inspirational leadership

Again, courage is achieved through the constant struggle against fear. Whatever you use in this struggle to provide yourself courage (again things we have mentioned like duty, honor, sense of purpose, cohesion, loyalty to each other, will to win, commitment, religion, patriotism), whatever you use, you just have to fight through it and you have to help your people fight through it. *You* have to provide them the "something else."

Prepare the best you can, because one thing we know for sure is that coping with fear and coping with stress are different challenges. My research revealed two strong methods that deal with reducing stress and fear:

Direction: eliminate threat-causing stress; correlate information to decrease uncertainty over data; revise plans to reduce risk to command; adjust defensive posture or position to reduce vulnerability; retreat.

Palliation: reduction of intensity; inform subordinates of decisions when practicable, involve subordinates in a critical decision when appropriate and practicable; apprise subordinates of risks where appropriate.

I recounted the points of the SA in the gun magazine:

- Just waiting during GQ, sometimes training but not really knowing what is happening, or what might happen and why.

- For knowledge to be useful it must be shared.

- Important to keep your people connected to the big picture.

Take a good look too at the medical information sheet at appendix D. Used by the Army in the treatment of combat stress, it highlights the common signs:

Trembling
Sweating
Nausea
Frequent urination
Frequent diarrhea
Pounding heart.
Stomach pains
Anxiety
Agitation

These are *common* signs and no special treatment is necessary. The information sheet also lists the following signs:

Not moving
Blank expression

Seems without emotion

Apathy

Moodiness

Unable to concentrate on the job

Decreased appetite

Overactive

Emotional outburst

Loss of self-control

Argumentative

Aggressive

Unable to sleep

The sheet then walks through the required treatment. The point is that military units have been dealing with this critical issue for a long time, but I don't ever remember talking about it until attending CLS.

From my research: six basic ways typically use to reduce palliation. You have probable seen all of these one time or another:

1. Denial: a "this is not happening" approach.

2. Hard work: "I'm not going to worry about it, I'm just going to keep working."

3. Superstition: "I've got my lucky rabbit's foot right here."

4. Fatalism: the "who wants to live forever" approach.

5. Religion: "his will be done."

6. Humor: "they should run out of ammo soon," or "good thing they are bad shots."

We have seen many or all of these at one time or another. In the end, the decision to be courageous comes from within, and drives to the concept of the next slide:

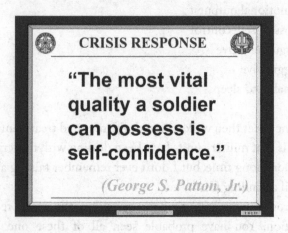

From Lord Moran, Anatomy of Courage, "he was not sure of his job, so he was uncertain of his temper."

Why does the leader who is a screamer scream? Studies show that can work for the officer in command also. You have got to figure out how to get over the effect of fear, and cross the line.

But how do you build this confidence for yourself and for your people?

Here is T.E Lawrence's take, in <u>The Science of Guerrilla Warfare:</u>

"Nine-tenths of tactics are certain, and taught in books; but the irrational tenth is like the kingfisher flashing across the pool, and that is the test for generals. It can only be ensured by instinct, sharpened by thought, practicing the stroke so often that at the crisis it is as natural as a reflex."

One way to reduce fear and stress is to lead with initiative and instinct. Let's discuss this concept and view a quick video to illustrate it. *(I would take a break at this point, four hours into the lesson)*

Introduce the Chamberlain video.

While watching this video, think about the sequence:

1. Did the leader:

    *   Understand the mission?

    *   Communicate it effectively?

    *   Accomplish the mission?

2. How did the leader inspire his men to willingly face the stress and danger of battle?

3. What leadership principles discussed in the course were applied by the leader?

Show Chamberlain Video from the movie Gettysburg.
Post-video discussion questions:

I cannot do the movie justice by writing the scene in this book. It is readily available in numerous venues. It is the battle scene where they are about out of ammunition. Chamberlain understands the situation and as he sees the panic in his men and their eyes turn to him, he creates the now famous "swinging gate tactic." I have provided a picture of that thought.

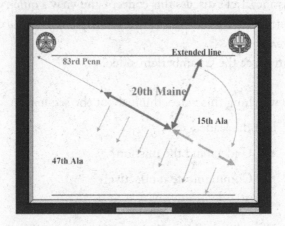

"The fight at Little Round Top took place on 2 July 1863 between the 20th Maine and two Alabama regiments, the 15th and the 47th. It provides a case study of leadership and unit cohesion in battle in one of the most significant small-unit actions in the Civil War.

Chamberlain said that at times there were more of the enemy around him then his own troops. Squads of attacking Confederate soldiers bayoneted their way through the defenses, but somehow his Maine men threw them back. A lull in the battle came after the sixth violent charge. Chamberlain knew he was outnumbered. He ordered his soldiers to fix bayonets and charge, not for heroics, but because it was the best chance for success. He reasoned his unit would have the advantage of attacking downhill.

On the way down the hill, at point blank range, a confederate officer fired his pistol at Chamberlain, but missed. With Chamberlain's sword at his throat, he surrendered.

It was said the General Lee was never so close to victory as on that day on Little Round Top. They had captured about 400 prisoners from four different regiments. The 20th Maine started the battle with 358 riflemen; they suffered 90 casualties. Forty were killed or died of wounds. Moreover, they were led by a colonel who was a seminary graduate and had been a professor of languages less than a year before the battle."

John J. Pullen, The Twentieth Maine

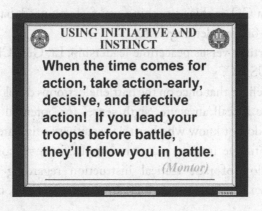

USING INITIATIVE AND INSTINCT

When the time comes for action, take action-early, decisive, and effective action! If you lead your troops before battle, they'll follow you in battle.

(Mentor)

Further insights:

Liddell Hart, <u>Thoughts of War,</u> used to describe both Chamberlain and Cdr. Evans:

"Creative intelligence is and always has been the supreme requirement of the commander…coupled with moral character… the best hope of tilting the scales and overcoming the resistance inherent in conflict lies in originality–to provide something unexpected that will paralyze the opponent of action."

Throughout combat historical readings are numerous examples of this idea of a sixth sense of a combat leader. Examples are—Facilitate a discussion on the concepts of <u>Sixth Sense of the Combat Leader</u>

What is a sixth sense? Knowing something is not right, a feel for the right thing to do at the right time.

Some relate this intuitive combat ability as significantly important and others discount it.

As a CO, is this something you feel you need, have, will develop or consider hogwash?

Wartime versus peacetime leadership, Lt. Gen. Clyde D. Dean, USMC:

"I believe that once on the battlefield, troops develop what I choose to call an acute "sixth sense" for potential danger areas. I do not know whether this sensitivity originates from some intuitive instinct or, more simply, from subconscious application of past tactical instruction regarding terrain and other combat expectations. In any event, I'm convinced it's there. I tend to think this results more from sensing 'something's not right' rather than 'something's wrong'; perhaps from activity or sounds in a given area not being as they usually are, or should be. Whatever the reasons, and thankfully so, our physical senses seem to communicate to us much more readily when enemy contact is imminent.

The luxury of time is not there in combat; as a result I feel that leaders in combat make decisions much more comfortably based on intuition and immediate assessment."

I believe he knows what he is talking about. He gets to the importance of being able to make time-critical decisions, the need and ability to act.

Studies are inconclusive but most couple intuition and coup d'oeil as key combat characteristics. These concepts are in many military organizations, often known by different names, but basically describing the same concept of a sixth sense.

- Coup d'oeil–French–stroke of eye–ability to intuitively assess the battlefield situation and know what needs to be done (according to Napoleon, but note an earlier quote that said it wasn't genius just hard work).

- Ishin Denshin–ability claimed by WWII Japanese fighter pilots to communicate, or at least know what the other would do during violent combat maneuvering.

- Intuition–Direct perception of truth, fact, etc. independent of any reasoning process.

- Fingerspitzengefuehl—that finger-tip feeling or instinctive sense of matching terrain with doctrine and weaponry.

Soviet Armed Forces Manual:

"Intuition is close to quickness of thought and it is nothing more than an unique mental activity reduced to the limit in time. Intuition is possible only as a result of profound knowledge and enormous personal experience."

Some Commanders given credit for these attributes:

- Alexander The Great
- Hannibal
- Frederick The Great
- Napoleon Bonaparte
- The Duke of Wellington
- General Ulysses S, Grant
- Winston Churchill
- Field Marshall Rommel
- General Douglas Macarthur
- CDR. Evans—in Harm's Way

How can it be built?

Build it through constant exposure to doctrine, derivative, simulations, war games, and exercises. Intuition can be cultivated.

Sometimes the toughest part of leadership in this decision-making and managing risks is knowing when you must ACT, when you can no longer wait for a better solution.

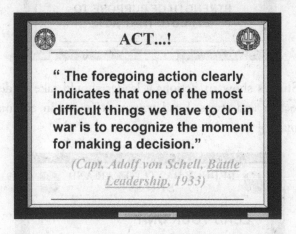

ACT...!

" **The foregoing action clearly indicates that one of the most difficult things we have to do in war is to recognize the moment for making a decision.**"

(Capt. Adolf von Schell, Battle Leadership, 1933)

Act, again the significant role time plays in decision-making. You must do something or fear mounts to panic. The eyes turn, and we know now how long they will wait.

This next slide is a good one that combines those points of creative intelligence/initiative and instinct/sixth sense and this requirement to ACT!

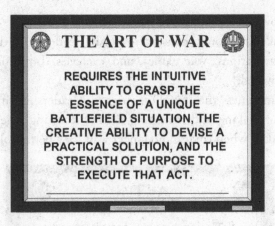

THE ART OF WAR

REQUIRES THE INTUITIVE
ABILITY TO GRASP THE
ESSENCE OF A UNIQUE
BATTLEFIELD SITUATION, THE
CREATIVE ABILITY TO DEVISE A
PRACTICAL SOLUTION, AND THE
STRENGTH OF PURPOSE TO
EXECUTE THAT ACT.

Studies show six actions a leader should take to defeat battle fear and stress. Lead your unit (when in command, command)!

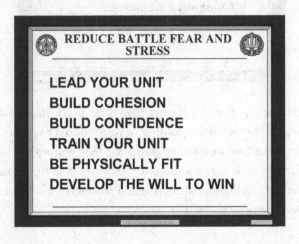

REDUCE BATTLE FEAR AND STRESS

LEAD YOUR UNIT
BUILD COHESION
BUILD CONFIDENCE
TRAIN YOUR UNIT
BE PHYSICALLY FIT
DEVELOP THE WILL TO WIN

The toughest challenge is knowing when to act, how to build confidence and reduce stress and fear, as well as the idea of building a will to win.

"The essential thing is action. Action has three stages: the decision born of thought, the order or preparation for execution, and the execution itself. All three stages are governed by the will. The will is rooted in character, and for the man of action character is of more critical importance than intellect. Intellect without will is worthless, will without intellect is dangerous."

Hans von Seekt, <u>Thoughts of Soldier</u>, trans. G, Waterhouse (London: Ernest Benn Ltd., 1930) p. 123

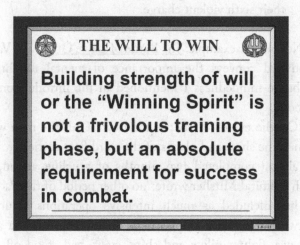

THE WILL TO WIN

Building strength of will or the "Winning Spirit" is not a frivolous training phase, but an absolute requirement for success in combat.

This slide gets to the heart of the last of four main elements that affect performance during combat or crisis. Time, fear, stress and now the last one, fatigue.

Let's recap some examples already seen in this course:

- The last attack of the 54th in "Glory." They had been marching non-stop for several days. While they did not take the fort, their courage was unmatched.

- The attack made by King Henry's men stood at 5-to-1 odds against winning the day.

- Chamberlain's men at Little Round Top withstanding their sixth violent charge.

Now a navy example: The Battle of Leyte Gulf by C. Vann Woodward conveys the importance of mental toughness and battle-mindedness I mentioned in the introduction to this book.

"On the eve of the battle for Leyte Gulf the men who manned the ships and planes of the third fleet carrier groups had almost completed two months of grueling action, of which Admiral Mitsher wrote: 'no other period of the Pacific war has included as much intensive operations.' During the two previous weeks of strikes on Luzon, Formosa and Okinawa, fighter pilots and ships' crews had stood off the heaviest series of air attacks the enemy had launched against our naval forces up to that time. These strikes came at the end of a period of ten months of operations in the tropics throughout which men had been living between steel decks and bulkheads, under constant pressure, and in large part under actual combat conditions. Shore leave, except for a few hours on some barren atoll, was very rare. 'Probably 10,000 men have never put a foot on shore during this period of ten months,' reported Mitsher. 'No other force in the world has been subjected to such a period of constant operation without rest or rehabilitation." p.43.

Gen. George C. Marshall underscored in his talk to the first graduating class of officers at Fort Benning, Georgia, in September 1941 "When you are commanding, leading men under conditions where physical exhaustion and privations must be ignored, where the lives of men may be sacrificed, then, the efficiency of your leadership will depend only to a minor degree on your tactical ability. It will primarily be determined by your character, your reputation, not much for courage—which will be accepted as a matter of course—but by the previous reputation you have established for fairness, for that high-minded patriotic purpose, that quality of unswerving determination to carry through any military task assigned to you."

In short, you need to have a plan that will provide your command this "winning spirit" and the determination to prevail. You can build it in yourself by your guts and determination. You build it in your command through your inspirational leadership.

Discussion then followed on the mental toughness required in order to have this will to win. We talked about the concept of the ability to go to the well, to dig deep and follow through, to be able bounce back from adversity, to just gut it out because it's too important not to.

Mental and physical toughness are not accomplished by accident. Doing what must be done until it is over, and how best to prepare ourselves and our people for that, are what we have been talking about today and for the last two weeks.

Success in combat is described as an end state of all the positive building terms we have talked about, courage, self-discipline, self-confidence, cohesion and so on.

<u>Lesson summary.</u>

Determination and the <u>will to win!</u>

Admiral Mahan describing Farragut, from <u>Command of the Sea, 4th edition, Combat Ops)</u>.

"It is in the strength of purpose, in the power of rapid decision, of instant action, and if need be, of strenuous endurance through a period of danger or of responsibility, when the terrifying alternatives of war are vibrating in the balance, that the power of a great captain mainly lies. It is in the courage to apply knowledge under conditions of exceptional danger; not merely to see the true direction for effort to take, but to dare to follow it, accepting all the risks and all the chances inseparable from war, facing all that defeat means in order to secure victory if it may be had. It was upon those inborn moral qualities that reposed the conduct which led Farragut to fame. He had a clear eye for the true key of a military situation, a quick and accurate perception of the right thing to do at a critical moment, a firm grasp upon the leading principles of war; but he might have had all these and yet miserably failed. He was a man of most determined will and character, ready to tread down or fight through any obstacles which stood in the path he sought to follow."

History talks about the responsibility of the combat leader to develop in himself and his people, the "warrior's soul."

New slide: (Spartans, Italian condollier, French Foreign Legion. Gurkha troops, Roman legions, Cdr. Evans, all built this).

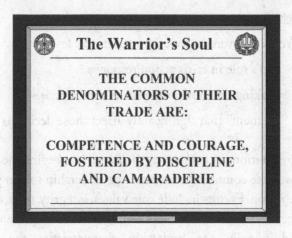

The Warrior's Soul

THE COMMON DENOMINATORS OF THEIR TRADE ARE:

COMPETENCE AND COURAGE, FOSTERED BY DISCIPLINE AND CAMARADERIE

Essence of Leadership, Preparing Command. Gen. S.L.A. Marshall and all my research sums up the essence of leadership.

ESSENCE OF LEADERSHIP

In these things lie a great part of the essence of leadership, for they are the constituents of that kind of moral courage that has enabled one man to draw many others to him in any age.

·Quiet Resolution

·The Hardihood to Take Risks

·The Will To Take Full Responsibility for Decisions

·The Readiness to Share Rewards With Subordinates

·An Equal Readiness to Take the Blame When Things Go Adversely

·The Nerve to Survive the Storm and Disappointment and to Face Toward Each New Day With the Scoresheet Wiped Clean, Neither Dwelling on One's Successes Nor Accepting Discouragement From One's Failures

Discussion:

We have covered a lot of ground in this lesson.

- CO's role in crisis action response
- Making decisions with risk in combat/crisis
- Elements that significantly affect those decisions

Preparation for combat, or the first crisis, begins the first day you take command or assume the leadership role in your organization. Factors include core values, integrity, trust, confidence, courage, command philosophy, command presence.

Additionally, the leadership characteristics the CO brings to the table, such as intelligence, judgment, initiative, force, cooperation, loyalty, communications, perseverance, endurance, maturity, enthusiasm, military bearing and sense of humor.

Your success in command will be based on your own warrior's soul and your personal effort and determination.

We have all talked about all the variables, elements and these attributes in both good leaders and good commands. The difficulty is not in our ability to recognize and understand their importance, but in the understanding of the kind of leadership skills, effort, energy, and example that is required to achieve them. *In essence, it is a matter of commitment, honor, courage and inspiration.*

As I started with this quote in my preface, let me begin to finish this, our final session, with it, hopefully having provided a better and deeper operational understanding of the true value of inspirational leadership.

THE COMMANDER AS A WARRIOR: success in war lurks invisible in that vitalizing spark, intangible, yet as evident as lightning—the warrior's soul....it is the cold glitter of the attacker's eyes, not the point of the questing bayonet, that breaks the line. It is the fierce determination of the driver to close with the enemy, not the mechanical perfection of the tank that conquers the trench. It is the cataclysmic ecstasy of conflict in the flier, not the perfection of the machine gun, which drops the enemy in flames. Yet volumes are devoted to arms; only pages to inspiration.

Gen. G.S. Patton, <u>Success in War, Infantry Journal, January, 1931, p.23</u>

To paraphrase Patton, I hope you will be both a good leader and an inspiration to your people and live up to your responsibilities under the law.

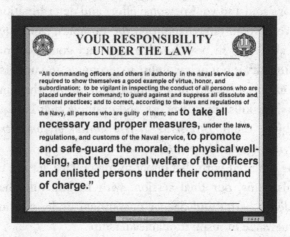

YOUR RESPONSIBILITY UNDER THE LAW

"All commanding officers and others in authority in the naval service are required to show themselves a good example of virtue, honor, and subordination; to be vigilant in inspecting the conduct of all persons who are placed under their command; to guard against and suppress all dissolute and immoral practices; and to correct, according to the laws and regulations of the Navy, all persons who are guilty of them; and to take all necessary and proper measures, under the laws, regulations, and customs of the Naval service, to promote and safe-guard the morale, the physical well-being, and the general welfare of the officers and enlisted persons under their command of charge."

Thanks for your participation and attention throughout.

As I said early in the book, we always opened and closed the school with Arleigh Burke. This quote was on the occasion of his retirement as Chief of Naval Operations.

CHIEF OF NAVAL OPERATIONS 10 JULY 1961
THE OFFICERS AND MEN OF THE UNITED
STATES NAVY

There comes a time in every man's life when he must attempt to evaluate what he has done to better his country, his service, his family and his group. This review can very well comprise the legacy a man bequeaths to his successors.

I have now—with more than a twinge of reluctance—reached this stage, and in retrospect I find it impossible to single out any one item which I can truthfully say was exclusively and inalienable mine. This is a truism which most men recognize eventually because they learn that major accomplishments can be achieved only with the cooperation of friends and shipmates.

In the forty-two years of naval service I have had a unique opportunity to serve my country which I deeply appreciate. I have also been blessed by the loyalty, support and friendship of the most dedicated people I have ever known, not least of whom is my devoted wife. Experience has brought me a full appreciation of the prize cargo a man can hoist aboard.

To this beloved Navy I do commend:

Love of country, overshadowing all other loves, including service, family and the sea.

Individual desire to excel, not for aggrandizement of self, but to increase the excellence of the Navy.

Devotion—perhaps consecration—to personal integrity in oneself, in one's service, in one's country.

Courage to stand for principle, regardless of efforts to dilute this courage through comprise or evasion.

My service life has been rich and rewarding, and no man can ask for more.

May you, too, find satisfaction and throughout your careers experience fair winds and following seas.

ARLEIGH BURKE

Being a part of creating the old Command Leadership School from scratch, being involved in the writing and facilitating of the earlier school were together by far my greatest accomplishment and contribution to my Navy. I hope this book has provided an opportunity to prepare you yourself for that truest test of character, to cross the line between fear and courage, and to deliver up what is most required in those most challenging of times, honor.

TOPIC 8-1
LEADERSHIP IN COMBAT/ CRISIS SITUATIONS

A. INTRODUCTION:

Topic 8-1 discusses the leadership perspective in the combat and crisis environment. Preparing for crisis situations and contingency planning are discussed. Factors which affect performance and strategies to deal with them are introduced.

B. TOPIC PREPARATION:

The following required readings and instruction sheets should be read prior to the lesson.

1. <u>Required Readings and references:</u>

   a) Ash, Leonard D. and Martin Hill. *In Harm's Way*, <u>The Retired Officer Magazine</u>, October 1994, 50, No. 10, pages 42-47.

b) Friedman, Norman. *The Vincennes Incident*, Proceedings, Naval Review, 1989, pages 72-79.

c) Holmes, Richard. Acts of War; The Behavior of Men in Battle. New York NY: The Free Press, 1986, pages 223-244.

d) Mack, Vice Admiral William P. and Commander Albert H. Konetzni. Command at Sea, Annapolis, MD: Naval Institute Press, 1982, appendix VII, pages 474-475.

e) Marshall, S.L.A. *Leaders and Leadership*, Military Leadership in Pursuit of Excellence, chapter 4, pages 37-48.

f) Montor, Karel, et al. Naval Leadership: Voices of Experience. Annapolis, MD: Naval Institute Press, 1987, pages 78 through 82.

g) Rosenbach, William E. and Robert L. Taylor, editors. Contemporary Issues in Leadership. Boulder, CO: Westview Press, chapter 4.

h) Slim, Field Marshal Sir William. Higher Command in War.

i) Tritten, Dr. James J. *Navy Combat Leadership and Doctrine*, essay, 1994, page 6.

j) U.S. Navy Regulations, page 60, article 0851.

2. Instruction Sheets:

Information Sheet 8-1-1

C. SUPPLEMENTAL READINGS and references: These readings are provided as additional information. Although not required, you are encouraged to review these readings to broaden your perspective of the lesson.

1. Armed Forces Staff College. Pub-1.

2. Armed Forces Staff College. <u>The Joint Staff Officer's Guide 1993</u>. Norfolk, VA: Armed Forces Staff College, 1993, chapter 7.

3. Evans, David C. and Mark R. Peattie. <u>Kaigun: Doctrine and Technology in the Imperial Japanese Navy, 1887-1941</u>. Draft book manuscript, chapter 11.

4. Hersey, Paul. *Situational Leadership, A Summary*, <u>Leadership Studies Inc.</u>, pages 1-3.

5. Hoyt, Edwin P. <u>Blue Skies and Blood, The Battle of the Coral Sea</u>. New York: Paul S. Eriksson, Inc., 1975.

6. Hoyt, Edwin P. <u>Men of the Gambier Bay</u>. Middlebury, VT: Paul S. Eriksson, Inc., 1979.

7. Mitroff, Ian I. <u>Crisis Management; A Diagnostic Guide for Improving Your Organization's Crisis</u>

Preparedness. San Francisco, CA: Jossey Buss Inc., 1993.

8. Hassen, John E. and Carol F. Denton, Naval Training Systems Center, Fred Reis CAPT USNR, John R. Ronchetto, CDR USNR, Navy Military Personnel Command (PERS-62). Technical Report 92-005, Effective Navy Combat Leadership: Lessons Learned From Desert Storm, (unpublished) Jan 1992.

9. Headquarters, Department of the Army. Military Leadership, Field Manual No. 22-100. July 1990, pages 69-70.

10. Headquarters, Department of the Army. Operations Field Manual No. 100-5. June 1993, pages 2-10, 2-12.

11. Naval Doctrine Publication 1, Naval Warfare. 1994, pages 50-51.

12. NAVSAFECEN Risk Management Lesson Guide, pages 1-13 and 1-14.

13. The Random House Dictionary of the English Language. New York: Random House, 1966 page 747.

14. Webster's Ninth New Collegiate Dictionary. Springfield, MA: Merriam-Webster Inc., 1991, page 407.

15. Woodward, Vann C. <u>The Battle for Leyte Gulf</u>, New York, NY: McGraw-Hill Book Co., 1947, page 175.

Outline Sheet 8-1

1. Information Sheet 8-1-1

2. Combat/crisis versus routine/non-combat
   a. The military leadership challenge
   b. Four factors
   a) Led
   b) Leader
   c) Situation
   d) Communications
   c. Foundation of leadership
   d. Responsibilities of the leader in combat/crisis
   e. Time factor
   f. CO's role change

3. Preparation for combat/crisis
   a. Training
   b. Organization/planning
   c. Factors affecting performance during combat/crisis
   a) Stress: A physical, chemical, or emotional factor that causes bodily or mental tension that tends to alter an existing equilibrium.
   b) Fear: An unpleasant, often strong, emotion caused by anticipation or awareness of danger, anxious concern.

1) Fatigue
2) Time

    d. Can you prepare yourself for combat/crisis?

    e. How can you prepare your command members?

4. Combat/crisis response

    a. Two methods to reduce stress

1) Direction: Eliminating threat-causing stress, correlating information to decrease uncertainty over data, revising plans to reduce risk to command, adjusting defensive posture or position to reduce vulnerability, retreating.

2) Palliation: Inform subordinates of decisions when practicable, involve subordinates in a critical decision when appropriate and practicable, apprise subordinates of risks where appropriate.

    b. Six actions to defeat battle stress

1) Lead your unit.

2) Build cohesion.

3) Develop confidence.

4) Train your unit.

5) Be physically fit.

6) Develop will to win.

    c. Video 8-1-1.

1) Discussion points.

    d. Role of initiative and instinct

1) Coup d'oeil: Ability to intuitively assess the battlefield situation and know what needs to be done (according to Napoleon).

2) *Inshin denshin*: Ability claimed by WWII Japanese fighter pilots to communicate, or at least know what the other would do during violent combat maneuvering.

3) Intuition: Direct perception of truth, fact, etc., independent of any reasoning process.

    e. Commander Evans's discussion

    f. Will to win

5. Summary

    a. Questions in review

1) Can combat/crisis leaders be developed in peacetime?

2) What are some common personality traits to combat effective naval leaders?

3) Is there a difference between combat leadership and non-combat leadership?

4) Is leadership an integral element of combat power?

5) What is the role of vision, empowerment, and communication in a combat/stress environment?

6) Risk-taking and realistic training in peacetime—a dilemma or a necessity?

APPENDICES

Appendix A:

1. Initial Thoughts on Command Policy and Standards: USS *Callaghan* (DDG-994)

2. USS *Callaghan* (DDG-994) Standing Goals

3. USS *Hewitt* (DD-996) Command Philosophy and Standards

Appendix B: General Douglas MacArthur's Farewell Speech (May 12, 1962)

Appendix C: Vision Statement

Appendix D: Combat Stress and Treatment

Appendix E: List of Additional References

APPENDICES

APPENDIX A

Initial Thoughts on Command Policy and Standards: USS CALLAGHAN DDG-994

Commanding Officer, USS CALLAGHAN (DDG 994)
28 Jan 1992 All Hands
INITIAL THOUGHTS ON COMMAND
POLICY & STANDARDS

1. Purpose. The purpose of this letter is to provide all hands in CALLAGHAN some of my thoughts on command policy and standards while I am in command of CALLAGHAN. I plan to update this letter from time to time while I am aboard to ensure that everyone understands clearly my expectations for CALLAGHAN and for each of you personally in the wardroom and crew.

2. Command Goals and Priorities. To augment these thoughts on command policy and standards, I will also provide on at least a quarterly basis, written state-

ment of my command goals and priorities—to assist all hands in planning and focusing their efforts in the months ahead. Our focus this quarter is clear: "The true worth of any warship is her ability to give and take hard knocks." We will be ready to enter the Gulf!

3. CALLAGHAN is a Warship. Above all else, CAL-LAGHAN is a warship. CALLAGHAN exists to support the interest of the United States and our Navy. We, the crew, make CALLAGHAN what she is. Our primary task is to maintain CALLAGHAN ready in all respects to go to war—not only the Equipment, but also in every facet of training.

4. The Standard is Excellence. The standard for CAL-LAGHAN is excellence. This means striving to do everything we do the right way, the first time. Quality control is a function of every level of the chain of command. Remember, that it takes less time to do something right the first time than it does to do it twice. If something is worth doing, it is worth doing right. In meeting these standards I expect an atmosphere of open honesty. I will accept honest mistakes from a man trying to do well. (However, let us strive to learn from the mistakes of others—it is not necessary to do all our learning by making mistakes!) Every man doing his best has my complete backing and respect.

5. Know your Men. High standards begin with knowing your men. I expect every leader to know the men under his charge—every-thing from his hometown and details about his family, to his progress in watch qualifications and toward advancement.

6. Know your Equipment. Every man must know his own equipment cold! This includes its proper operation, all its safety features, and how it relates to the other systems in the ship. Use the Technical Manuals. Know the standards to which the Equipment must be maintained and its proper operational parameters. Maintain the equipment so that the standards and parameters are met. Sincerity is not enough—deeds, not just good intentions, are what matters. Know things!

7. My basic philosophy. "Every job is important. Every system is a combat" system. There is no such thing as an unimportant job on CALLAGHAN. The ability of CALLAGHAN to perform as a fighting warship depends totally on the combined performance of each member of the crew. In this sense, every system in CALLAGHAN is a combat system. For example, without the engineering plant, CALLAGHAN is useless as a warship. Without a healthy and properly fed crew, CALLAGHAN would quickly become a less effective warship. The points here are: every man

aboard is an important factor in CALLAGHAN's readiness and sustainability in combat and every system and function aboard CALLAGHAN can directly affect the ability of CALLAGHAN to fight and win.

8. What's the CO's Job? My duties and responsibilities are clearly defined in Navy Regulations. As described therein, I am utterly accountable, for the condition and performance of CALLAGHAN in all its aspects. However, I feel strongly that Navy Regulations are only part of the story. I consider that a key aspect of the duties of a Commanding Officer is to see that every man in CALLAGHAN has what he needs to perform his duties properly—including training, materials and time. Another key duty of the Commanding Officer is to be the ship's long-range planner—looking downstream at the ship's schedule, reducing uncertainty in everyone's planning and eliminating to the maximum extent possible the need for "crisis management."

9. You make your own Luck. While being lucky is handy, I believe strongly that you make your luck, through careful planning and lot of hard work. The harder you work the luckier you get! We've all heard the motto "prior planning prevents poor performance."

10. Safety is Key. Safety is an absolutely vital consideration in every evolution—including routine ones—in a Navy Warship. Safety precautions are written in the

blood of sailors who failed to heed them. I expect each of you to be intimately familiar with the safety precautions and features associated with the equipment you operate and to ensure that they operate properly. I am the only man onboard who can authorize the bypassing of any safety feature or procedure.

11. On PMS. The Planned Maintenance System has my complete support. The goal is to accomplish all required PMS actions each quarter. The PMS should be continuously validated against the equipment onboard. If the PMS coverage in your work center does not match your equipment or the PMS action seems to be incorrect, submit a feedback and get it fixed. Do Not Gundeck PMS! You will not fool the equipment. Do it right the first time. If you don't have the tools or special material that you need to perform the PMS, let your LPO, Chief, Division Officer and Department Head know—and get what you need to do your maintenance properly.

12. On Procedures. As mentioned earlier, program procedures shall be followed with any operation related to equipment or machinery. Where it exists, always use EOSS, CSOSS, etc. Never "wing it." If you need more time to review a procedure before operating equipment, ask.

13. On PQS. Our Personnel Qualification Standards (PQS) program is only as good as our standards, and the qualifications of our senior qualifiers. All qualifications will be pursued as though they will soon be experienced in combat.

14. On ESWS. Our Enlisted Surface Warfare Specialist (ESWS) program will be the capstone of our shipboard PQS qualification program in CALLAGHAN. It is my policy that every sailor, E-4 and above will pursue ESWS qualification in accordance with the current program. I believe that is important for a number of reasons, including enormously increasing the combat readiness of the ship, adding extensive additional damage control and firefighting expertise crew-wide and generally making every ·man in the crew better able to understand where he fits into the ship's organization as part of a smoothly operating combat team. The emphasis here is on "warfare specialist."

15. On Mutual Respect, Cooperation and Teamwork. There will be no "unions" on CALLAGHAN. There is only one crew and we will all work together to meet our standards of excellence. Every man in CALLAGHAN is on the "first team." Our lives in combat will depend on every man doing the right thing without having to be told—This is the essence of teamwork. The crew of a modern warship is the "ultimate team". Every man

doing his job to the best of his ability no matter what the level of the job within the team deserves the support, cooperation and respect of every other shipmate.

16. On "I" Division. For new men onboard, the quality of our "I" Division Indoctrination is a key element in how quickly they can come aboard as a contributing member of the CALLAGHAN "first string." Making new crew members feel welcome, and showing them the ropes, is the responsibility of all hands, not just those men giving the indoctrination briefings. And if you have any good ideas 'on ways' that the current "I" Division Indoctrination could be improved' (based on your own experiences with "I" Division), be sure to pass your ideas to the Command Master Chief.

17. On Guests and Visitors aboard CALLAGHAN. Any guest and visitor (yes, even inspectors) aboard CALLAGHAN will be treated as though they were my own personal guests. They will be afforded every courtesy that you would provide me. They will be made to feel comfortable and welcome in CALLAGHAN. Treat visitors, in other words, as you would like to be treated if you were aboard another ship helping to accomplish a task. A little courtesy can go a very long way toward making activities "outside the life lines" aid and want to help CALLAGHAN. Courtesy and thoughtfulness

cost nothing, but can provide enormous dividends—and have a large impact on the reputation of the ship.

18. On Recognition. I strongly believe in the value of recognition for excellent performance. Crew members in positions of leadership should ensure that proper recognition, at the proper level is given to performance above the norm—to exceptional efforts that deserve special merit. Every man wants to do a good job; every man doing a good job wants to feel that his superiors have noticed just how hard and effectively he is working. Be sure that your top performers get the recognition that they have earned.

19. On Retention. It is the responsibility of every man in a leadership position to strive to retain in the naval service their best and most effective sailors. Our Navy and the Navy of the future, deserves nothing less. The command will do whatever efforts are necessary to obtain the best possible choice of duty for those who decide to make the Navy a career.

20. On Keeping the Crew Informed. I will strive to keep all hands informed concerning the current and future operations of the ship, recognizing that the uncertain and volatile nature of the world's operational environment means that we can expect changes in our projected future from time to time. To the extent possible, I will seek to reduce the uncertainty about the future

for both your work planning aboard the ship and for your family. To put the word out, I will use the Site TV, 1MC, periodic Captain's Calls and such tools as the Plan of the Day. When I know, you will know.

21. On the Appearance of the Ship and Cleanliness. First impressions of the ship, in addition to personal courtesy are most often built upon the visitor's impressions of the ship's seamanship appearance and general cleanliness. Our standards will be an immaculate appearance, both topside and inside the ship. Every space should be ready to "show off" to a visitor at all times. We should never have to go into a "crisis mode" to prepare for a distinguished visitor; rather, our standards will be such that we are always ready to receive outside visitors. Run we must; shine we will.

22. Keep me Informed. To plan and direct the near and long-term activities of CALLAGHAN, I need to understand completely the capabilities and limitations of the ship. In order to do this, I need continual feedback from the chain of command. I do not like surprises. I need to know everything related to the ability of CALLAGHAN to fight, in all her missions' areas. If you are in doubt whether I would want to know something—pass it up the chain of command. 'Err in excess—you will not be able to tell me too much. In particular, let me know where there's an area where I

need to apply my influences "outside the lifelines" to help someone in the ship to do his job.

23. On watchstanding. I expect all watches to be stood in a proper and formal manner. We stand no unimportant watches! For example, most "disasters" that occur to Navy ships in port are directly attributable to sloppy watchstanding procedures—like flooded spaces unnoticed by Sounding and Security or Cold Iron Watches. When on watch, know your duties and carry them out to the best of your abilities. Take pride in doing a job well Done—it's important.

24. On Supervision and Following Up. It is the responsibility of men in leadership positions in Callaghan not only to supervise the work of the men under them, but to follow up on the proper execution of orders made. Proper supervision and follow—up can't be conducted from the Wardroom, chief's quarters or First Class lounge. I expect the leadership of the CALLAGHAN to be visible and available in their working spaces often throughout the working day. Such attention to detail is vital if our efforts are to be done the right way the first time—rather than supervise only after inexperienced men have made a preventable mistake had there been proper supervision in the first place. Management without proper supervision and follow-up is one of the primary causes of "crisis management." Don't let it happen to your workcenter...

25. On the Chain of command. The chain of command must work up as well as down the line. The command will provide help to any crewmember or dependent who seeks it. Each member of the crew is encouraged to keep his superiors advised of problems that he may be facing. Each man should feel free to discuss personal problems with me or others in the chain of command at any time. If you need to discuss personal matters, matters of official nature, or to air a grievance, I urge you to apply for request mast via the chain of command if you feel that the chain of command is not responding effectively. The chain of command requires the cooperation of all hands to work properly. Without it, a warship cannot function in combat.

26. Personal Qualities I Value. The following are a few personal leadership qualities which I particularly value, and look for in each man in a leadership position.

    - Loyalty
    - Military Bearing
    - Intelligence
    - Judgment
    - Initiative
    - Force
    - Moral Courage
    - Cooperation
    - Perseverance

- Stability under Fire
- Endurance.
- Industry Enthusiasm

27. Things I will not Tolerate. The following are a few of the things I will not tolerate as Commanding Officer:

    - Sloppy or informal watchstanding

    - Disrespect to a superior (or any other crew member)

    - Disobedience of a lawful order

    - Any form of drug abuse, including alcohol abuse

    - Anything other than professional and gentle-manly behavior ashore

    - Any form of discrimination—religious, racial or otherwise

    - PMS gundecking

    - Lying, cheating or stealing

    - Initiations not approved by me.

28. Things I don't Like. The following—are a few things I don't like as a naval officer and that all hands should strive to avoid:

    - Unauthorized absence or lateness

    - Laziness or shirking of assigned duties

    - Dirty spaces

- Unshined brightwork

- Sloppy, dirty uniforms

- Sloppy paperwork

- Shaggy hair

- Water and oil in bilges (or any place else where it does not belong)

- Incomplete homework, sloppy preparation

- Uncooperative attitudes

29. Summary Thoughts. In summary, to make CALLA-GHAN an effective, efficient warship, we must:

   - Operate CALLAGHAN smartly and skillfully, meeting every inport and operational commitment on time

   - Exercise every design capability regularly

   - Be ready for combat on short notice

   - Maintain CALLAGHAN in the highest possible state of material and training readiness

   - For each man in the crew, actively encourage personal and professional growth; provide each man and his family with fair and human treatment

   - Retain every crew member who meets our high standards of naval service.

30. I expect every member of the crew to:

- Develop the practice of initiative doing the right thing without having to be told

- Develop and exercise leadership, including setting a good example for others

- Use standard procedures, the ship's organization and the chain of command to get things done

- Delegate responsibility to those who can do the job

- exercise authority at the lowest possible level

- Never exceed the boundaries of safety—only I can order that

As I mentioned in my remarks at the change of command, I am proud and honored to be a member of the crew of USS CALLAGHAN. The men of CALLAGHAN have proven themselves as first-rate destroyermen and proud professionals. I intend for us to continue that great tradition. Our duty in the Persian Gulf is fast approaching. We will be ready.

APPENDIX A2
USS *CALLAGHAN* (DDG 994) STANDING GOALS

USS CALLAGHAN (DDG 994) INSTRUCTION 3120.1

Subj:

Ref:

USS CALLAGHAN (DDG 994) STANDING GOALS

(a) OPNAVINST 3120.328, Chapter 8

(b) CALLAGHANINST 3120.328 (SORM)

1. <u>Purpose</u>. To establish those goals for USS CALLA-GHAN which are of a continuing nature to be used as a foundation and framework to prioritize the efforts of all hands.

2. <u>Discussion</u>. Clearly defined goals are an essential element to the proper focus of our planning, management, and leadership efforts aboard USS CALLA-GHAN (DDG 994) in accordance with reference (a). There are two categories of goals, standing and emerging. Standing goals are those to be fulfilled on a regular and continuing basis and are independent of the ship's schedule; they should always be considered in your near term planning. Emerging goals are those specifically related to the ship's schedule of training and major evolutions (e.g. deployment, SRA, major inspections such as OPPE and CSA, etc.) which

require special preparatory efforts to excel; Emerging goals will be provided quarterly.

3. <u>Primary Goals</u>. USS CALLAGHAN's (DDG 994) primary goal, and indeed our normal responsibility to the United States, is to be a combat ready unit fully prepared to employ the full capabilities of this warship. Combat readiness means that CALLAGHAN is ready to fight and win, whenever called, wherever needed. It is built upon a triad of supporting goals: material readiness effective training, and safety. These supporting goals, working in concert with each other, form the proper foundations to combat readiness and are amplified as follows:

 a. Material Readiness. The equipment and systems of the ship must function to their design capabilities if CALLAGHAN is to meet her combat missions. As Admiral Arleigh A. Burke has said,

> All that good equipment has to work the way it ought to, or it is simply excess baggage. Busted equipment won't help in battle. If your gear won't work, it's no good to anybody. If the systems operators know how to use their equipment, if they have kept the equipment in operating condition, there is a good chance we can win naval battles.

All systems aboard CALLAGHAN are combat systems—they all contribute to the combat effectiveness of the ship. Relentless pursuit of 100 percent operational equipment is the only standard of material readiness on CALLAGHAN. Two essential components of material readiness are:

(1) PMS. The PMS system is the bedrock upon which we maintain our equipment. PMS will be intelligently scheduled and promptly completed. The goal for PMS accomplishment will be a 95 accomplishment rate with a 100 confidence factor. This goal will be achieved by an aggressive spotcheck program. PMS will be accomplished by a trained maintenance man using the proper materials in exact accordance with the Maintenance Requirement Card (MRC). If the MRC doesn't fit the installed equipment, then submit a feedback report through administrative channels. This is a zero deviation goal. Shortcuts and gundeck will not be tolerated. Perform your equipment maintenance as if your life depended upon it—in combat it will!

(2) Cleanliness. Dirty spaces lead to broken equipment. The lack of pride and attention to detail that leads to poorly cleaned spaces leads to poorly maintained equipment. Each space has a man assigned, and the appearance of that space is a direct reflection of his pride and the professionalism and that of his chain of command. Spaces with proper preservation, clean decks, spotless bulkheads, angle irons free of dust, and brightwork shined are the only acceptable standards. These standards will be maintained by a zone inspection schedule which will ensure that each space is inspected at least once every quarter.

b. Effective Training. CALLAGHAN is the most sophisticated surface warfare platform afloat today, and as such it requires a highly trained crew to fully exploit its combat potential. A vigorous, thorough, and well documented training program in accordance with the provisions of reference (b) is essential to our combat readiness. Effective training is also an important contributor to crew morale, ensuring that each crewmember is challenged to achieve his personal and professional development goals. It is each man's obligation to work towards professional development goals. It is each man's obligation to work towards professional and personal improvement through both formal and informal study. Essential components to an effective training program include:

(1) Intelligent scheduling. Training must be scheduled to support the ships' near and long term schedule. It is not by accident that reference (b) requires each divisional training notebook to contain the ship's long range and quarterly schedules. These training notebooks will be reviewed by the Executive Officer or Training Officer at least once each quarter. Scheduling appropriate training to support the ship's schedule ensures safe and efficient performance, giving a purpose and motivation to the training that would otherwise be lacking.

(2) PQS. The PQS system is the primary means of setting training goals, guiding professional improvement, and watchstation qualification aboard CALLAGHAN. It provides a time-tested structure and rigor to training, and is the official method of documenting watchstation qualification. New personnel will be assigned goals upon checking aboard and their progress will be closely monitored.

Personnel will maintain their completion percentage rates within 20 percent of the time completed for each assigned item. For PQS to be effective, clear goals must be assigned, steady progress must be achieved, and high standards of qualification required. The following PQS qualification priorities are established:

(a) General Damage Control

(b) Battle Bill assigned watchstation(s)

(c) 3M Maintenance

(d) Warfare qualification (SWO, ESWS)

(3) Realism. To be effective, training must be as realistic as possible. Realistic training is the result of thorough preparation by a knowledgeable training supervisor, and is whenever possible conducted in the space and on the equipment that is the subject of the training. A careful review of authorized simulations prior to each training evolution will ensure that simulations are kept to an absolute minimum within the confines of safety.

(4) Assessment. Most of the benefits of training that have been outlined above are wasted

unless there is a proper assessment after training. Assessments (or wash-ups, critiques, post-ex's, tests, etc.) are necessary to evaluate the effectiveness of training, to reinforce training lessons, to correct mistakes, and to ensure that the pace of training is not too slow or fast. It is the responsibility of not only the training supervisor, but also all of those being trained, to ensure that a complete assessment is conducted after all training evolutions. Assessments should always be done in accordance with the requirements of the appropriate FXP.

c. Safety. Taking ships to sea is, and always has been, an inherently dangerous calling. We cannot control the elements of wind and sea, and therefore must respect them and accommodate ourselves to them. A warship, laden with fuel and armament, designed to fight, can be unforgiving to those not alert to safety. Safety must permeate everything that we do aboard USS CALLAGHAN (DDG 994). In a peacetime environment there is nothing associated with our mission which requires us to disregard known safety rules. It is every crewmember's responsibility to be a safety supervisor, and to take immediate corrective action when an unsafe condition is noted. Hazard reports should be frequently submitted in a prompt fashion. A lack of hazard reports does not indicate a lack of hazards. Essential components to a safe ship included, but are not limited to:

(1) procedures and written in the blood for your strict observance of established operational safety rules. Most of these rules have been written in the blood of our predecessors—don't rewrite them in successors!

(2) Thorough planning and preparation for all evolutions. Such preparations will preclude the shortcuts and "crisis management" that often create unsafe situations.

(3) Systems knowledge. A thorough knowledge of the system to be operated on the part of a trained and qualified operator is the best assurance of a safe evolution.

(4) Supervision. There is no greater responsibility that can be assigned to a crewmember than that of safety observer. His shipmates are literally putting their lives into the safety observer's hands. It is also the explicit responsibility of all seniors to supervise their subordinates to ensure a safe working environment is always maintained.

(5) Alert people. Each of us is, ultimately, responsible for our own safety. "One hand for the man, one hand for the ship," is a traditional Navy adage that summarizes this requirement well.

4. <u>Supplemental goals</u>. Supplemental goals are those which we must, on a steady strain basis, excel every day. Supplemental goals will include, but should not be limited to the following items:

   a. Efficient administration of all Command and Department tickler files. Without up to date tickler files which are actively in use, accomplishment of the remaining supplemental goals becomes impossible.

   b. Well run administrative programs. These are essential in that they support a wide variety of broad goals. In addition to those previously mentioned, programs which should see a steady day to day emphasis are as follows:

      (1) Money Audit Programs (wardroom mess, postal effects, flight deck/hazardous duty, etc.)

      (2) CMS Administration

      (3) Tag-out Program

      (4) Equipage Inventory and Accountability

    (5) Personnel Records

    (6) Classified Material Control

    (7) Engineering Administrative Programs

    (8) Technical Publication Management

    (9) Retention Program

    (10) Execution of Departmental or task specific POA&M's (NTPI, Medical POAM INSURV, OPPE, act.)

    (11) Supply Administrative Programs

c. Efficient and timely administration of collateral duties. Proper attention to collateral duties will ensure the smooth day to day operation of command programs without a need for "crisis management."

d. Timely submission of thorough and accurate performance evaluations, including:

    (1) Officer Fitness Reports

    (2) Enlisted Performance Evaluations

    (3) Mid-term Evaluation Sheets

    (4) Performance Counseling Sheets

    (5) Letters of Instruction

(6) Letters of Appreciation

(7) Letters of Commendation

(8) Award Recommendations (Flag Officer Letters of Commendation, Navy Achievement Medals, Command Advancement Program, etc.)

5. <u>Action</u>. The above goals are best achieved in a command environment of calm, confident professionalism based upon demonstrated excellence in all mission areas, team spirit, and the personal pride of each crewmember in doing his job well. It is impossible to list everything that must be done; this instruction is designed to convey the general philosophy and priorities, not specify every action. The bottom line is for all of us aboard CALLAGHAN to do our jobs and do them to the absolute best of our ability. You are contributing to the defense of your country and the preservation of peace while continuing the traditions of excellence and victory that have characterized our Navy for over 200 years. It should be both fun and rewarding to perform such an important job well. The final priority is just that, to have fun while performing this important job of ours well.

Distribution:
DDG994INST 5216.1
List I, Case A

APPENDIX A3
USS *HEWITT* (DD-996) COMMAND PHILOSOPHY
AND STANDARDS

DEPARTMENT OF THE NAVY
USS HEWITT (DD–966)
FPO AP 96667-1204
15 August 1992

MEMORANDUM

From: Commanding Officer, USS HEWITT (DD–966)
To: All Hands
Subj: **COMMAND PHILOSOPHY AND STANDARDS**

1. There is plenty of guidance already officially promulgated from higher authority that directs, regulates, and controls many of the things we do on a daily basis. The purpose of outlining my command philosophy and standards for HEWITT is to explain how I intend to comply with those directives while at the same time establishing a standard for HEWITT that allows us to confidently perform any assigned mis-

sion. My philosophy can be broken down into three major categories and are listed in order of priority:

a. <u>TAKE CARE OF YOUR PEOPLE</u>. HEWITT cannot complete her mission without a well trained, well led, motivated, and happy crew. To that end, all personnel in a supervisory position must look after their assigned personnel in both a personal and professional manner. On the personal side, that includes: ensuring newly reporting personnel have active sponsors, departing personnel are properly recognized for their contribution to HEWITT; there is equal opportunity in the work center; berthing compartments are clean and well maintained; families are well taken care of; special request chits are processed rapidly; there is zero tolerance for drug/alcohol abuse and sexual harassment; personal problems are dealt with in a caring manner; each man feels he belongs and is a contributor to HEWITT; treating everyone as a shipmate; and generally looking after the welfare of each crewman. On the professional side that includes: ensuring all eligible personnel are advancement ready; progress towards watch qualifications are satisfactory; encouraging qualification as an Enlisted Surface Warfare Specialist; assignment of tasks to only qualified people; maintaining an effective training program to include cross training where applicable; insisting on compliance with all existing safety programs such as tagout, hearing conservation, heat stress, electrical safety; and encouraging pursuit of educational opportunities. What I have listed is by no means all inclusive, but is provided to illustrate how existing programs fit into my command philosophy with respect to how we take care of our people. Fundamental to the success of this is an effective chain of command that works both ways and provides a conduit for a constructive flow of information between all levels of the command.

b. <u>REMEMBER OUR MISSION</u>. HEWITT is a warship. Simply stated, our mission is to be able to conduct prompt, sustained combat operations at sea. In order to complete our mission, HEWITT needs to be 100 percent combat ready at all times. Everything we do should be geared towards fulfilling our mission. Here, PMS and PQS go hand in hand in ensuring both our equipment and people are ready to fight. We will train to fight in all conditions of readiness against all types of expected threats. Training is the key! In the heat of battle, when you are both tired and under a great deal of stress, it is your level of training that determines whether we carry the day. We will! To that end, each HEWITT sailor is a major contributor to our ability to fight this ship. Your input on how to best operate equipment and systems is vital to developing effective battle orders and corresponding equipment configurations. You are the experts.

c. <u>KNOW YOUR EQUIPMENT</u>. For us to succeed, we must fully understand how our equipment and systems work in all modes and in various degrees of degradation. You must know not only how your equipment works under normal conditions, but also its safety features, how it relates to other systems, and how to extract its full capability in all conditions. Technical manuals and PMS are the fundamental sources of information to ensure our equipment and systems function properly. We must also become self-sufficient. It is our gear—we fix it!

2. My standard for HEWITT is excellence. We should endeavor to do things right the first time. That means that the equipment must be well maintained; operators trained and qualified to operate the equipment; watch qualifications complete; evolutions fully prebriefed, executed smartly, then debriefed to determine ways to improve upon performance; and qual-

ity control procedures in place and followed to insure maintenance actions are performed correctly the first time. I fully intend to operate this ship the way it was designed to be operated. We are destroyer men, a cut above the rest, and we will carry out our mission swiftly and with style. The ship's motto sums up the way I want each and every HEWITT sailor to feel on a daily basis–BE JUST AND FEAR NOT.

J. C. MEYER

APPENDIX B

GENERAL DOUGLAS MACARTHUR'S FAREWELL SPEECH (MAY 12, 1962)

General Douglas MacArthur's Speech to West Point

United States Military Academy
West Point, New York
May 12, 1962

General Westmoreland, General Groves, distinguished guests, and gentlemen of the Corps: As I was leaving the hotel this morning, a doorman asked me, "Where are you bound for, General?" and when I replied, "West Point," he remarked, "Beautiful place, have you ever been there before?"

No human being could fail to be deeply moved by such a tribute as this. [Thayer Award] Coming from a profession I have served so long, and a people I have loved so well, it fills me with an emotion I cannot express. But this award is not intended primarily to honor a personality, but to symbolize a great moral code—the code of conduct and chivalry of those who guard this beloved land of culture and ancient descent. That is the meaning of this medallion. For all eyes and for all time, it is an expression of the ethics of the American soldier. That I should be integrated in this way with so noble an ideal arouses a sense of pride and yet of humility which will be with me always.

Duty—Honor—Country. Those three hallowed words reverently dictate what you ought to be, what you can be, what you will be. They are your rallyingpoints: to build courage when courage seems to fail; to regain faith when there seems to be little cause for faith; to create hope when hope becomes forlorn. Unhappily, I possess neither that eloquence of diction, that poetry of imagination, nor that brilliance of metaphor to tell you all that they mean. The unbelievers will say they are but words, but a slogan, but a flamboyant phrase. Every pedant, every demagogue, every cynic, every hypocrite, every troublemaker, and, I am sorry to say, some others of an entirely different character, will try to downgrade them even to the extent of mockery and ridicule. But these are some of the things they do. They build your basic character, they mold you for your future roles as the custodians of the nation's defense, they make you strong enough to know when you are weak, and brave enough to face yourself when you are afraid. They teach you to be proud and unbending in honest failure, but humble and gentle in success; not to substitute words for actions, nor to seek the path of comfort, but to face the stress and spur of difficulty and challenge; to learn to stand up in the storm but to have compassion on those who fall; to master yourself before you seek to master others; to have a heart that is clean, a goal that is high; to learn to laugh yet never forget how to weep; to reach into the future yet never neglect the past; to be serious yet never to take yourself too seriously; to be modest so that you will remember the simplicity of true greatness, the open mind of true wisdom, the meekness of true strength. They give you a temper of the will, a quality of the imagination, a vigor of the emotions, a freshness of the deep springs of life, a temperamental predominance of courage over timidity, an appetite for adventure over love of ease. They create in your heart the sense of wonder, the unfailing hope of what next, and the joy and inspiration of life. They teach you in this way to be an officer and a gentleman.

And what sort of soldiers are those you are to lead? Are they reliable, are they brave, are they capable of victory? Their story is known to all of you; it is the story of the American man-at-arms. My estimate of him was formed on the battlefield many, many years ago, and has never changed. I regarded him then as I regard him now—as one of the world's noblest figures, not only as one of the finest military characters but also as one of the most stainless. His name and fame are the birthright of every American citizen. In his youth and strength, his love and loyalty he gave—all that mortality can give. He needs no eulogy from me or from any other man. He has written his own history and written it in red on his enemy's breast. But when I think of his patience under adversity, of his courage under fire, and of his modesty in victory, I am filled with an emotion of admiration I cannot put into words. He belongs to history as furnishing one of the greatest examples of successful patriotism; he belongs to posterity as the instructor of future generations in the principles of liberty and freedom; he belongs to the present, to us, by his virtues and by his achievements. In 20 campaigns, on a hundred battlefields, around a thousand campfires, I have witnessed that enduring fortitude, that patriotic self-abnegation, and that invincible determination which have carved his statue in the hearts of his people. From one end of the world to the other he has drained deep the chalice of courage.

As I listened to those songs of the glee club, in memory's eye I could see those staggering columns of the First World War, bending under soggy packs, on many a weary march from dripping dusk to drizzling dawn, slogging ankle-deep through the mire of shell-shocked roads, to form grimly for the attack, blue-lipped, covered with sludge and mud, chilled by the wind and rain; driving home to their objective, and, for many, to the judgment seat of God. I do not know the dignity of their birth but I do know the glory of their death. They died unquestioning, uncomplaining, with faith in their hearts, and on their lips the hope that we would go on to victory. Always for them—Duty—Honor—Country; always their blood and sweat and tears as we sought the way and the light and the truth. And 20 years after, on the other side of the globe, again the filth of murky foxholes, the stench of ghostly trenches, the slime of dripping dugouts; those boiling suns of relentless heat, those torrential rains of devastating storms; the loneliness and utter desolation of jungle trails, the bitterness of long separation from those they loved and cherished, the deadly pestilence of tropical disease, the horror of stricken areas of war; their resolute and determined defense, their swift and sure attack, their indomitable purpose, their complete and decisive victory—always victory. Always through the bloody haze of their last reverberating shot, the vision of gaunt, ghastly men reverently following your password of Duty–Honor–Country. The code which those words perpetuate embraces the highest moral laws and will stand the test of any ethics or philosophies ever promulgated for the uplift of mankind. Its requirements are for the things that are right, and its restraints are from the things that are wrong. The soldier, above all other men, is required to practice the greatest act of religious training–sacrifice. In battle and in the face of danger and death, he discloses those divine attributes which his Maker gave when he created man in his own image. No physical courage and no brute instinct can take the place of the Divine help which alone can sustain him. However horrible the incidents of war may be, the soldier who is called upon to offer and to give his life for his country, is the noblest development of mankind.

You now face a new world—a world of change. The thrust into outer space of the satellite, spheres and missiles marked the beginning of another epoch in the long story of mankind—the chapter of the space age. In the five or more billions of years the scientists tell us it has taken to form the earth, in the three or more billion years of development of the human race, there has never been a greater, a more abrupt or staggering evolution. We deal now not with things of this world alone, but with the illimitable distances and as yet unfathomed mysteries of the universe. We are reaching out for a new and boundless frontier. We speak in strange terms: of harnessing the cosmic energy; of making winds and tides work for us; of creating unheard synthetic materials to supplement or even replace our old standard basics; of purifying sea water for our drink; of mining ocean floors for new fields of wealth and food; of disease preventatives to expand life into the hundred of years; of controlling the weather for a more equitable distribution of heat and cold, of rain and shine; of space ships to the moon; of the primary target in war, no longer limited to the armed forces of an enemy, but instead to include his civil populations; of ultimate conflict between a united human race and the sinister forces of some other planetary galaxy; of such dreams and fantasies as to make life the most exciting of all time. And through all this welter of change and development, your mission remains fixed, determined, inviolable—it is to win our wars. Everything else in your professional career is but corollary to this vital dedication. All other public purposes, all other public projects, all other public needs, great or small, will find others for their accomplishment; but you are the ones who are trained to fight: yours is the profession of arms—the will to win, the sure knowledge that in war there is no substitute for victory; that if you lose, the nation will be destroyed; that the very obsession of your public service must be Duty–Honor–Country. Others will debate the controversial issues, national and international, which divide men's minds; but serene, calm, aloof, you stand as the nation's war guardian, as its lifeguard from the raging tides of international conflict, as its gladiator in the arena of battle. For a century and a half you have defended, guarded, and protected its hallowed traditions of liberty and freedom, of right and justice. Let civilian voices argue the merits or demerits of our processes of government; whether our strength is being sapped by deficit financing, indulged in too long, by federal paternalism grown too mighty, by power groups grown too arrogant, by politics grown too corrupt, by crime grown too rampant, by morals grown too low, by taxes grown too high, by extremists grown too violent; whether our personal liberties are as thorough and complete as they should be. These great national problems are not for your professional participation or military solution. Your guidepost stands out like a ten-fold beacon in the night–Duty–Honor–Country.

You are the leaven which binds together the entire fabric of our national system of defense. From your ranks come–the great captains who hold the nation's destiny in their hands the moment the war tocsin sounds. The Long Gray Line has never failed us. Were you to do so, a million ghosts in olive drab, in brown khaki, in blue and gray, would rise from their white crosses thundering those magic words–Duty–Honor–Country. This does not mean that you are war mongers. On the contrary, the soldier, above all other people, prays for peace, for he must suffer and bear the deepest wounds and scars of war. But always in our ears ring the ominous words of Plato that wisest of all philosophers, "Only the dead have seen the end of war."

The shadows are lengthening for me. The twilight is here. My days of old have vanished tone and tint; they have gone glimmering through the dreams of things that were. Their memory is one of wondrous beauty, watered by tears, and coaxed and caressed by the smiles of yesterday. I listen vainly for the witching melody of faint bugles blowing reveille, of far drums beating the long roll. In my dreams I hear again the crash of guns, the rattle of musketry, the strange, mournful mutter of the battlefield. But in the evening of my memory, always I come back to West Point. Always there echoes and re-echoes Duty–Honor–Country. Today marks my final roll call with you, but I want you to know that when I cross the river my last conscious thoughts will be-of The Corps, and The Corps, and The Corps. I bid you farewell.

APPENDIX C

PERSONAL VISION

PERSONAL VISION (by Cdr, William Landay)

I want every member of the crew to leave the command feeling that this tour was one of the most positive experiences of their lives. I want them to look back on their time on Paul Hamilton with a sense of pride, accomplishment, and personal growth. I hope that their ball cap, coffee mug, or plaque figure prominently in their collection of personal mementos. To accomplish that vision, I intend to focus on the following values.

Professionalism. I want us to believe that we are the best surface warriors in the world. That we know our profession, technically and tactically, that we have trained ourselves as well as possible and that there is no doubt in anyone's mind that we will accomplish the mission assigned. Part of that professionalism is a quiet sense of confidence. I want us to be utterly confident that each member of the crew is capable of doing his job and will do it in any situation and that the command itself will succeed. I want to let our actions speak for themselves. We don't need to tell anyone how good we are, they will already know.

Honesty and Integrity. I want us to have a deep rooted sense of honor and integrity in everything we do. I want to encourage and strengthen the basic traits of goodness, honesty and courtesy that I believe exists in everyone. I want this to become an automatic response to every action we take. I don't want anyone to wonder if it is ok to tell a "little white lie", but rather to know what is right and to do it. I want the crew to truly believe that if they do the "right thing", that I will stand by them 100%, no matter what the consequences.

Enthusiasm and Pride. I want us to have a great sense of enthusiasm for what we are about. While there will be some tough days, as a whole I want us to be excited about what the command is doing, and what each person contributes. I want us to feel that this is where they belong and where they want to be. That they are accomplishing something good for themselves; their ship and their country. I want every crew member to be proud to be a sailor and especially proud to be a Paul Hamilton sailor. When they walk down the pier, I want each one, from the newest deck seaman to the XO, to know that the rest of the pier is looking at them wondering how they do it and how each would measure up to the Paul Hamilton standards.

Camaraderie and a Sense of Family. I want us to have a great sense of camaraderie within the crew. To believe that everyone is important and that everyone contributes to our success. I want there to be true pride in the accomplishments of others in the crew. I want to develop a tremendous loyalty to the ship and each other. In the end, I believe this will carry us through many hardships, however I never want that sense of loyalty to overcome our sense of honesty and integrity. I encourage good natured competition and rivalry between divisions and departments. I think it is part of the spirit of who we are, our will to win and be the best. I want to ensure however that we never lose sight of the fact that in the end it is the success of the group that is the goal. I want to extend this sense of camaraderie beyond the lifelines and ensure it includes the families. I want them to feel that they are an integral part of who we are as a command, that they are a foundation of our success, and that they have the same sense of pride about being a Paul Hamilton family as we do.

Personal Worth and Growth. I want each member of the crew to have a great sense of personal worth as a result of being in this crew. They should feel that they are important, that they are contributing to a greater good and that the ship, Navy, and country are a little bit better because of them. I want to ensure that we are sensitive to constantly reinforce that sense of worth and are on the lookout for any indication that they are losing it. This is an extraordinarily difficult and stressful profession we have chosen. The opportunities to be knocked down are plentiful. I want to ensure we minimize those opportunities and as a group we pickup those who may be down, reinforce their sense of worth, and set them back on their feet. That is our responsibility as comrades and shipmates. Additionally, I want to foster an atmosphere of personal growth. I want to challenge everyone to improve themselves during their time on board. To grow professionally, spiritually, mentally, and in character. I want to provide every opportunity and every day examples for each member to take advantage of. Where necessary I will push, as well as encourage, for this is one of the most critical achievements of the command. Not every sailor will stay in the Navy, but we want to ensure that we give the Navy and society a stronger person back than the one we received.

Steady Strain and Balance. I want to constantly operate on an even keel. While we are always subject to the taskings of our seniors, I want us to make the routine be routine. To do the daily business of our profession as a matter of course and to always be one step ahead of everyone else. As a result, we will be able to handle the unexpected/short fused tasker with a minimum of turmoil. In this way we can keep a sense of balance in managing all of our requirements. I want to be able to balance the needs of the command, the individual and their families.

There will be many ways to measure the extent to which we lived these values. Probably one of the most telling will be years later, after we have all left the command, when someone will come up to me at a movie, restaurant or on the street and tell me that he was on Paul Hamilton with me and wanted to introduce me to his son, daughter, wife, or parents. When that person says" I am glad to meet you. He has told me so much about the time he spent on that ship…"That's when I'll know!

APPENDIX D

....

COMBAT STRESS AND TREATMENT

Most soldiers have these reactions No special treatment necessary

> Trembling, sweating, nausea, frequent diarrhea, frequent urination, pounding heart, stomach pains, anxiety, agitation Not moving or talking, blank expression, seems without emotion, apathy, cannot be bothered, moodiness, unable to concentrate on job, decreased appetite, overreaction, emotional outbursts, loss of self-control, argumentative, aggressive, unable to sleep

Look out for these reactions

Give on-the-spot treatment
Do not over react.
Remain calm yourself.
Do not ridicule.
Calm the soldier.
Reassure the soldier.
Show understanding.
Team up with him for a while.
If possible, give him a warm drink/cigarette.
Give him a specific task to accomplish

Severe reactions

Keep soldier with unit but away from battle.
Allow him to sleep.
Treat him as a soldier not as a patient.
Have someone stay near him; supervise.
Have members of his unit interested in his welfare.
Return him to unit after about two days.
Unit treatment is necessary.

If reactions persist or become more severe, report to your superior.

> Repeated nausea and vomiting.
> Inability to use some parts of the body.
> Unable to perform his job.
> Feelings of guilt.
> Excessive use of alcohol/tobacco.

APPENDIX E

Clinton, William J. *A National Security Strategy of Engagement and Enlargement.* The White House, February, 1995. Read preface pages I-iii, Introduction 1–5, Conclusions page 33.

Dalton, John H. *Forward...From the Sea*, *Proceedings*, December, 1994, page 1–2 and scan the rest.

Naval Doctrine Publication 1, *Naval Warfare*, 1994, page 26. "Control of the Sea Concept" page 22, International Law. Article 51.

Owens, William A. *Naval Voyage to an Uncharted World*, *Proceedings*, December, 1994, pages 30–34.

Shalikashvili, John M. *National Military Strategy of the United States.* March, 1995. Executive Summary pages 1–5 and conclusion.

Shalikashvili, John M. *A Word from the Chairman*, Joint Forces Quarterly Autumn/Winter, 1994–1995, pages 4–8.

Armed Forces Staff College. *The Joint Staff Officer's Guide 1993*. Norfolk, VA: Armed Forces Staff College, 1993, pages 1–13.

Clinton, William J. *A National Security Strategy of Engagement and Enlargement*. The White House, July, 1994.

Dalton, John H. et al. *Forward… From the Sea, Proceedings*, December, 1994, pages 46–49.

Joint Pub 1, *Joint Warfare of the US Armed Forces*, 1991, pages 5–6.

Joint Publication 1-02. *DOD Dictionary of Military and Associated Terms*, pages 80, 252–254, 364, and 380.

Joint Publication 0-2, *Unified Action Armed Forces*, pages 2–6 and 7.

Kilpatrick, C. W. *The Naval Night Battles of the Solomon's*. Pompano Beach: Exposition Press of Florida, 1987, page 133.

Naval Doctrine Publication 1, *Naval Warfare*, 1994, pages 31–33, 50–57.

Powell, Colin J., Chairman Joint Chiefs of Staff. *National Military Strategy of the United States*, January, 1992.

CHAPTER 6 REFERENCES

Dalton, John H. *The Character of Readiness: The Ethics of Moral Behavior, Vital Speeches of the Day*, January 1994, pages 296–298.

Landenberg, Rear Admiral William H. *1972: The Nadir of the Navy, Professionalism, Shipmate*, January/February, 1995, Volume 58, No. 1, pages 35–36.

Lynch, Major General J. D. *Nobody Asked Me But … Fish Rot from the Head*, Proceedings, February 1995, page 73.

Montor, Karel, et al. *Naval Leadership: Voices of Experience*. Annapolis, MD: Naval Institute Press, 1987, pages 26–32, Components of Integrity.

Raspberry, William. *Ethics Without Virtue, The Washington Post*, 16 December 1991, page A23.

Stockdale, James B. *Leadership in Response to Changing Societal Values: What is Today's Skipper of a Destroyer, Submarine or Aircraft Squadron Up Against?* May 25, 1987.

Stockdale, James B. *Taking Stock, Naval War College Review*, fall, 1978, "Right and Wrong Changed to Legal and Illegal."

Excerpts from Leadership Jazz by Max Depree.

A Report Prepared For Navy Senior Officers: Command Excellence Seminar (undated).

Blanchard, Kenneth and Norman Vincent Peale. *The Power of Ethical Management*. New York: William Morrow and Company, 1988, page 80.

CNO 281746Z OCT 92. *Core Values of the United States Navy*.

Common Sense and Everyday Ethics. Washington, DC: Ethics Resource Center, 1980.

Covey, Stephen R. *Principle-Centered Leadership*. New York: Fireside Edition, Simon & Schuster, 1992, pages 101–108, 141, 171.

Covey, Stephen R. *The Seven Habits of Highly Effective People*. New York, NY: Fireside Edition, 1989, pages 15–34 and 195–197.

Dalton, John H. *The Character of Readiness: The Ethics of Moral Behavior, Vital Speeches of the Day*, January, 1994, pages 296–298.

Forward…From the Sea, A Navy/Marine Corps White Paper.

Handout from SLS, "Senior Leader Responsibilities for Leading Process Management."

Montor, Karel. *Ethics for the Junior Officer*, Annapolis, MD: Naval Institute, 1994.

NAVOP 030/92, *Core Values of the United States Navy*.

Navy's *Core Values Instructor Guide*.

NPRDC, *Senior Leader's Seminar Guide*, 1994.

Raspberry, William. *Ethics Without Virtue, The Washington Post*, 16 December 1991, page A23.

SECNAVINST 5370.2J, Standards of Conduct and Government Ethics.

Stockdale, James B. *A Vietnam Experience: Ten Years Reflection*. Stanford, CA: Hover Institute, 1984.

TQLO Publication #93-05, *TOL in the Fleet: From Theory to Practice*.

TQLO Publication #93-04, *A Briefing Package for Senior Leaders*.

Warner, Oliver. *Command at Sea: Great Fighting Admirals From Hawke to Nimitz*. New York: St. Martin's Press, 1976.

Webster's Ninth New Collegiate Dictionary. Springfield, MA: Merriam-Webster Inc., 1991, page 407.

Whiteside, David E. *Command Excellence: What it Takes to Be The Best!* Washington, DC: Department of the Navy, 1985.

Additional References

Metz, E. J. "Managing Change: Implementing Productivity and Quality Improvement," *National Productivity Review*, 1984, 3(3), pages 303–314.

Tichy, Noel M. and Mary Anne Devanna. *The Transformational Leader*. New York: John Wiley & Sons, 1990, pages 3–6, 27–33, 48–57 (How to Start Transformational Change), and pages 198–213.

Forward … From the Sea: Preparing the Naval Service For the 21st Century. Washington, DC: Department of the Navy, 1993, chapters 1 and 2.

Kantor, Rosabeth Moss. *The Change Masters*. New York, NY: Simon & Schuster, 1983, chapters 2 and 10.

Rosenbach, William E. and Robert L Taylor. *Contemporary Issues in Leadership*. Boulder, CO: Westview Press, 1993, page 117.

Scholtes, Peter. *The Team Handbook: How to Use Teams to Improve Quality*. Madison, WI: Joiner Associates, Inc., 1988, page iv.

Total Quality Leadership Office. *Senior Leader's Seminar Guide*. Washington, DC: Department of the Navy, 1994, chapters 1, 3.2, 5.2, and 6.2.

Wasik, Judy K. and Bobbie Ryan. *TQL in the Fleet: From Theory to Practice*. Arlington, VA: TQLO Publication 93-05, 1993.

Blanchard, Kenneth H. *SLII, A Situational Approach to Managing People*. Blanchard Training and Development, Inc., pages 1-10.

Hersey, Paul and Kenneth H. Blanchard. *Management of Organizational Behavior: Utilizing Human Resources*. Sixth Edition. Englewood Cliffs, NJ: Prentice Hall, 1993, pages 5-6, 93-97, and 111-113.

Locke, Edwin A. and Associates. *The Essence of Leadership: The Four Keys to Leading Successfully*. New York: Lexington Books, 1991, pages 6-11.

Tichy, Noel M. and Mary Anne Devanna. *The Transformational Leader*. New York: John Wiley & Sons, 1990, pages xi-xv, 3-6, 27-33, and 44.

Whiteside, David E. *Command Excellence: What it Takes to Be The Best!* Washington, DC: Department of the Navy, 1985, pages 11–28.

Blanchard, Kenneth H. *Leadership and the One-Minute Manager*, New York: William Morrow and Company, 1985.

CNO 281746Z Oct 92, *Core Values of the United States Navy*.

Covey, Stephen R. *Principle-Centered Leadership*. New York: Fireside Edition, Simon & Schuster, 1992, pages 13–25.

Stockdale, James B. *A Vietnam Experience: Ten Years of Reflection*. Stanford, CA: Hoover Institution, 1984.

Stockdale, James B. *In Love and War*. Annapolis, MD: Naval Institute Press, 1990.

The Heart of an Officer, comments by Secretary of the Navy, Sean O'Keefe, Annapolis, MD, 24 September 1992.

Dalton, John H. *The Character of Readiness: The Ethics of Moral Behavior, Vital Speeches of the Day*, January, 1994, pages 296–298.

Langenberg, Rear Admiral William H. *1972: The Nadir of the Navy, Professionalism, Shipmate*, January/February, 1995, Volume 58, No. 1, pages 35–36.

Lynch, Major General J. D. *Nobody Asked Me But… Fish Rot from the Head*, Proceedings, February, 1995, page 73.

Montor, Karel, et al. *Naval Leadership: Voices of Experience*. Annapolis, MD: Naval Institute Press, 1987, pages 26–32, Components of Integrity.

Raspberry, William. *Ethics Without Virtue, The Washington Post*, 16 December, 1991, page A23.

Stockdale, James B. *Leadership in Response to Changing Societal Values: What is Today's Skipper of a Destroyer, Submarine or Aircraft Squadron Up Against?* May 25, 1987.

Stockdale, James B. *Taking Stock, Naval War College Review*, Fall, 1978, "Right and Wrong Changed to Legal and Illegal."

Excerpts from Leadership Jazz by Max Depree.

Covey, Stephen R. *The 7 Habits of Highly Effective People*. New York: Fireside Edition, Simon & Schuster, 1989, pages 147–149.

Tichy, Noel M. and Mary Anne Devanna. *The Transformational Leader*. New York: John Wiley & Sons, 1990, pages 137—top of 140.

Bennis, Warren and Burt Nanus. *Leaders, The Strategies for Taking Charge*. New York: Harper & Row, 1985.

Covey, Stephen R. *Principle-Centered Leadership*. New York: Fireside Edition, Simon & Schuster, 1992.

Covey, Stephen R. *The 7 Habits of Highly Effective People*. New York: Fireside Edition, Simon & Schuster, 1990. Drucker, Peter. *Leaders, The Strategies for Taking Charge*. New York: Harper & Row, 1985.

Huse, Edgar F. and Thomas Cummings. *Organization Development and Change*. St Paul, MN: West Publishing Company, 1985, pages 360–366.

Tichy, Noel M. *Managing Strategic Change*. New York: John Wiley & Sons, 1990, pages 117–138.

Tichy, Noel M. and Mary Anne Devanna. *The Transformational Leader*. New York: John Wiley & Sons, 1990, pages 48–57.

Total Quality Leadership Office. *Department of the Navy Total Quality Leadership Glossary*. Washington, DC: Department of the Navy, 1994.

Total Quality Leadership Office. *Senior Leader's Seminar*. Washington, DC: Department of the Navy, 1994, pages 193–197.

Mack, Vice Admiral William P. and Commander Albert H. Konetzni, *Command at Sea*. Annapolis, MD: Naval Institute Press, 1982, pages 18–28.

Whiteside, David E. *Command Excellence: What It Takes To Be The Best!* Washington, DC: Leadership Division, Bureau of Naval Personnel, 1985, page 17.

Covey, Stephen R. *The 7 Habits of Highly Effective People*. New York: Fireside Press, 1989, pages 23–45.

Locke, Edwin A. and Associates. *The Essence of Leadership: The Four Keys to Leading Successfully*. New York: Lexington Books, 1991, pages 88–93.

Whiteside, David E. *Command Excellence: What It Takes To Be The Best!* Washington, DC: Department of the Navy, 1985, pages 37–55.

OPNAVINST 1306.2B, *Fleet, Force, and Command Master Chief Program*, 1994, Section D, pages 7–9.

Whiteside, David E. *Command Excellence: What It Takes To Be The Best!* Washington DC: Leadership Division, Bureau of Naval Personnel, pages 15-35, 47-50, and 63–65.

OPNAVINST 1306.2B, *Fleet, Force, and Command Master Chief Program*, 1994, Section D, pages 7–9.

Whiteside, David E. *Command Excellence: What It Takes To Be The Best!* Washington DC: Leadership Division, Bureau of Naval Personnel, pages 15–35, 47–50, and 63–65.

Byham, William C. and Jeff Cox. *Zapp! The Lightening of Empowerment.* **Pittsburgh, PA: Development Dimensions International Press, 1989**, pages 55, 56, 59, 60, 98, 104, 105, 111, 126.

Joint Pub 1, *Joint Warfare of The U.S. Armed Forces*, 11 November 1991, page 36.

Kirkland, Farris R. *Combat Leadership Styles: Empowerment Versus Authoritarianism, Parameters: Journal of the U.S. Army War College*, Vol. XX, No. 4, December 1990, pages 61–72.

Montor, Karel, et al. *Naval Leadership: Voices of Experience.* Annapolis, MD: Naval Institute Press, 1987, pages 213 through 278, only sections 36, 47, 51, and pages 242 through 245.

Ackoff, Russell L. *Creating the Corporate Future.* New York: John Wiley & Sons, 1981, pages 34–45.

Buckles, Brian K. *What is This Mentor Stuff?*, *Marine Corps Gazette*, Vol. 78 No. 10, October 1994.

Chief of Naval Operations. *The United States Navy Policy Book*. Washington, DC: Department of the Navy, 1992, chapter 4.

Hersey, Paul and Kenneth H. Blanchard. *Management of Organizational Behavior: Utilizing Human Resources*, Sixth Edition. Englewood Cliffs, NJ: Prentice Hall, 1993, pages 8, 248–268, and 314–316.

Aubrey II, Charles A. and Patricia K. Felkins. *Teamwork: Involving People in Quality and Productivity Improvement*. Milwaukee, WI: Quality Press, 1988, pages 70–74.

Blanchard, Kenneth, Donald Carew, and Eunice Parisi-Carew. *The One Minute Manager Builds High Performing Teams*. New York: William Morrow and Company, Inc., 1991, pages 19–27, 33–67.

Chief of Naval Education and Training. *Team Skills and Concepts, Instructor Guide*. Washington, DC: Department of the Navy, 1992, pages 6–3 to 6–41.

Chief of Naval Education and Training. *Implementing Total Quality Leadership, Student Guide*. Washington, DC: Department of the Navy, 1993, Modules 2 and 4.

Covey, Seven R., *The 7 Habits of Highly Effective People.*, New York: Fireside Edition, Simon and Schuster, 1990, pages 205–234.

Mitchell, Howard E. *A Classic Case of "Group Think" at NSC, The Philadelphian Inquirer*, August 9, 1987.

Norton, CDR Richard J. *Human Factors in National Security Decision Making, Naval War College.*

Chief of Naval Education and Training. *Team Skills and Concepts, Instructor Guide.* Washington, DC: Department of the Navy, 1992, chapter 6.

Hersey, Paul and Kenneth H. Blanchard. *Management of Organizational Behavior, Sixth Edition.* Englewood Cliffs, NJ: Prentice Hall, 1993, pages 353–355.

Kohn, Alfie. *No Contest: The Case Against Competition.* Boston: Houghton Mifflin, 1986.

Gabarro, John J. and John P. Kotter. *Managing Your Boss, Harvard Business Review*, May/Jun 93, Vol. 71 Issue 3, pages 150–157.

Atkinson, Rick. *Crusade: The Untold Story of the Persian Gulf War.* Boston: Houghton Mifflin, 1993, pages 148–150 and 237–240.

Covey, Stephen R. *The 7 Habits of Highly Effective People*, New York: Fireside Edition, Simon & Schuster, 1989, pages 233–260.

Hersey, Paul and Kenneth H. Blanchard. *Management of Organizational Behavior: Utilizing Human Resources*, Sixth Edition. Englewood Cliffs, NJ: Prentice Hall, 1993, pages 166–168, 220–224, and 325–343.

Montor, Karel, et al., ed., *Naval Leadership: Voices of Experience*. Annapolis: Naval Institute Press, 1987, pages 108–113, and 320–321.

Rogers, Carl R. and F. J. Roethlisberger. *Barriers and Gateways to Communication*, Harvard Business Review, Nov/Dec 91, Vol. 69 Issue 6, page 105.

Schwarzkopf, H. Norman with Peter Petre. *It Doesn't Take a Hero*. New York: Linda Grey, 1992, page 437.

Dobyns, Lloyd and Clare Crawford-Mason. *Thinking About Quality*. New York: Random House, 1994, chapter 1, pages 1-27. This has a distinctly business/management flavor, but the concepts are valid. Think about how they might apply to navy situations for discussion in class.

Garrett, H. Lawrence, III. *DON Executive Steering Group Guidance on Total Quality Leadership (TQL)*. Washington, DC: Department of the Navy, June 6, 1991, page 1.

Garvin, David A. *What Does "Product Quality" Really Mean?*, Sloan Management Review, 26(1), pages 29–33.

Ishikawa, Kaoru. *What is Total Quality Control? The Japanese Way*. (David J. Lu translator). Englewood Cliffs, NJ: Prentice-Hall, 1985, page 45.

Scholtes, Peter R. *The Team Handbook*. Madison, WI: Joiner Associates, Inc., 1988.

Total Quality Leadership Office. *Senior Leader's Seminar Guide*. Washington, DC: Department of the Navy, 1994, pages 50–59, 441–442.

Wheeler, Donald J. *Understanding Variation, The Key to Managing Chaos*. SPC Press, Inc., Knoxville, TN, 1993, pages 1 through 78 and 81 through 113.

Commander Cruiser Destroyer Group Three Message 280858Z OCT 94, *TQL in Carl Vinson Battle Group*.

Deming, W. Edwards. *Out of the Crisis*. Cambridge, MA: MIT/Center for Advanced Engineering Studies, 1986, pages 169 and 276.

Garvin, David A. *What Does "Product Quality" Really Mean?*, *Sloan Management Review*, 26(1), pages 29–33.

Ishikawa, Kaoru. *What is Total Quality Control? The Japanese Way*. (David J. Lu, translator.) Englewood Cliffs, NJ: Prentice-Hall, 1985, page 17.

Scholtes, Peter R. *The Team Handbook*. Madison, WI: Joiner Associates, Inc., 1988, pages 2–28.

Total Quality Leadership Office. *Senior Leader's Seminar Guide*. Washington, DC: Department of the Navy, 1994, pages 59–69, 70–76, 79–90.

Deming, W. Edwards. *Out of the Crisis*. Cambridge, MA: Massachusetts Institute of Technology/Center for Advanced Engineering Studies, 1986, pages 3–6.

Deming, W. Edwards. *The New Economics for Industry, Government, Education.* Cambridge, MA: Massachusetts Institute of Technology/Center for Advanced Engineering Studies, 1993, page 96.

Rummler, Geary A. and Alan P. Brache. *Improving Performance: How to Manage the White Space on the Organization Chart.* San Francisco, CA: Jossey-Bass, 1990, pages 116–123.

Schein, Edgar H. *Organizational Culture, American Psychologist,* February 1990, volume 45, issue 2, page 111.

Total Quality Leadership Office. *Senior Leader's Seminar Guide.* Washington, DC: Department of the Navy, 1994, pages 97–98.

Boardman, Thomas J. and Eileen C. *Don't Touch That Funnel, Quality Progress.* Dec 1990.

Brassard, Michael. *Memory Jogger +.* Methuen, MA: GOAL/QPC, 1989.

Total Quality Leadership Office. *Senior Leader's Seminar Guide.* Washington, DC: Department of the Navy, 1994, pages 249 through 295.

Total Quality Leadership Office. *Systems Approach to Process Improvement.* Washington, DC: Department of the Navy, 1993, Lesson 4.

Total Quality Leadership Office, *Basic Tools for Process Improvement.* Washington, DC: Department of the Navy, Draft, 1995

Juran, J.M. *Juran on Leadership for Quality*. New York: The Free Press, 1989, pages 153–156.

The Air Force Metric Handbook, First Edition, 1991.

Total Quality Leadership Office. *Senior Leader's Seminar Guide*. Washington, DC: Department of the Navy, 1994, pages 65, 68–69, 280–283.

Total Quality Leadership Office. *Systems Approach to Process Improvement*. Washington, DC: Department of the Navy, 1993, pages 1–37 to 1–45, 2–19 to 2–20, 2–50 to 2–60.

Wheeler, Donald J. and David S. Chambers. *Understanding Statistical Process Control*. Knoxville, TN: SPC Press, 1992.

Wheeler, Donald J. *Understanding Variation: The Key to Managing Chaos*. Knoxville, TN: SPC Press, 1993.

Brassard, Michael. *Memory Jogger +*. Methven, MA: GOAL/QPC, 1989.

Thomson and Roberts. *"Leading Total Quality"*, *Journal for Quality and Participation*, Jul/Aug 1992.

Total Quality Leadership Office. *Senior Leader's Seminar Guide*. Washington, DC: Department of the Navy, 1994.

Wheeler, Donald J. *Understanding Variation, The Key to Managing Chaos*. Knoxville, TN: SPC Press, Inc., 1993, pages 117–121.

NPRDC-TN-94-11, *Command Assessment Team Survey System (CATSYS) User Guide*. Navy Personnel Research and Development Center, San Diego, CA, December, 1993.

SECNAVINST 5300.26, *Policy on Sexual Harassment*. Washington, DC: Department of the Navy.

Tichy, Noel M. and Mary Anne Devanna. The Transformational Leader. New York: John Wiley & Sons, 1990, pages 222–223, 225–226, and 242–243.

FY94 National Defense Authorization Act.

NAVEDTRA 7524D, *Navy Rights And Responsibilities Workshop, Instructor Guideu*. Naval Aviation Schools Command, NAS Pensacola, 1990.

NAVEDTRA 7540, *CMEO Users Guide*.

Navy Regulations, Article 1165.

OPNAVINST 5354.1C, *Navy Equal Opportunity*.

Schein, E.H. *Organizational Culture. American Psychologist*, 1990, pages 109–119.

Tichy, Noel M. and Mary Anne Devanna. *The Transformational Leader*. New York: John Wiley & Sons, 1990, pages 222–243.

Uniform Code Of Military Justice (UCMJ), Article 134.

Bluejackets Manual, Twenty-first Edition, Annapolis, Maryland: U.S. Naval Institute Press, 1990. *U. S. Navy Regulations*, 1973.

Hersey, Paul and Kenneth H. Blanchard. *Management of Organizational Behavior; Utilizing Human Resources*, Sixth Edition. Englewood Cliffs, NJ: Prentice Hall, 1993, pages 31–33.

Lynch, Rick, and Sue Vineyard. *Secrets of Leadership*. Downers Grove, IL: Heritage Arts Publishing, 1991, pages 27–30.

Mack, Vice Admiral William P. and Commander Albert H. Konetzni. *Command at Sea*. Annapolis, MD: Naval Institute Press, 1982, pages 171–176.

Deming, W. Edwards. *The New Economics*. Cambridge: Massachusetts Institute of Technology, 1993, pages 110–118.

Hersey, Paul and Kenneth H. Blanchard. Management of Organizational Behavior: Utilizing Human Resources, Sixth Edition. Englewood Cliffs, NJ: Prentice Hall, 1993, pages 18–49, 51–82, 209–217.

Lynch, Rick and Sue Vineyard. Secrets of Leadership. Downers Grove, IL: Heritage Arts, 1991, pages 27–34.

Kohn, Alfie. No Contest: The Case Against Competition. Boston, MA: Houghton Mifflin, 1986, pages 49–51, 59–61.

Montor, Karel, et al. *Ethics for the Junior Officer*. Annapolis, MD: Naval Institute, 1994, pages 37, 191.

Schermerhorn, John R., et al. *Managing Organizational Behavior*. New York: John Wiley & Sons, Inc., 1994.

Scholtes, Peter R. *The Team Handbook*. Madison, WI: Joiner Associates, 1988, pages 6.24–31.

U.S. Naval Academy. *Fundamentals of Naval Leadership*. New York: American Heritage, 1994, chapter 8.

Mack, VADM William P. and LCDR Royal Connell. Naval Ceremonies, Customs, and Traditions. Annapolis, MD: Naval Institute Press, 1980, pages x, 3–7, and 16–17.

Mack, Vice Admiral William P. and Commander Albert H. Konetzni. *Command at Sea*, Annapolis, MD: Naval Institute Press, 1982.

OPNAVINST 1710.7, *Social Usage and Protocol Handbook,* 1979. USS. Navy Customs and Traditions. Navy Regulations, 1990.

OPNAVINST 3120.23C, *SORM*.

OPNAVINST 3120.32C, *Standard Organization and Regulations of the U.S. Navy*, chapters 1 and 3. *U.S. Navy Regulations*, 1990.

CHAPTER 12 REFERENCES

Moran, Lord. *The Anatomy of Courage,* Garden City Park, New York

Ash, Leonard D. and Martin Hill. *In Harm's Way, The Retired Officer Magazine*, October 1994, 50, No. 10, pages 42–47.

Friedman, Norman. *The Vincennes Incident, Proceedings, Naval Review*, 1989, pages 72–79.

Holmes, Richard. *Acts of War; The Behavior of Men in Battle*. New York NY: The Free Press, 1986, pages 223–244.

Mack, Vice Admiral William P. and Commander Albert H. Konetzni. *Command at Sea*, Annapolis, MD: Naval Institute Press, 1982, appendix VII, pages 474–475.

Marshall, S.L.A. *Leaders and Leadership, Military Leadership in Pursuit of Excellence*, chapter 4, pages 37–48.

Montor, Karel, et al. *Naval Leadership: Voices of Experience*. Annapolis, MD: Naval Institute Press, 1987, pages 78 through 82.

Rosenbach, William E. and Robert L. Taylor, editors. *Contemporary Issues in Leadership*. Boulder, CO: Westview Press, chapter 4.

Slim, Field Marshal Sir William. *Higher Command in War*.

Tritten, Dr. James J. *Navy Combat Leadership and Doctrine*, essay, 1994, page 6.

U. S. Navy Regulations, page 60, article 0851.

Armed Forces Staff College. Pub-1.

Armed Forces Staff College. *The Joint Staff Officer's Guide 1993*. Norfolk, VA: Armed Forces Staff College, 1993, chapter 7.

Evans, David C. and Mark R. Peattie. *Kaigun: Doctrine and Technology in the Imperial Japanese Navy, 1887-1941*. Draft book manuscript, chapter 11.

Hersey, Paul. *Situational Leadership, A Summary, Leadership Studies Inc.*, pages 1–3.

Hoyt, Edwin P. *Blue Skies and Blood, The Battle of the Coral Sea*. New York: Paul S. Eriksson, Inc., 1975.

Hoyt, Edwin P. *Men of the Gambier Bay*. Middlebury, VT: Paul S. Eriksson, Inc., 1979.

Mitroff, Ian I. *Crisis Management; A Diagnostic Guide for Improving Your Organization's Crisis Preparedness*. San Francisco, CA: Jossey Buss Inc., 1993.

Hassen, John E. and Carol F. Denton, Naval Training Systems Center, Fred Reis CAPT USNR, John R. Ronchetto, CDR USNR, Navy Military Personnel Command (PERS-62). Technical Report 92-005, Effective Navy Combat Leadership: Lessons Learned From Desert Storm, (unpublished) Jan 1992.

Headquarters, Department of the Army. *Military Leadership, Field Manual No. 22-100.* July 1990, pages 69–70.

Headquarters, Department of the Army. *Operations Field Manual No. 100-5.* June 1993, pages 2-10, 2–12.

Roger H. Nye. *The Challenge of Command.* Reading for military Excellence. Avery publishing group Inc., Garden City Park, New York.

Naval Doctrine Publication 1, *Naval Warfare.* 1994, pages 50–51.

NAVSAFECEN Risk Management Lesson Guide, pages 1–13 and 1–14.

The Random House Dictionary of the English Language. New York: Random House, 1966 page 747.

Webster's Ninth New Collegiate Dictionary. Springfield, MA: Merriam-Webster Inc., 1991, page 407.

Woodward, Vann C. *The Battle for Leyte Gulf,* New York, NY: McGraw-Hill Book Co., 1947, page 175.